Always a River

ALWAYS
A RIVER
The Ohio River
and the
American Experience

Always a River

THE OHIO RIVER AND THE AMERICAN EXPERIENCE

Edited by ROBERT L. REID

Indiana University Press

BLOOMINGTON & INDIANAPOLIS

PUBLICATION OF THIS VOLUME WAS AIDED BY A GRANT
FROM THE NATIONAL ENDOWMENT FOR THE HUMANITIES
IN THE FORM OF HONORARIA TO THE CONTRIBUTORS.

The paper used in this publication meets the minimum requirements of American National Standard for Information Sciences—Permanence of Paper for Printed Library Materials, ANSI Z39.48-1984.

Manufactured in the United States of America

Library of Congress Cataloging-in-Publication Data

Always a river : the Ohio River and the American experience / edited by Robert L. Reid.
p. cm.
ISBN 0-253-34958-3 (alk. paper). — ISBN 0-253-20645-6 (pbk. : alk. paper)
1. Ohio River. 2. Ohio River Valley. I. Reid, Robert L., date.
F516.A5 1991
977—dc20 90-25293
CIP

1 2 3 4 5 95 94 93 92 91

CONTENTS

Foreword

It was Woodrow Wilson who wrote: "A spot of local history is like an inn upon a highway; it is a stage upon a far journey; it is a place the national history has passed through." There is no place in which Wilson's insight is more true than the Ohio River Valley.

Yet, for more than a generation, historical scholarship in and about the Ohio River Valley has lacked the vigor, depth, and perspective which illuminated such work before the last Great War. Whereas in a previous generation the Ohio River was, as one scholar puts it, "a pregnant term with which to conjure," we seem to have largely lost a regional consciousness in our own time.

Because of this loss, the state humanities councils of the Ohio Valley are collaborating on a major initiative to re-ignite and sustain public education and dialogue about the history and culture of the Valley. The product of this collaboration is a multifaceted series of projects operating under the title **Always a River: The Ohio River and the American Experience.** The centerpiece of the project is a "floating exhibition" which will tour the river valley beginning the spring of 1991. **Always a River** also includes library programs, a public history conference, teacher training seminars, media productions and a number of publications.

The work of our humanities councils on this project has been animated by the belief that the study of regional, state and local history is an important element in developing the understanding and perspective necessary to civic literacy. The starting place for such study has always been the work of original and perceptive observers and scholars. The success of our river project will, in large part, depend on its capacity to capture and engage those who can help all of us in the region better see and understand the place we call home.

In this work the state humanities councils of the Ohio River region have been supported by major grants from the National Endowment for the Humanities. The Endowment has been particularly interested in encouraging new scholarship and publications about the Ohio River.

The collection you hold before you now represents the first fruits of this enterprise. As you will see from your reading, the volume is also a significant and original contribution to Ohio River scholarship. It is a new start on interpreting the Ohio River and its relationship to all those who live on its banks, work on its waters, or cross its powerful currents.

The river has many lessons to teach. This book of essays, published here for the first time, is a great way to begin our schooling.

Kenneth L. Gladish
Project Director: Always A River
Executive Director: Indiana Humanities Council
For the Humanities Councils of Illinois, Indiana
Kentucky, Ohio, Pennsylvania and West Virginia

Acknowlegments

Each contributor to this book is a "river rat." Undismayed by the pejorative nature of most applications of rat (for example, "rat fink," "rat race," or just plain "rat") we take pride in this riverine form of the term. Our associations with the Ohio River have many sources including childhood experience, geographic location, work activity, recreational orientation, and scholarly enthusiasm. As editor, it was my pleasure to work with seven authors whose sense of place and love for the Ohio rings true in the pages of their essays.

Special thanks are due to Leland Johnson who read the entire manuscript and offered many useful corrections and suggestions. Hubert Wilhelm contributed ideas for the outline, Sandra Hermann read portions of the text with care, David Hoppe helped guide the book toward publication, and Bobbi Diehl copyedited the manuscript. Others who assisted include Rita Kohn, the Project Coordinator for "Always a River," and Charles Parrish, Historian in the Louisville District Office of the U.S. Army Corps of Engineers. From the beginning, John Gallman, Director of the Indiana University Press, and Ken Gladish, Executive Director of the Indiana Humanities Council, have been enthusiastic supporters; all merit the appellation, "river rat."

Robert L. Reid

Robert Reid

INTRODUCTION

The Iroquois called the river the "Oyo," which early French explorers interpreted as *la belle rivière,* "the beautiful river." In the eighteenth century, a British army captain named Harry Gordon described the Ohio country as the "most healthy (as no sort of chronic disorder ever prevailed in it), the most pleasant, the most commodious, and most fertile spot of Earth known to European people." The bible for early Ohio River travelers, Zadock Cramer's *The Navigator,* pictured it as "the most beautiful river in the universe." In the Jacksonian era, the astute French observer Alexis de Tocqueville wrote that the Ohio "waters one of the most magnificent valleys in which man has ever lived." From the perspective of 1991, such paeans of praise seem exaggerated, perhaps even hyperbole; however, to those who experienced the Ohio Basin as the new nation's first "West," these romantic descriptions swelled their sense of regional pride.[1]

While some saw the Ohio as a river of beauty, others viewed it as a river of opportunity. To Christopher Gist, a land agent for the Ohio Company of Virginia, the abundant basin lacked only "Cultivation to make it a most delightfull Country." In 1753, Gist accompanied the twenty-one-year-old George Washington, who traveled to the forks of the Ohio to warn the French against further encroachment. Washington, whose career was intimately involved with the Ohio country as messenger, military officer, and land speculator, envisioned the region as a haven for the poor, the needy, and the oppressed "as in the Land of promise, with milk and honey." A traveler in 1803 likened the clearing of the forests to changing "the desert into a fruitful field" and cheered the replacement of "the silence of nature" with the buzz of human activity. Another visitor, Caleb Atwater, wrote in 1831 that the wood and coal of the Ohio

Valley were sufficient to fuel the nation "as long as the sun shines upon the globe."[2] Whether described in terms of settlement, agriculture, or industry, the Ohio River Basin was virgin territory awaiting humanity's shaping influence.

This wilderness, then, was welcomed as an area of abundance, not to preserve and protect, but to develop and transform. The instruments of change were science and technology in forms ranging from steamboats, movable dams, and puddling furnaces to massive steel mills, huge chemical complexes, and major cities. Log cabins and Pennsylvania barns gave way to new imprints on the landscape—the gigantic electricity generating plants powered by fossil fuels and nuclear energy that are scattered along the rivers of the Ohio Basin. This collection of essays, *Always a River,* is about our relationship with the river of opportunity.

Unlike other major rivers, whose origins often are described in terms of long-sought, near-legendary sources, the Ohio is born at the convergence of two established rivers, the Allegheny and the Monongahela. From this meeting place at Pittsburgh, the new river flows in a westerly direction for nearly one thousand miles, then doubles the volume of water of the Mississippi when it enters the mighty river at Cairo, Illinois.

The Ohio and its eighteen major tributaries (a musical litany including the Muskingum, Kanawha, Scioto, Miami, Kentucky, Wabash, Cumberland and Tennessee) make up a drainage basin encompassing 203,910 square miles. The Ohio Valley is a term which refers to the area along the main channel or mainstream and is limited to the six border or valley states: Pennsylvania, West Virginia, Ohio, Kentucky, Indiana, and Illinois. But the broader drainage basin or watershed of the Ohio and its tributaries reaches portions of fourteen states, including large parts of these six and smaller areas of Alabama, Georgia, Maryland, Mississippi, New York, North Carolina, Tennessee, and Virginia. Rich in natural resources, agricultural products, and industrial enterprises, critical to the development of the United States, the Ohio River Basin continues to play a vital part in the nation's story.

Sometimes called "the valley of democracy" in recognition of its critical role in the shaping of the American experience, the Ohio country was of little importance in the early phases of the imperial struggle which kept Europe at war from 1689 to 1815. However, the New World's emerging role became evident during the 1750s. Military clashes at the forks of the Ohio started the French and Indian War, or the Seven Years War as it was known in Europe. The Treaty of Paris of 1763 ended this "Great War for Empire." But the newly won British supremacy in North America soon turned into conflict over administrative authority and economic responsibility. The result was the War for Independence between Great Britain and its colonies (1776–1783). In the course of that struggle, American victories in the Ohio country secured that region for the new United States.

The Ohio River was our first interstate highway, carrying men, women, and children to new opportunities, new homes, and new lives. They traveled down the river on all manner of craft, then struck out over land on horseback, in wagons, or simply on foot. Between the 1780s and 1820, this tide of settlement swept westward in an "epidemic of state making." New states, embracing principles unique in the history of the world, joined the union as equal partners with the original thirteen. Of the nine states admitted prior to the Missouri Compromise of 1820, four bordered the Ohio River—Kentucky, Ohio, Indiana, and Illinois—and three others, Tennessee, Mississippi, and Alabama, had portions within the Ohio River Basin.

In the nineteenth century, the Ohio continued to influence the nation's destiny. Among the provisions of the Northwest Ordinance of 1787 was the exclusion of slavery in the area north of the Ohio River. The river consequently became the dividing line between two cultures, one based on slavery, the other on free labor. In the 1830s the always-observant de Tocqueville noted that a traveler journeying down the river sails "between slavery and freedom; and he has only to glance around him to see instantly which is best for mankind."[3]

Abraham Lincoln, born in Kentucky and raised across the Ohio in Indiana on Little Pigeon Creek, understood the magnitude of both this vision and division. In his 1858 Illinois campaign for the U.S. Senate, he noted that the nation could not exist "permanently half slave and half free." Lincoln's election as president in 1860 led to southern secession. Four bloody years of Civil War were ended with the surrender of the Confederate Army at Appomattox Court House in April 1865. With the defeat of the principle of secession and the end of slavery, Lincoln's faith in the workings of democracy and the sanctity of Union was affirmed.

The late nineteenth century witnessed the settlement of the trans-Mississippi West, the development of new means of transportation, and the emergence of an urban society. While these forces diminished the concept of regional identity, the Ohio River Basin took on importance as the nation's industrial heartland. A major factor in this transformation from wilderness society to one of steel, asphalt, and concrete was inexpensive and abundant power made possible through energy sources such as water, wood, and coal. In the twentieth century during the New Deal years, the federally sponsored Tennessee Valley Authority produced vast quantities of electric power. This made possible the construction of the nation's first atomic plant at Oak Ridge, Tennessee, during World War II. Other uranium enrichment facilities were built in the Ohio valley at Paducah, Kentucky, and Portsmouth, Ohio, in the 1950s. Hundreds of power generating stations, both coal-burning and nuclear-based, including some of the largest power plants in the world, have been built in the region to meet the almost insatiable American demand for electricity.

Throughout the history of the United States, the Ohio Basin has steadily gained importance in both the economic and the environmental concerns of our energy-hungry nation. Today, problems related to the safe use of nuclear power, the disposal of nuclear waste, pollution caused by the burning of coal in massive electric power plants up and down the valley, water quality for urban dwellers along the river, and the preservation of wetlands focus national and world attention on the Ohio Valley. All of us must look more closely at the "Oyo," *la belle rivière,* the beautiful—and troubled—Ohio. Our solutions—or failure to find answers—will change human lives, not just for those who live and work in the Ohio River Basin, but for all the residents of Planet Earth.

The essays presented in *Always a River* illuminate the relationship between the Ohio River Basin and the people who live on the banks of its river systems. Seven authors here bring their perspectives—historical, political, geographical, and literary—to a vision and a comprehension of the river. They reaffirm the continuing significance of the Ohio Basin, not merely as a fascinating chapter in history, but as a force and a resource for our present and our future.

The authors of the first two essays draw on their experience as writers about the landscape of the Midwest. Scott Russell Sanders, English professor and writer by trade, melds descriptions of the natural setting with his own reflections on the meaning of the river. John Jakle, a geographer, is the author of the highly regarded *Images of the Ohio Valley*. He returns to the theme of travelers' impressions by comparing and contrasting the experiences of an eighteenth-century traveler, Nicholas Cresswell, with those of Reuben Thwaites, a historian who traveled down the Ohio in 1894. The third essay, by another geographer, Hubert Wilhelm, discusses the still-evident imprints of early settlement and landscape change and use, so evident to nineteenth-century travelers.

The next three contributions are by historians who use their understandings of the past to inform us about the present. Michael Allen writes about means of transportation—riverboats—drawing on his research as a scholar and his personal experience as a towboatman. Darrel Bigham provides us with a comprehensive overview of the economic development of the Ohio River ranging from colonial days to the twentieth century. Leland Johnson, a leading authority on our nation's interior waterways, in particular the role of the U.S. Army Corps of Engineers, tells us of the profound alterations we have made to improve the river highway. The final essay is written by Boyd Keenan, a political scientist who codirected the major federal project of the late 1970s known as the Ohio River Basin Energy Study (ORBES). Viewing the Ohio River Basin as "an ecopolitical system of global significance," he challenges us to understand its critical importance for our own present and hoped-for future.

Applying an understanding which is consistent with the writings of today's ecologists, John Jakle tells us that "change itself is the region's constant." As each essayist in *Always a River* holds his unique lens up to the Ohio, we see, through his careful observations, unique perspectives on a natural constant that is always changing. John James Audubon, one of America's most eminent artists, reflected on the extraordinary changes he found between two trips down the Ohio—one in 1830, the other, some twenty-two years earlier. Gone were the Native Americans, the vast herds of elk, deer, and buffalo, and much of the primeval forest. Villages, farms, and towns had sprung up in their place, swelled by "the surplus population of Europe." Hundreds of steamboats plied the river, "forcing commerce to take root and to prosper at every spot." Audubon was observing a change so profound that he could "scarcely believe its reality," the transformation from natural river to human artifact.[4]

This flow, flux, transformation has given the Ohio River and its basin a paradoxical—but somehow abiding—sense of place. In reflecting upon the history of the river, we are reminded of the often unanticipated consequences that result from humanity's impact on the environment. With these essays, we attempt to understand and interpret the extraordinary diversity that has characterized our relationship to the Ohio—always a river.

NOTES

1. Harry Gordon, "Extracts from the Journal of Captain Harry Gordon, Chief Engineer in the Western Department of North America, who was sent from Ft. Pitt on the River Ohio, down the said River to Illinois, in 1766," in Thomas Pownall, *A Topographical Description of Such Parts of North America as Are Contained in the (annexed) Map of the Middle British Colonies, &c., in North America* (London: Thomas Pownall, 1776), Appendix Number IV, 3; Zadok Cramer, *The Navigator: Containing Directions for Navigating the Monongahela, Allegheny, Ohio and Mississippi Rivers*, 8th ed. (Pittsburgh: Cramer, Spear, and Eichbaum, 1814), 24; Alexis de Tocqueville, *Democracy in America* by J. P. Mayer and Max Lerner (New York: Harper and Row, 1966), 317.

2. J. Stoddard Johnston, ed., "Colonel Christopher Gist's Journal," *First Explorations of Kentucky*, Filson Club Publication No. 13 (Louisville: The Filson Club, 1898), 133; quoted in R. E. Banta, *The Ohio* (New York: Rinehart and Co., 1949), 10; Thaddeus Harris, *Journal of a Tour into the Territory Northwest of the Allegheny Mountains; made in the spring of the year 1803* (Boston: Manning and Loring, 1805), 51; Caleb Atwater, *Remarks made on a Tour to Prairie DuChien; thence on to Washington City in 1829* (Columbus, Ohio: Isaac N. Whiting, 1831), 230.

3. Tocqueville, 318.

4. Maria R. Audubon, *Audubon and His Journals*, II (Boston: Charles Scribner's Sons, 1897), 206–207.

Always a River

Scott Russell Sanders **THE FORCE OF MOVING WATER**

I am one who is drawn to water. When it storms and the street is running like a creek, I go out barefoot or booted and slosh about while my wife and neighbors stare at me from the shelter of porches. I hike miles to see a real creek slide over limestone ledges, I gaze like a soothsayer into ponds, I slip into a daze from the sound of rain sizzling on the roof.

When my children were little, every cloudburst would tug us outdoors, and we took long shivery walks through the downpour. We built dams in the gutter, laid our ears against storm grates to hear the underground roar, raced sticks on the swollen brook in the park. I would come inside tingling. There are souls—including many of the saints—who feel at home in deserts, but I am not one of them. I am strictly a wetlands man. I crave the company of water, any water, above all the meander and surge of rivers.

The river I have come to know most deeply, the river that winds through the center of my imagination as it winds through my region, is the Ohio. I was born next to a larger one, the great brown flood into which the Ohio pours, the Old Man himself, the Mississippi. I remember dragging a gunny sack behind me down the rows of cotton in a field near Memphis, a toddler not much taller than the bushes, remember coming to the steep bank of a levee, climbing to the top and then finding spread before me the mile-wide muddy water. It might have been an ocean, for all I could see of the far shore. The very earth seemed to have turned liquid. I knew what it was, of course, because the slick brown river was my most famous neighbor, the Father of Waters. I knew stories about the way it sometimes stirred in its bed and cut a new channel or snatched houses and trees and unwary toddlers in its wet claws. I could even spell its long snaky name, chanting the jingle, "Em-I-ess-ess-I-ess-ess-I-pee-pee-I." Looking out over that rolling flood from the levee, I was mesmerized and terrified. Rivers still affect me that way. Anybody who is not a bit scared by a river has either not looked at a real one or not looked hard enough.

About the time I learned to shape the letters of Mississippi with a fat pencil, my family moved north into the vicinity of a new river. I dozed in Kentucky and woke to the rumble of our car tires on the bridge leading from Covington into Cincinnati. A bridge meant water, so I stuck my head out the window and peered down between steel girders. What I saw looked smaller than the Mississippi, tamer, less muddy, but for all that it was still impressive. My mother told me its name, only four letters, easy to spell: O-hi-o. Except for time spent elsewhere studying and traveling, I have lived ever since in the valley of this river. After all these years of riding beside or upon it, hearing and reading about it, carrying its great muscular body in my mind, there is a part of me that runs night and day with the Ohio.

Chances are, your own life and the history of your place are braided with the current of a river, as my life and place are braided with the Ohio. When we figure our addresses, we might do better to forget zip codes and consider where the rain goes after it falls outside our windows. As the poet Conrad Hilberry has written,

> Knowing rivers, you know the slope and bias
> Of the earth's body. You know how the land lies.[1]

We need such knowledge, need to feel as intimate with the branching and gathering of the earth's veins as we do with the veins in our own wrists. The tilt of land that snares the rain also defines where we *are* more profoundly than any state line or city limit. States often draw their borders along rivers, yet that is false to the land, because rivers join rather than divide their two shores. Nature ignores our political boundaries, while paying close attention to watersheds. Birds migrate up and down the valleys, seeds ride the currents, plants colonize outward from the banks, and all manner of beasts—including humans—seek homes and food and one another along the paths of rivers. A true map of our continent would show a pattern of curving watersheds stitched together along high ridges, like a paisley fabric.

The watershed of the Ohio stretches into fourteen states, including ones as far afield as New York, Maryland, and Alabama, draining an area that is roughly the size of France (204,000 square miles). The basin reaches from the Appalachian Mountains in the east to the Illinois prairies in the west, from the Great Lakes in the north to the Great Smoky Mountains in the south. Two sizable rivers, the Monongahela and Allegheny, give rise to the Ohio at Pittsburgh, and before it empties into the Mississippi at Cairo, almost a thousand miles later, it gathers in dozens of tributaries, including the Muskingum, Kanawha, Scioto, Big Sandy, Great and Little Miami, Kentucky, Green, Wabash, Cumberland, and Tennessee. Its width varies from 700 feet in the upper reaches to nearly a mile at the mouth. In low stages, it pours 22,000 cubic feet of water into the Mississippi every second, and in flood it pours 1,600,000, an amount that would cover a football field to the height of a four-story building. Those flood waters can be as muddy as the Old Man's, but generally the Ohio is clearer, slow to mix with the "thick and yaller" current of the Mississippi, as Mark Twain observed.[2] Depending on the light, the season, and the stage of the river, the water can remind you of coffee with cream, the amber of tobacco juice, the green of moss, the lavender of lilacs, or robin's egg blue; or the surface can become a liquid mirror, doubling the islands and hills.

Swimming in the Ohio, afloat on my back, I try to feel all the remotest creeks of that vast basin trickling through me, my body woven into a far-flung web of water. Cupping a handful of the river under my nose, I like to imagine I can smell the pines of the mountains, the oaks and hickories of the foothills, the blackberries and wildflowers of the bottomlands. What I'm likelier to smell is diesel oil, cotton poison, coal slurry, or sewage, for twenty-five million people live in the basin, and the watercourses are lined with towns, factories, mills, slag heaps, power plants, and refineries. Like the rest of our planet, the Ohio is caught in a tug-of-war between natural influences and human ones.

From bluffs along the river, you gaze down on a quintessential American landscape: a low island in mid-channel, half woods and half overgrown pasture surrounding the tumbled foundations of barns; coal-filled barges churning past, some headed for power plants whose cooling towers and smokestacks bristle around the next bend; other barges heaped with corn or steel or automobiles, lashed to docks for unloading by conveyors and long-armed derricks; beyond the docks, a scramble of railroad tracks, high tension wires, gas lines, roads, our own channels of power following the river's; in the bottomlands, clapboard farm houses, some in ruins and some in restored glory; dented trailers with dish antennas and woodpiles and cannibalized cars in the yards; inlets marked by the white blaze of sycamores; fields of tobacco and soybeans; a chemical plant spewing gray smoke; hills illumined by redbud and the blue pokers of larkspur; mud lots gouged by hogs, meadows grazed by cows; old cellar holes outlined by the persistent blooms of jonquils and forsythia; glacial sand and gravel pits; the spires and boxy shoulders of white frame churches; and on the ridge against the sky a whiskery fringe of trees. It is a landscape at once pastoral and industrial, wild and tame. The river is a sovereign power only half bound in the chains of our purposes. We exist as a people in that tension, loving wildness and fearing it, longing for contact with untrammeled nature and at the same time longing for control.

The Ohio has concentrated our desires and designs as it has concentrated the waters of a hundred streams. Because it was the principal avenue of settlement leading west from the colonies on the Atlantic seaboard, the history of our dealings with the Ohio epitomize our dealings with the continent as a whole. By dumping our wastes into the water, building dams and locks and bridges, raising floodwalls and levees, naming the tributaries, charting every point and riffle and bar, we have superimposed ourselves onto the river. Only by consulting old records and resorting to imagination can we glimpse what the Ohio must have been like apart from our tinkering.

Humans have lived beside the Ohio for virtually all of its history. It is not very old as rivers go, only some ten or fifteen thousand years. When the last glaciers crunched down over the Midwest, they blocked the north-flowing rivers. These trapped streams and the glacier's own meltwater scoured westward, cutting through ridges of limestone and sandstone and coal-rich shale, gouging fresh channels and joining together pieces of ancient riverbeds, eventually producing the modern Ohio, which is a sort of twisted rag rope of old and new. And I do mean twisted: while the river drifts generally southwest, there are stretches where within a few miles it flows toward every point of the compass. Get a map and look at the stretch between Pomeroy, Ohio, and Parkersburg, West Virginia, or look at the section upriver from Owensboro, Kentucky. If it were a crow instead of a stream, the Ohio would cover the distance between Pittsburgh and Cairo in only half as many miles. The other half it spends meandering.

In cutting through bedrock, the turbulent new river exposed to view the fossils of sea creatures—dazzling corkscrews, hinged shells like the wings of angels, armored trilobites, entire coral reefs. Rambling along the Ohio in 1810, Zadok Cramer—author of *The Navigator*, the standard early guide to the river—noticed "the very singular manner in which the rocks were filled with appearances of animal and vegetable substances, marine shells, particularly the cockle; the whole shape of a bird, in form like the bat; the butterfly, &c." Well before geologists explained these mysterious shapes, Cramer was shrewd enough

> to suppose this country was once a great sea or lake, either of fresh or salt water, and that these substances, after the great convulsion of nature which occasioned dry land to appear, were thrown together in the struggle, and being exposed to a different element, from animated and soft vegetable bodies, Time, the moulder of Nature's matter, has shaped them into massy rocks, as we now find them.[3]

Indeed, a shallow ocean had occupied the heart of the continent for tens of millions of years, and the newly spawned Ohio carved a channel through the ancient sediments.

After the ice vanished, the river remained, and soon plants flung their net of green over the boggy shores, arborvitaes and sedges, spruces and firs. Pockets of those cold-loving species can still be found in the valley on north-facing slopes and in frosty hollows. The plants were followed by animals, including such lumbering brutes as musk oxen, giant beavers, saber-toothed tigers, and woolly mammoths. The remains of these creatures show up dramatically at Big Bone Lick, just south of the river below Cincinnati, a spot that intrigued explorers from the earliest days. On a mapping journey for the British in 1766, Thomas Hutchins visited "the Licks in which Elephants' bones are found," a visit that left him puzzled "[f]rom whence these animals came, and the cause of their Extinction."[4] Half a century later, the ornithologist Alexander Wilson

> found numerous fragments of large bones lying scattered about. In pursuing a wounded duck across this quagmire, I had nearly deposited my carcass among the grand congregation of mammoths below, having sunk up to the middle, and had hard struggling to get out.[5]

Fossils from Big Bone Lick were exhibited in America's first museum of natural history, the gallery of Charles Willson Peale, which opened in Philadelphia just after the Revolution.

Less respectful travelers used the gigantic ribs and tusks for tent poles or gate posts. Ever-curious about the western lands, President Jefferson sent William Clark to perform a dig there in 1807—very likely the first paleontological expedition in the western hemisphere—and Clark, who had returned only the previous year from his epic journey to the Pacific with Meriwether Lewis, duly shipped three hundred bones to the White House. Some of the prize specimens made their way into collections in Europe, where they provoked naturalists to speculate anew about the history of life on earth. More recent digs at Big Bone Lick have turned up the remains of mastodons, peccaries, ground sloths, tapirs, and gigantic elk.

The dumb beasts were succeeded by the smart ones, the hunters and fishers and planters. Through overzealous hunting, in fact, these two-legged newcomers may well have contributed to the extinction of the great mammals. The earliest human settlers along the Ohio were descendants of those who crossed over from Asia, the original American immigrants hungry for land. I like to think of them in their skins and shrewdness coming upon the raw swollen river while the retreating wall of ice was still visible on the horizon. Over millennia they created in this northern valley a civilization that rivaled the more famous ones (more famous thanks to Spanish chroniclers and gold) of the Aztecs, Mayas, and Incas farther south. Their great earthen fortifications, temple plazas, and tombs, along with the jewelry, carvings, and tools they buried with their dead, speak of complex and sophisticated cultures. From shells and flints and other materials found in their villages, we know their trade networks extended north beyond the Great Lakes, south to the Gulf of Mexico, east to the Atlantic, and west to the desert. Known collectively (and crudely) as the Mound Builders because of their impressive earthworks, these primordial settlers flourished along the Ohio from at least 1000 B.C. until roughly 1500 A.D., dates that encompass the golden age of Greece as well as the lifespans of the Assyrian, Persian, and Roman Empires.

When I was a kid growing up in Ohio, where these industrious people left more than ten thousand mounds, I suspected every hillock of hiding beartooth necklaces and freshwater pearls and the seven-foot-long skeletons of giants. Although I walked the creek beds and farm fields with head bowed, on the lookout for arrowheads, some primitive awe kept me from digging into these humps of earth. But others were not so shy—after all, why respect the graves of heathens?—and gradually cupboards and museum shelves filled with the broken leavings of these vanished tribes. Early in the last century, for example, the huge tomb that gave a name to the river town of Moundsville, West Virginia, was gouged with tunnels to allow passage for the curious, and its bones and burial goods were unceremoniously scattered. In our own century, a few sites have been carefully excavated. At Angel Mounds, for instance, on the Indiana side just upriver from Evansville, archaeologists have traced the outlines of a fortified town. One can go there and lean against the reconstructed palisade, peer into the shadows of a circular hut, gaze up at the central mound where high priests may have lived, and one can almost hear the voices of those river people.

What did the Ohio mean to the Mound Builders? The early white settlers, who rifled the tombs and leveled earthworks to clear the way for plows, did not care; and now it is too late for us to know for sure. But I would guess that the river was a god to them, a brawny presence, a strong back to ride through the forest, a giver of fish and mussels, flowing always and flooding when it took a notion. If you look at the most stunning of all the earthworks, the sinuous, quarter-mile-long Great Serpent Mound in southern Ohio, with its coiled tail and gaping mouth, and then look at the twisty Ohio itself, you can see that the river is a snake, the snake a river. In many mythologies, and even in the cellars of our own post-mythic minds, the serpent is the raw intimidating power of nature itself, the pure energy of creation and destruction made visible. My hunch is that the Mound Builders felt this, worshipping the brown sinewy god and placing their villages on high ground to give the serpent room for writhing. If you are going to survive in the land, you must know and honor the local powers, and nothing in this region is more steadily, unignorably powerful than the river.

No one knows what happened to the Mound Builders. They may have died out from epidemics or warfare, may have been forced out of the region by tribes invading from elsewhere or by their own overpopulation, or may have lived on to become one or another of the peoples known to history, such as the Shawnee. In any event, well before Europeans reached the Ohio, the elaborate ceremonial practices of the Mound Builders had dwindled away. The valley was thinly settled by tribes that relied on hunting, fishing, the gathering of seeds and nuts, and the cultivation of corn, beans, and squash. Because the Ohio was prone to flood, they built most of their villages on the tributaries instead of the main channel. By the eighteenth century, as traders and soldiers filtered into the valley, the principal tribes included the powerful Iroquois north and east of the Forks of the Ohio, the Delawares and Wyandots along the Muskingum, the Shawnees on the Scioto, the Miami on the twin rivers that bear their name and on the Wabash, the Illinois on the Illinois, the Cherokees and Chickasaws on the Tennessee and Cumberland. Much of what is now Kentucky and West Virginia was hunting territory, the Bloody Ground, without permanent settlements. The Wyandots had a village at the mouth of the Muskingum that survived into the period of European exploration. But high waters forced the Shawnees to remove their town from the mouth of the Scioto upriver to what is now Chillicothe. Visiting there in 1750, a commercial agent reported finding three hundred people living prosperously in bark huts.

On a steamboat trip down the Ohio in 1841, Charles Dickens met a Choctaw chief who presented him with a calling card and then conversed with him, in English, about the poetry of Sir Walter Scott. Describing the incident in *American Notes* (1842), Dickens clearly intended for his readers to lift their eyebrows at the spectacle of a savage become civilized.[6] By 1841, however, the "savages" had already maintained a civilization in the Ohio valley for several thousand years, far longer than descendants of Europeans and Africans have yet managed to survive here.

If, say in the year 5000, *our* descendants are still living beside the Ohio in peace and prosperity, without having exhausted the soil or poisoned the river, then there will be cause for boasting. For now, we are still sojourners in the land, our wisdom untested, the durability of our ways unproved.

A good deal of ugly frontier history is compressed into one stanza of an early folk song about the river:

> Those blood thirsty Indians you need not fear,
> We will all united be and we will be free from care,
> We'll march into their towns and give them their deadly blow,
> And we'll fold you in our arms in the pleasant Ohio.[7]

Native presence along the Ohio effectively came to an end in the mid-nineteenth century, when the last Wyandots and Shawnees withdrew to the west. What these people thought about the river we can gather from an Iroquois creation myth, which tells how, in the beginning, muskrat brought mud between its paws to Manitou, who lives in the river beneath the great falls. Manitou took the mud and made Earth. As Earth cooled it took the shape of a pumpkin, and all creatures grew upon it. Waters ran down the valleys of the pumpkin and became rivers. Where the Iroquois traveled to fight their enemies and to kill buffalo and deer, the river was called the beautiful one, Ohio.

Anyone who has seen the river in flood can understand how the gathering of mud from the deeps and the emergence of land above the waters might stand for the mystery of creation itself.

Thanks in part to the Iroquois, who cleared out much of the upper Ohio, when the French and English entered the valley in the seventeenth century they found a sparsely settled land for the taking. And of course they took. What else was the wilderness for? The name of the river itself was adopted and probably garbled from an Iroquois word, something like "Oyo," which the French translated as "beautiful river," but which later authorities have rendered as "great white water," "river of the white foam," or "bloody river." There is truth in all the names, even the claim of whitecaps, for the water is periodically whipped into froth by the prevailing westerly winds.

Authorities also disagree about which European first "discovered" the Ohio. Most say the honor goes to Réné Robert

Cavelier, Sieur de La Salle, who is supposed to have paddled downstream along with a Seneca guide and two dozen voyageurs as far as the falls in the winter of 1669–70; others say no, he never made the trip. No indisputable record of the journey has turned up. La Salle certainly *wanted* to find the river, for he believed that it led to the western sea, and thence to the Orient and riches. He was so intent upon finding a quick route to the Far East that comrades named his Canadian estate "La Chine." Like many who followed him, he saw the Ohio not as a place-in-itself to be understood and respected, but as a pathway to somewhere more profitable. Trapping beaver as he went, he paid his bills with furs. Whatever the truth of La Salle's claim, white hunters and traders and scalawags whose names have been lost to us were visiting the river well before 1700, some venturing out from the French settlements on the Mississippi, others crossing the mountains from the English colonies. In any case, identifying which European first laid eyes on the Ohio, and when, has never seemed a burning question to me. The river was in no need of discovery, since the native people already knew precisely where it was.

The question mattered a great deal to France and England, however, for they spent a century spatting and warring over who owned the river. One of the most revealing episodes in this long tussle occurred in 1749, when a French captain named Céleron de Bienville deposited in the mouths of several tributaries engraved lead plates, like miniature tombstones, which announced that the Ohio and all the streams flowing into it and all the uncharted lands drained by those waters belonged to King Louis XV. It was a brazen gesture, akin to planting a flag on the moon. With a handful of words, a single vainglorious potentate who had never so much as glimpsed North America laid claim to a realm that was nearly as large as his entire kingdom. If the purpose of Céleron's journey was, as the plates declared, "to restore tranquillity in certain villages of these cantons," then his mission failed.[8] The European rivals kept fighting for control of the forks of the river until 1758, when the British emerged victorious. The fort they built at the confluence of the Monongahela and Allegheny would evolve into Pittsburgh, a center for boat-building, a terminus for roads, a supply depot for settlers, the gateway to the Ohio.

Had the local tribes been consulted about Céleron's lead plates, they might well have scratched their heads. The notion of owning a river would have made no sense to the native peoples, but it made perfect sense to the Europeans. The Old World viewed the New as unclaimed real estate. The history of our approach to the Ohio, like that of our approach to the whole continent, might be summed up as the scramble to convert wilderness into property.

Although bewildered by European notions of ownership, the Iroquois and other tribes understood that forts and farms and log cabins were a threat to their own use of the land. During the eighteenth century, their rallying cry was, "White man shall not plant corn north of the Ohio." Partly to mollify these tribes, partly to confine the colonists within an easily patrolled region, the British government, by a proclamation of 1763, forbade settlements west of the Appalachian Mountains. It was a decree widely ignored, even before the Revolution annulled all British proclamations. Families hungry for land, investors eager for profit, and scamps fleeing debts or crimes or foul reputations, all looked eagerly toward the Ohio valley.

Among the first observers to record their impressions of the river in detail were English traders and land company agents, men such as Christopher Gist and George Croghan. They were "bold and enterprising," wrote the nineteenth century historian Francis Parkman:

> These and other chief traders hired men on the frontiers, crossed the Alleghanies [sic] with goods packed on the backs of horses, descended into the valley of the Ohio, and journeyed from stream to stream and village to village along the Indian trails, with which all this wilderness was seamed, and which the traders widened to make them practicable. More rarely, they carried their goods on horses to the upper waters of the Ohio, and embarked them in large wooden canoes, in which they descended the main river, and ascended such of its numerous tributaries as were navigable.[9]

As an agent for the Ohio Land Company of Virginia, Gist explored the Ohio in 1750–51, noting soils, timber, minerals, game, and the disposition of the natives. Thus, below the mouth of the Great Miami, he noticed

> fine, rich level Land, well timbered with large Walnut, Ash, Sugar Trees, Cherry Trees, &c, it is well watered with a great Number of little Streams or Rivulets, and full of beautiful natural Meadows, covered with Wild Rye, blue Grass and Clover, and abounds with Turkeys, Deer, Elks and most Sorts of Game particularly Buffaloes, thirty or forty of which are frequently seen feeding in one Meadow: In short it wants Nothing but Cultivation to make it a most delightfull Country.[10]

That closing note was struck repeatedly in early accounts of the river: here was a raw abundance needing only shrewd investment and determined labor in order to be turned into wealth.

As another example of the proprietary outlook, consider George Washington's traffic with the Ohio. While still a teenager, he surveyed land near the forks at the behest of an English lord. The same year in which Céleron deposited his lead plates, two of Washington's brothers helped form a company for the colonization of the Ohio country. Soon after, Washington visited the French troops near the headwaters, warning them in the name of the Governor of Virginia to abandon their fort and yield all claims to the river. The French scoffed, war broke out, and Washington led troops into battle for control of the valley. When at length the British won, the king gave Washington 5,000 acres on the Ohio as a reward for his services. In a letter of 1770 to Jefferson, Washington suggested opening up a path between the Potomac and the Ohio, to provide a "channel of conveyance of the extensive and valuable trade of a rising empire."[11] He kept adding to his holdings until, by the eve of the Revolution, he was one of the grandest landowners in the western country, amassing some 60,000 acres near the mouth of the Great Kanawha. His real estate, plus his ambitions for the new nation, led him to keep pushing after the Revolution for the settlement of the Ohio country by Americans.

How did Washington see the river? Reading the journal from a trip he made downstream in 1770, we find ourselves in the company of a shrewd-eyed speculator. He assessed the fertility of bottomlands ("in many places very rich, in others somewhat wet and pondy; fit for meadow, but upon the whole exceeding valuable, as the land after you get out of the rich bottom is very good for grain"); the likely yield of meat ("This country abounds in buffaloes and wild game of all kinds; as also in all kinds of wild fowl, there being in the bottoms a great many small, grassy ponds, or lakes, which are full of swans, geese, and ducks"); the convenience of navigation ("When the river is in its natural state, large canoes, that will carry five or six thousand weight or more, may be worked against stream by four hands, twenty or twenty-five miles a day; and down, a good deal more"); and the mood of the natives ("The Indians who reside upon the Ohio . . . view the settlement of the people upon this river with an uneasy and jealous eye").[12] In 1773 he placed an ad in a Baltimore paper for homesteads on the Ohio, a place "abounding with fine fish and wild fowl of various kinds, as also in most excellent meadows, in their present state, almost fit for the scythe."[13]

The buying and selling of this vast new territory was made easier by the comprehensive survey provided for in the Ordinance of 1785. All land north of the river was divided into 640-acre, mile-square parcels, with the sides of the squares running north-south and east-west, a mathematical grid that would have pleased Sir Isaac Newton. The Northwest Ordinance of 1787 had an even more profound influence on the region, providing for the creation of new states and prohibiting slavery north of the river. That ban would make the river a symbol of freedom for slaves escaping from the South (near Ripley, Ohio, you can still drive on Free Soil Road); it would dot the northern shore with stops on the Underground Railroad; and, three-quarters of a century after passage of the Ordinance, the ban on slavery would make the Ohio a highway for troops and supplies during the Civil War.

One of the drafters of the Northwest Ordinance was the Rev. Manasseh Cutler, who also wrote a "Description of Ohio" in 1787. Reflecting on that pristine valley from his home in long-settled Massachusetts, Cutler remarked:

> Besides the opportunity of opening a new and unexplored region for the range of natural history, botany, and the medical sciences, there will be one advantage which no other part of the earth can boast, and which probably will never again occur—that, in order to begin *right*, there will be no *wrong* habits to combat, and no inveterate systems to overturn—there is no rubbish to remove, before you can lay the foundation.[14]

Like a new Eden, the valley of the Ohio offered natural bounty and the chance of a fresh start.

Journeying down the wild river, early observers marveled over that plenitude. "The country hereabouts abounds with buffalo, bears, deer, and all sorts of wild game, in such plenty, that we killed out of our boats as much as we wanted," wrote George Croghan in 1765. Voyagers were still killing as much as they wanted half a century later, according to John James Audubon, who lived beside the Ohio for a dozen years: "The margins of the shores and of the river were . . . amply supplied with game. A Wild Turkey, a Grouse, or a Blue-winged Teal, could be procured in a few moments." A traveler in 1807, who relished the sight of numerous bald eagles circling overhead, noted that in one season a hunter killed two hundred deer and eighty bears. There were panthers and wildcats, fox and lynx, otters and minks, herds of elk, packs of wolves, whooping cranes by the thousands, ducks and geese and partridges and pheasants by the millions.[15]

Well into the nineteenth century, it was common for travelers to see large animals swimming across the river. Here, for example, is an encounter from 1820:

> Near midnight, one of the men and myself being up, we discovered something near us, which we took for a log, and began pulling from it, when we found our mistake; it was a bear swimming in the river; he came close to that part of the boat where I was standing, and then made off up the river in great haste. We could hear him blow in the water longer than we could see him.[16]

Boat passengers watched otters sliding on the banks, or beavers and muskrats churning in the shallows, or deer with gleaming antlers and frightened eyes wedging the current. Migrating squirrels crossed the water in such numbers that they formed thick gray rafts, blocking traffic.

More than a hundred species of fish lived in that early, unpolluted stream, including white and black bass, crappie, sturgeon, sunfish, rockfish, and several varieties of catfish—mud cats, channel cats, Mississippi blues—as well as mullet, perch, and carp. Even allowing for the proverbial exaggeration of fish stories, the size of some catches was astounding. Audubon reported that a friend caught from the river below Louisville a catfish "in which was found the greater part of a sucking pig."[17] Further downriver, near Henderson, Kentucky, using trot-lines baited with toads, Audubon himself landed catfish weighing up to a hundred pounds. Frogs, turkey, the entrails of venison, any bait would do, the fish were so plentiful. Settlers could gather enough for their own tables using nets, or they could wade into the river at night carrying torches of pine knots or hickory bark and spear enough to feed the neighbors and the hogs as well.

Grapevines, heavy with fruit in season, laced tree to tree along the banks, and mistletoe clotted the branches. Sometimes a tree, chopped through at the base, would be held upright by the entangling vines. Where the river admitted sunlight to the forest floor, the undergrowth was so dense it made the shores almost impassable. Those uncut shores were lined with beech and maple and oak, ash and hickory (ideal for ax-handles), tulip poplar (logs for cabins), locust and cedar (fence posts), sassafras (tea), elm and chestnut, cottonwood, buckeye, juniper, the luminous dogwood and redbud and magnolia, the fruiting persimmon and mulberry, the lithe willows and—my favorite—the fat, gnarly, white-flecked sycamores. "The *Sycamore*," Zadok Cramer noted, "seems to be the king of the forest on the banks of the Ohio. Their monstrous growth, towering height, and extended branches really fill the beholder with awe and astonishment." He described one specimen "into whose hollow thirteen men rode on horse back, June 6, 1808, the fourteenth did not enter, his horse being skittish and too fearful to advance into so curious an apartment, but there was room enough for two more." On a mapping expedition in 1766, Thomas Hutchins found islands covered with "the tallest of Timber," and the river "inclosed with the finest Trees of different kinds, of various verdures and leaves of the largest soils." Then as now, you could judge the fertility of the soil by the dominant species: walnut, maple, buckeye, elm, and papaw grew on the richest land; and on the poorest grew hickory and black and white oak. Avoid beech forests, George Washington advised, "as their roots spread over a large surface of ground and are hard to kill." Then as now, open ground would be swiftly reclaimed by red cedar, locust, and sumac. Then as now, wildflowers licked up like flames from the earth, trout-lilies and trillium, rosy columbine and fire pinks, celandine poppies and spring beauties, phlox, goldenrods, mullein, Solomon's seal—a dazzling array.[18]

As the Rev. Cutler noted, the opening of the valley did offer "a new and unexplored region for the range of natural history." The great Philadelphia botanist John Bartram went on a collecting trip down the Ohio in 1761, soon after the British troops had won control of the headwaters from the French. Over the next century, Bartram was followed by one distinguished naturalist after another, each one eager to claim this fresh country for science.

Alexander Wilson, selling subscriptions to his book on American birds and gathering information on new species, set out from Pittsburgh in a skiff dubbed the *Ornithologist* just after the clearing of ice in 1810.

> The current went about two and a half miles an hour, and I added about three and a half miles more to the boat's way with

> my oars. I could only discover when I was passing a clearing by the crowing of cocks, and, now and then, in more solitary places, the big horned owl made a most hideous hollowing, that echoed among the mountains. In this lonesome manner, exposed to hardships all day, and hard berths all night, to storms of rain, hail, and snow—for it froze severely almost every night—I persevered.[19]

Wilson traveled with a portfolio of his bird paintings, a flute, and a parakeet named Poll which he had winged with a shot from the boat. In Cincinnati he met Dr. Daniel Drake, a physician who had founded a library and museum to celebrate the river's wildlife and lore. At Shippingport, just above Louisville, Wilson tried in vain to sell a subscription to a shopkeeper who was busy making his own paintings of Ohio Valley birds, a young man with a heavy French accent, John James Audubon.

A few years later, Audubon would again play host to a wandering naturalist, one Constantine Rafinesque, who scoured the river with avid eye. During his first night in the household, by Audubon's account, Rafinesque shattered Audubon's favorite violin while trying to kill a bat, which Rafinesque believed might be a species never before described. Altogether, during his tour of the Ohio, Rafinesque supposed that he had found

> Abt 25 new species of Bats, Rats and other quadrupeds, abt. 20 N. Sp of Birds. Abt. 15 N. Sp of snakes, turtles, lizards, and other reptiles, 64 N. Sp of fishes of the Ohio: more than 80 N. Sp of shells, besides some new worms and many fossils. And in Botany I have collected more than 600 Sp of Plants of which one-tenth part at least are new.[20]

Even allowing for Rafinesque's capacity for exaggeration, which was gargantuan, his claims suggest the enthusiasm stirred in naturalists by this wild, uncatalogued country.

While serving as the first professor of natural history at Transylvania University in Lexington, Rafinesque went to confer with the scientists at New Harmony, on the banks of the Wabash a few miles upriver from its junction with the Ohio. For more than a decade, beginning in 1825, this community was a hotbed of research. The Scottish industrialist Robert Owen had purchased the town from a German religious society with the aim of establishing there an experiment in utopia. Together with his partner, William Maclure, he persuaded some of the country's most distinguished scientists and educators to move to the wilds of southern Indiana and join that experiment. The most noteworthy influx of talent made its way down the Ohio on a single keelboat in the winter of 1825–26. Known as the "Boatload of Knowledge" from a phrase in one of Owen's speeches, the craft bore an architect, a physician, workmen skilled at various trades, artists and musicians, as well as three celebrities from Philadelphia's Academy of Natural Sciences, each man a leader in his field: Maclure in geology, Thomas Say in entomology and conchology, Charles Alexandre Lesueur in zoology.[21]

Another passenger on that intellectual keelboat was Robert Owen's eldest son, Robert Dale Owen, who would later become a state and federal legislator, a diplomat, and a founder of the Smithsonian Institution. The journal Robert Dale kept during the trip reveals a young man divided between two passions, one for utopian speculation and the other for hunting. In the evenings he read social philosophers and discussed plans for the ideal commonwealth. By day, he pursued turkeys, woodpeckers, doves, pheasants, partridges, squirrels, and above all deer:

> Dr. Price discovered a deer on the ice and we went out immediately after it. But the ice was too weak to bear us, and the deer too far off to enable us to shoot it. In the meantime another deer crossed: immediately after it came out of the water I fired at it without effect. It recrossed passing down opposite our keelboat and was shot on the other side.[22]

The deer and other game emerged from a forest that was closer to pure wilderness than anything the younger Owen had ever seen: "The appearance of the woods is wild and magnificent in the extreme, immense trees lying across one another, and everything, apparently, in a perfect state of nature."[23] Lesueur's sketches from the journey show river banks that, except for clearings around homesteads and towns, were still uncut. The prospect of entering a valley that was indeed still close to "a perfect state of nature," this as much as Robert Owen's visionary experiment lured scientists to the Ohio country, as it lured traders, explorers, tourists, and settlers.

For settlers, those early years along the river were often lean and grim. Francis Parkman captured something of the mood of that time and place in his sketch of the frontier:

> Buried in woods, the settler lived in an appalling loneliness. A low-browed cabin of logs, with moss stuffed in the chinks to keep out the wind, roof covered with sheets of bark, chimney of sticks and clay, and square holes closed by a shutter in place of windows; an unkempt matron, lean with hard work, and a brood of children with bare heads and tattered garments eked out by deerskin,—such was the home of the pioneer in the remoter and wilder districts. . . . If the country had been an open one, like the plains beyond the Mississippi, the situation would have been less frightful; but the forest was everywhere, rolled over hill and valley in billows of interminable green,—a leafy maze, a mystery of shade, a universal hiding-place, where murder might lurk unseen at its victim's side, and Nature seemed formed to nurse the mind with wild and dark imaginings.[24]

In spite of the menacing woods, in spite of the Indians and snakes and wolves, settlers poured into the valley, one great wave coming after the Revolution and another after the War of 1812. Songs wooed them with promises of the river's abundance:

> The land it is good my boys you need not to fear
> 'Tis a garden of Eden in North America:
> Come along my lads and we'll altogether go
> And we'll settle on the banks of the pleasant Ohio.
>
> There's all kind of fish in that river for our use,
> Besides the lofty sugar trees that yields us their juice,
> There's all kinds of game besides the buck and doe,
> And we'll range through the wild woods and hunt the buffalo.[25]

For Audubon, the most astonishing abundance of all was that of passenger pigeons. Riding along the Kentucky bank upstream toward Louisville in 1813, he tried counting the flocks as they passed overhead, but gave up out of weariness. "The air was literally filled with Pigeons; the light of noon-day was obscured as by an eclipse; the dung fell in spots, not unlike melting flakes of snow; and the continued buzz of wings had a tendency to lull my senses to repose." When he reached Louisville, some fifty miles later, "The Pigeons were still passing in undiminished numbers, and continued to do so for three days in succession." The dung beneath their roosting places was several inches deep, and stout trees broke under their weight.[26]

Who would have imagined that such riches could ever be exhausted? After describing the wholesale slaughter of pigeons in the beech forests along the river—heaps larger than haystacks rolling away on wagons, boatloads floating to city markets, hogs devouring the leftovers—Audubon added that "Persons unacquainted with these birds might naturally conclude that such dreadful havock would soon put an end to the species. But I have satisfied myself, by long observation, that nothing but the gradual diminution of our forests can accomplish their decrease."[27] He was only half right; while clearing of the forest did contribute to the decline of the passenger pigeon, it was the "dreadful havock" wrought by hunters that pushed the bird to extinction.

The pattern of habitat destruction and relentless hunting has been repeated for species after species. Bison, whose wide traces offered routes through the woods for the first roads, were still counted in hundreds and thousands at salt licks near the river on the eve of the Revolution, and yet within a few years they had been killed off. The green parakeet vanished, along with the lynx, wildcat, panther, elk, otter, bear, and wolf. The whooping cranes dwindled almost to extinction, and so did the bald eagles. By 1900, coal slurry and oil slicks from wells and mines on the upper river had killed off untold species of fish.

The vigorous cane, a jointed grass that shot up over a dozen feet, with stalks as thick as your arm, once flourished along the banks, providing color as well as fodder all year long. Cramer noted that "from its ever-green foliage, it has a pleasant effect on the imagination, when all the surrounding vegetable matter is locked up in the winter's frost."[28] And yet the cane was soon eradicated through burning, clearing, and over-grazing. By sheer good luck, as the ecologist Aldo Leopold pointed out,

> the cane-lands, when subjected to the particular mixture of forces represented by the cow, plow, fire, and axe of the pioneer, became bluegrass. What if the plant succession inherent in this dark and bloody ground had, under the impact of these forces, given us some worthless sedge, shrub, or weed? Would Boone and Kenton have held out? Would there have been any overflow into Ohio, Indiana, Illinois, and Missouri?[29]

Land will not always recover so generously. Although you can still see log trucks and steaming piles of sawdust on the shore, especially in West Virginia and Indiana, the old growth timber is gone. We replant only the fastest growing and most profitable varieties of trees, so that our new forests are puny imitations of the original ones. Like the old timber, most of the oil and gas and iron ore within easy reach of the Ohio was used up in less than a century, a brief time in the life of a river or a civilization.

When you look at the filth and squalor along parts of the Ohio, when you consider the annihilation of the forests and the disappearance of wildlife, you have to ask whether such brief profit justifies so much desolation. James Wright, from Martins Ferry, Ohio, wrote of burying a dead swan in the river he mourned and loved:

> Here, carry his splintered bones
> Slowly, slowly
> Back into the
> Tar and chemical strangled tomb,
> The strange water, the
> Ohio river, that is no tomb to
> Rise from the dead
> From.[30]

Since the earliest days, the river had been used as a dump, receiving offal from slaughterhouses, mash from breweries, manure from livestock pens, sewage from towns, waste from factories and mines. Little was done to control pollution of the Ohio until about 1950, and we are still a long way from having cleaned up our own mess. This, too, is part of the river's history, the tar and chemicals, the oil slicks, the "strange water," the squandering within a few generations of an unforeseen, unearned bounty.

Despite George Washington's optimism about the convenience of navigation, the natural Ohio was an imperfect highway on several counts. Over its 981 miles, the river dropped (and still drops) only 430 feet, an average of less than six inches a mile. In low water, it was so shallow in places that a child could wade across. It remained low in the dry months of summer and in winter before the snow melt, rising high enough for ready passage only in the rainy months of spring and fall. On his way down the Ohio to rendezvous with William Clark in 1803, Meriwether Lewis had to pay local draymen two dollars to haul his boat over riffles—an exorbitant fee, he complained—and at gravel bars his men often had to climb out and shovel a passage, until the languid current swept a channel clear. Even in high water, sunken trees, rocks, sand bars, and the wrecks of earlier boats made travel hazardous. Drift ice was a problem most winters, and about once in every ten years the river froze solid.

For the first half of the nineteenth century, voyagers carefully studied the latest editions of Zadok Cramer's *Navigator* to learn how to negotiate the endless obstacles. Here, for example, was the advice in 1814 concerning Dead-man's Island:

> The channel is somewhat difficult and serpentine in very low stages of the water. A bar extends upwards from the head of the island, which forms a ripple, and which you avoid by pulling for the right shore as soon as you get near it, leaving the head of the bar and island to the left. After the first chute to the right, bear towards the island, then again to the right shore, and then again incline to the left, which puts you clear of Dead-man's ripple just below the island, where the water, from a rocky bottom, is rough, and looks formidable, but is not dangerous.[31]

If the river was to become a highway, something would have to be done about these nuisances, especially about the falls at Louisville. (Actually, the "falls" were a series of rapids tumbling over limestone ledges, dropping only twenty-odd feet in three miles.) There were schemes afoot to dig a canal past the falls as early as 1787, and by 1825 the Kentuckians were actually digging one. About the time that canal opened for traffic, in 1830, the Army Corps of Engineers began hauling out snags and wrecks, blasting troublesome rocks, and dredging channels all up and down the Ohio. They built stone "training dikes" to narrow and deepen the river. But still, boats and barges could only travel in the high water of spring and fall. Why not build a series of locks and dams, backing up enough water to guarantee, say, a year-round depth of six feet? And once you get six feet, why not go for nine?

This grandiose scheme, proposed in 1875, was only carried out in our own century, after the scare of World War I and the near-breakdown of the railroads pried the necessary funding from Congress. When the nine-foot channel was opened in 1929, Herbert Hoover declared: "While I am proud to be the President who witnesses the apparent completion of its improvement, I have the belief that some day new inventions and new pressures of population will require its further development."[32] He was right about the unrelenting pressures. Before long the original fifty-one dams were replaced by nineteen new ones, each fitted with locks and steel doors for opening and shutting the river. It is easy to forget this when you sit on the bank and watch the splayed roots of a tree creep by, or when you drift downstream in a skiff, but the Ohio has become, in fact, a chain of lakes, a grand canal for barges. I could quote you figures about tonnage shipped (more passes along the Ohio than through the Suez or Panama Canals) until your eyes glazed over; but my point is about the drive to "improve" the river. Most picture-books about the Ohio feature human works—dams and locks, boats and barges, highways and railroads, power plants, canals, levees, bridges, docks.

With rare exceptions, those who have left us records of their thinking about the Ohio and its valley have seen it as the raw material for human shaping, as if the landscape did not truly exist until we came along to transform it. I give three examples from hundreds that might serve. First, a tourist in 1803:

> When we see the forest cleared of those enormous trees . . . we cannot help dwelling upon the industry and art of man, which by dint of toil and perseverance can change the desert into a fruitful field . . . when the silence of nature is succeeded by the buzz of employment, the congratulations of society, and the voice of joy.[33]

Next, a minister in 1849 celebrating the newfangled train that hugged the shore:

> What music for the forest is a railroad train! . . . We dashed along through these forest scenes . . . intent only upon our mission of progress, though it should oblige us to cut down all the trees in the universe, disturb the repose of nature in her lair, and quench the lights of heaven by the smoke of our civilizing chimneys.[34]

Last, a Kentucky Congressman speaking in 1900:

> And I tell you that I am neither a prophet nor the son of a prophet, but one of the results of this movement of river improvement will be that along the valley of the Ohio, God's Eden restored, will spring up on this great canal when it is completed, as it will be completed, the peer of any city in this or any other country on the reeling earth.[35]

One is left reeling along with the earth after plowing through such booster rhetoric. Dizzying as it may be, it goes to the heart of our relationship with the river, and with the entire continent. It is a relationship founded on *use* and *possession*. The wild valley was a "desert" awaiting our activity, a silence awaiting our noise, a botched attempt at Eden that we in our wisdom would perfect.

While engineers saw the Ohio as a problem in plumbing, and explorers and merchants saw it as a highway to somewhere else, and politicians saw it as an avenue for power, and speculators saw it as an investment, there have always been others who looked at the river and found that most intangible of commodities, fine scenery. Mapping the river in 1766, Thomas Hutchins admired how "The stillness of the current and a calm sunshine put a Trace on the Water, from which was reflected the most beautiful objects of simple nature, that I ever beheld." In his *Notes on the State of Virginia* (1784–85), Thomas Jefferson declared that "The *Ohio* is the most beautiful river on earth." The author of *The Navigator* outdid even that tribute by describing the Ohio as "beyond all competition, the most beautiful river in the universe." Many others have echoed these sentiments. In fact, when you scan the volumes of purple prose, it seems that every traveler who could wield a pen must have written impressions of the Ohio.[36]

Early European visitors generally praised the scenery while regretting that much of the valley was still so wild. Thus the Englishwoman Frances Trollope in 1832: "Often a mountain torrent comes pouring its silver tribute to the stream, and were there occasionally a ruined abbey, or a feudal castle, to mix the romance of real life with that of nature, the Ohio would be perfect."[37] Now as it happens, mountain torrents are as scarce on the Ohio as feudal castles; yet no literary river could do without them, so Mrs. Trollope put them in. Her hasty gaze is less disturbing than her assumption that the life of nature is false, and only human life is "real." Dickens, the first great urban writer in our language, was uneasy in this raw country:

> For miles, and miles, and miles, these solitudes are unbroken by any sign of human life or trace of human footstep; nor is anything seen to move about them but the blue jay, whose color is so bright, and yet so delicate, that it looks like a flying flower. At lengthened intervals a log-cabin, with its little space of cleared land about it, nestles under a rising ground, and sends its thread of blue smoke curling up into the sky.[38]

Here is a German visitor writing in 1852 (in syntax more twisted than the river):

> If someday the forest primeval which now crowds and shades it is cleared a bit more, if its hills are crowned with country homes, if its bush-covered islands are adorned by little white cabins, and if its side valleys are cleared for views into the distance—then . . . a

total impression will be formed in the mind of the observer that will be inferior to that of our Rhine only because it lacks memories of historical significance.[39]

Like the minister willing "to cut down all the trees in the universe" to make way for our "mission of progress," many visitors seemed eager to clear the shores. George Washington complained that "the sides of the river were a good deal incommoded with old trees, which impeded our passage." Frances Trollope, as usual, minced no words: "I never found the slightest beauty in the forest scenery. Fallen trees in every possible stage of decay, and congeries of leaves that have been rotting since the flood, cover the ground and infect the air."[40]

Even American travelers, who often praised the very wildness that troubled Europeans, could not look at the river for long without celebrating what humans had made of it. Thus Charles Fenno Hoffman, a New Yorker, wrote in 1835 that one's "first view of the lovely river of the west is worth a journey of a thousand miles," but quickly added a tribute to the "deeds done upon its banks—the wild incidents and savage encounters of border story." Hoffman tempered his admiration for the scenery with a regret that there was so much of it:

> The windings of the river present, at every turn, some of the most beautiful views in the world; but the regular alternations of "bluff" and "bottom" give such a sameness to the landscape, that unless familiar with the points of the country around, one might be dropped in a dozen different places along the river, and not be aware of a change in his situation. Nature seems to have delighted in repeating again and again the same lovely forms, which she first moulded in this favourite region.[41]

And Walt Whitman, an enthusiast who was disappointed by very few features of the American landscape, found the Ohio less beautiful than its reputation:

> Like as in many other matters, people who travel on the Ohio, (that most beautiful of words!) for the first time, will stand a chance of being somewhat disappointed. In poetry and romance, these rivers are talked of as though they were cleanly streams; but it is astonishing what a difference is made by the simple fact that they are always and altogether excessively muddy—mud, indeed, being the prevailing character both afloat and ashore.[42]

In our own time, the Ohio poet James Wright, who moved away from the river, kept returning there in imagination:

> Tossing aside the worry of the place,
> As someone threw an apple core across
> A wall I walked beside, I sought delight
> Pebble by pebble, song by song, and light
> By light, singly, among the river boats.
> Down to the river at the end I came.[43]

Another modern celebrant who never tired of the river, mud and pollution and floods and all, was Harlan Hubbard. He and his wife, Anna, lived on the Ohio for decades, first on a shantyboat and then in a cove on the Kentucky shore, just downriver from Madison, Indiana. Hubbard painted the Ohio in watercolor and oil, wrote of it in journals, and chronicled his river way of life in two eloquent books, *Shantyboat* and *Payne Hollow*. In the latter book he declared his purpose:

> To achieve more perfect harmony with the river and at the same time to live close to the earth and free from entanglement with this modern urban world, I became a shantyboater. Although this was a natural consequence, it came about surprisingly late in my life. I was old enough to be called middle-aged before I ceased being a dilettante and took to the river in earnest.[44]

Taking to the river became for him a spiritual discipline as well as a right way of living. Thus, rowing out in his johnboat after midnight to set trot-lines, he caught more than fish:

> I felt I was fishing with the One who made the river and set it flowing. I felt its length and sinuous curving, fed by swift streams in the wooded mountains, and somewhere, after a long course through country unknown to me except by hearsay, past the mouths of new rivers and strange towns, it would at last enter an ocean and lose its identity, as I would, too, at the end of my devious drifting.[45]

Like his master Thoreau, Harlan Hubbard traveled extensively in his own territory, all senses alert, a witness to nature and to his own responsive moods.

Although the history of our dealings with the Ohio has been, for the most part, one long saga of "improvement," not everyone has felt easy about the triumph of human will over the river. Here for example is Audubon, writing in the 1830s about his impressions from a quarter of a century earlier:

> When I . . . call back to my mind the grandeur and beauty of those almost uninhabited shores; when I picture to myself the

> dense and lofty summits of the forests, that everywhere spread along the hills and overhung the margins of the stream, unmolested by the axe of the settler; . . . when I see that no longer any aborigines are to be found there, and that the vast herds of Elk, Deer, and Buffaloes which once pastured on these hills, and in these valleys, making for themselves great roads to the several salt-springs, have ceased to exist; when I reflect that all this grand portion of our Union, instead of being in a state of nature, is now more or less covered with villages, farms, and towns, . . . I pause, wonder, and although I know all to be fact, can scarcely believe its reality.

"Whether these changes are for the better or for the worse," Audubon mused, "I shall not pretend to say."[46]

No one can escape this doubleness of vision. The river we see today is in part the offspring of a glacier and of a million rains, in part our own creation. I feel closest to the primordial river at dawn or dusk, when twilight erases our handiwork, or in fog, when the hills wear white rags and the water slides by, arriving from a mystery and vanishing into a fullness and confusion of light.

I still try to dig down through all our inherited images of the Ohio—as real estate, as highway, as plumbing, as scenery—to the river-in-itself. Thinking of the Mississippi that surges past his native St. Louis, but speaking a truth about all great rivers, T. S. Eliot wrote in *Four Quartets*:

> I do not know much about gods; but I think that the river
> Is a strong brown god—sullen, untamed and intractable,
> Patient to some degree, at first recognised as a frontier;
> Useful, untrustworthy, as a conveyor of commerce;
> Then only a problem confronting the builder of bridges.
> The problem once solved, the brown god is almost forgotten
> By the dwellers in cities—ever, however, implacable,
> Keeping his seasons and rages, destroyer, reminder
> Of what men choose to forget.[47]

"The river is within us," Eliot adds a few lines later, "the sea is all about us." The Ohio can still speak to us of the holy, the non-human, as it spoke to the Mound Builders a millennium ago. What I feel when I ride on the water in a canoe or sit on the bank with my bare feet dangling, and I forget the dams, and I put the human buzz of barges and trucks and trains out of mind, is that the force driving the river also drives me. I do not mean simply gravity, but the whole thrust of the world that heaves us into existence and then draws us back to the source.

The river's movement is an outward show of the current that bears everything along. Wearing a groove in the earth, it reveals the grain of the universe. Herman Melville's narrator in *Moby Dick*, no doubt speaking for the sea-loving author himself, proposes an experiment: "Let the most absent-minded of men be plunged in his deepest reveries—stand that man on his legs, set his feet a-going, and he will infallibly lead you to water, if water there be in all that region." Why this attraction to water? Because, Melville explained, oceans and rivers are "the image of the ungraspable phantom of life; and this is the key to it all."[48] Quick or sluggish, all creation is a flow—rivers, mountains, trees, rocks, clouds, sun, Milky Way, each part driven at its own pace but all parts caught in the single current. When I look in the mirror each morning the face I see is familiar from the day before, yet subtly changed, shifted downstream, as the river sliding within its banks alters moment by moment.

Water is the medium of life. We are made of it, mostly. Our cells are tiny seas. Anyone who has held in the hand a freshly caught fish can see this streamlined shape as a bit of water with a temporary skin around it. So are we all. Near the river, you are reminded that water is the fundamental element on the surface of our planet; land is a latecomer, and everywhere vulnerable. The mountains are hustling, grain by grain, toward the oceans. Near the river, you see water in its metamorphoses: as liquid, as fog and steam, as ice and snow, the endless cycling of stuff through its many forms. Near the river you are never far from an awareness of time, vast and moody and inhuman. Is time an arrow or a loop? The river dissolves that puzzle, for it is both arrow and loop, a current that moves in a circle, from hills to sea and back through snow and rain to hills, and so on down again to the sea. Perhaps our lives are segments in such a larger circle. Just as we are born from a sack of waters, so, in our stories, we cross a river—Lethe, Styx, Jordan—after death.

The Ohio carries for me the lights of the sky and the colors of the shore. It is the marriage of earth and air. Even in its chastened, diminished state, it holds out the promise of abundance, cleansing, and renewal. In fall, the maples along the banks still light their torches. In spring, the new leaves flare like struck matches. Viewed in the long perspective of ecology or in the briefer perspective of the merely human future, issues of ownership and profit seem trivial. What matters is the durability of land and water, how they bear up under our use. President Hoover, in his speech celebrating the completion of the slackwater dams, made a high-sounding but optimistic claim about our relations with the Ohio: "It is the river that is permanent; it is one of God's gifts to man, and with each succeeding generation we will advance in our appreciation and our use of it. And with each generation it will grow in the history and tradition of our Nation."[49] We have not yet lived up to that promise of ever-increasing wisdom in our use of the river; but we might. We should.

If Audubon were to come back and have a look at the Ohio today, he might be able to make up his mind whether our tinkering with the river has been for the better or the worse. Without wanting to undo all of our work, I would relish a bit more wildness. Now that the river banks have been cleared, I would trade a thousand acres of parking lots for a single acre of "forest primeval," with cane growing thicker than teeth on the river's edge, grape vines snarling the treetops a hundred feet in the air, larkspur bristling purple among the roots, brilliant green parakeets in the limbs, flocks of pigeons spiraling down to roost, bears pawing the rotten logs for grubs, and sycamores fatter than silos. I have nothing against hogs, but I would swap a herd of them for a single unpastured bison, would swap a train load for a woolly mammoth. And since I don't ship coal or sail a yacht, I would be glad to do without the dams; failing that, I would be satisfied if the engineers were to open the gates once a month or so and let the river flow.

Riverness—the appeal of a river, the way it speaks to us—has to do with our craving for a sense of direction within the seeming randomness of the world. Narrative offers us the same pleasure, a shape and direction imposed on time. And so we tell stories and listen to them as we listen to the coursing of water.

One night I was telling my children stories about the Ohio. We were in Cincinnati's riverfront park, sitting on the curved, stairstepped levee they call the serpentine wall. It is the right shape for the river, the shape of the snaky brown god. I am glad the wall is there, a wise and handsome creation, a sign of what we can do when we have our wits about us. Tires whined overhead on the meshwork of a bridge, the same one from which, as a boy of five, I had first glimpsed the Ohio. Behind us, kids waded squealing in fountains and in front of us a dozen roaring boats crisscrossed the river. My children had heard the stories before, but they indulged me by pretending every word was news. I told them how the tusks of mammoths discovered at Big Bone Lick were ground up to make fertilizer. I told them about river catfish weighing more than the anglers who caught them, about hollow sycamores large enough to shelter families, about floods that lifted cows through the second-story windows of a Louisville hotel. I told them how, in the days before sonar and radar, travelers estimated their distance from shore in darkness or fog by heaving stones and listening for the splash or thud. I told them how the northern shore, the very shore on which we sat, had been known for a century as the Indian side, and how slaves crossed the river by night on their way to freedom, and how steamships raced with their safety valves tied down, and how pirates infested the cliffs in Illinois, and how in spring the thawing ice grumbled like cannon fire. I rattled on, because I wanted my children to grow up carrying the Ohio in their minds.

Then after a while I realized that, like the tourists and speculators, I was not speaking of the river but of us two-legged wonders. So I shut up. And as the darkness thickened, traffic thinned on the bridge. Boats put in for shore. The fountains stopped sputtering and the waders went home. Eventually there came a moment when the only sound was the shudder of the great muscular dragon body slithering in its bed. And that was the truest speech about the river.

NOTES

1. Conrad Hilberry, "Rivers," *Rust* (Athens: Ohio University Press, 1974), 59.
2. Mark Twain, *Life on the Mississippi* [1883], in Guy Cardwell, ed., *Mississippi Writings* (New York: Library of America, 1982), 245.
3. Zadok Cramer, *The Navigator*, 8th ed. (Pittsburgh: Cramer, Spear and Eichbaum, 1814; reprint: Readex Microprint, 1966), 246.
4. Thomas Hutchins, "*Journal from Fort Pitt to the Mouth of the Ohio in the Year 1766*," in Don Wallis, ed., *Oyo: An Ohio River Anthology* (Yellow Springs, Ohio: OYO Press, 1988), II, 22.
5. Quoted in Joseph Kastner, *A Species of Eternity* (New York: E. P. Dutton, 1978), 177.
6. Charles Dickens, *American Notes for General Circulation* [1842] (Gloucester, Mass.: Peter Smith, 1968), 191–93.
7. Richard E. Banta, *The Ohio* (New York: Rinehart, 1949), 266–67.

8. Francis Parkman, *France and England in North America* [1851–1892] (New York: Library of America, 1983), II, 875.

9. Parkman, II, 874.

10. Christopher Gist, "Colonel Christopher Gist's Journal," in *First Explorations of Kentucky*, ed. J. Stoddard Johnston, Filson Club Publications No. 13 (Louisville: Morton, 1898), 133.

11. George Washington, "Washington's Tour to the Ohio," *Old South Leaflets*, No. 41 (1893), 12.

12. Washington, 1–12.

13. Benjamin F. Klein, ed., *The Ohio River Handbook and Picture Album* (Cincinnati: Young and Klein, 1969), 67.

14. Manasseh Cutler, "Description of Ohio" [1787], *Old South Leaflets*, No. 40 (1892), 10–11.

15. George Croghan, *A Selection of Letters and Journals Relating to Tours into the Western Country* [1750–1765], in Reuben Gold Thwaites, ed., *Early Western Travels 1748–1846* (Cleveland: Clark, 1904), I, 131–32. John James Audubon, "The Ohio," in Maria Audubon, ed., *Audubon and His Journals* (New York: Scribner's, 1897), II, 205–206.

16. John Woods, *Two Years' Residence on the English Prairie of Illinois* [1822], ed. Paul M. Angle (Chicago: Lakeside Press, 1968), 93.

17. Audubon, "Fishing in the Ohio," in Maria Audubon, ed., *Audubon and His Journals* (New York: Scribner's, 1897), II, 215.

18. Cramer, 30; Hutchins, 21; Archer Butler Hulbert, *The Ohio River: A Course of Empire* (New York: Putnam's, 1906), 98.

19. Kastner, 177.

20. Kastner, 246.

21. Donald E. Pitzer, "The Original Boatload of Knowledge," *Ohio Journal of Science*, Vol. 89, No. 5 (December 1989), 128–42.

22. Robert Dale Owen, *To Holland and New Harmony: Robert Dale Owen's Travel Journal, 1825–1826*, ed. Josephine M. Elliott (Indianapolis: Indiana Historical Society, 1969), 255.

23. Owen, 242.

24. Parkman, II, 1073–74.

25. Banta, 266–67.

26. John James Audubon, "Passenger Pigeon," in *Audubon Reader*, ed. Scott Russell Sanders (Bloomington: Indiana University Press, 1986), 116–23.

27. Audubon, "Passenger Pigeon," 121.

28. Cramer, 127.

29. Aldo Leopold, *A Sand County Almanac and Sketches Here and There* [1949] (New York: Oxford University Press, 1987), 205.

30. James Wright, *Collected Poems* (Middletown, Conn.: Wesleyan University Press, 1972), 156.

31. Cramer, 75–76.

32. Klein, 373.

33. Thaddeus Harris, *Journal of a Tour into the Territory Northwest of the Alleghany Mountains; Made in the Spring of the Year 1803* (Boston: Manning and Loring, 1805), 51.

34. James Dixon, *Methodism in America* (London: Printed for the Author, 1849), 104.

35. Hulbert, 359.

36. Hutchins, 21; Thomas Jefferson, *Notes on the State of Virginia* [1784–5], ed. Thomas Perkins Abernethy (New York: Harper and Row, 1964), 8; Cramer, 24.

37. Frances Trollope, *Domestic Manners of the Americans* [1832] (New York: Dodd, Mead, 1901), I, 46.

38. Dickens, 185.

39. Moritz Busch, *Travels between the Hudson and the Mississippi, 1851–1852*, trans. and ed. Norman H. Binger (Lexington: University Press of Kentucky, 1971), 206.

40. Washington, 8; Trollope, I, 59.

41. Charles Fenno Hoffman, *A Winter in the West*. 2 vols. (New York: Harper and Brothers, 1835), I, 49–50, 57.

42. Walt Whitman, *The Uncollected Poetry and Prose of Walt Whitman*, 2 vols., ed. Emory Holloway (Garden City, N.Y.: Doubleday, 1921), I, 187.

43. Wright, 38.

44. Harlan Hubbard, *Payne Hollow* (Frankfort, Ky.: Gnomon Press, 1974), 34.

45. Harlan Hubbard, *Shantyboat: A River Way of Life* (Lexington: University Press of Kentucky, 1977), 74.

46. Audubon, "The Ohio," 206–207.

47. T. S. Eliot, *Four Quartets* [1943]. *The Complete Poems and Plays* (New York: Harcourt, Brace and World, 1952), 130.

48. Herman Melville, *Moby Dick* [1851], ed. Harrison Hayford and Hershel Parker, (New York: Norton, 1967), 13, 14.

49. Klein, 373.

John A. Jakle

THE OHIO VALLEY REVISITED: IMAGES FROM NICHOLAS CRESSWELL AND REUBEN GOLD THWAITES

Once the Ohio was the great river highway to a developing American West and the Ohio Valley was a vital place much respected in the American lexicon of regions.[1] As first railroads, then highways and air transport, completed the nation's urban networks, other notions of region—of a Midwest and of an American South—came to the fore. The Ohio Valley remained in people's minds primarily as an economic backwater not really midwestern and not fully southern. By the mid-point of the twentieth century, most Ohio Valley people had become backward-looking in contemplating themselves and their region. They acquired a kind of rearview mirror vision which was at best nostalgic. Its golden age behind it, the Ohio Valley was a place seen dominated by decaying factories, abandoned mines, and crumbling main streets. The region's forests had been cut, its mountains despoiled by strip mining and other abuses, and its rolling hills exhausted by exploitative farming. The river itself flowed polluted toward the sea. The images that Americans attached to the river and to its region, to the extent that images attached at all, tended to the negative.

One would like to think that the Ohio Valley as a place is coming back into American consciousness in a more favorable light. Over past decades the nation has shifted from a substantially industrial economic base to one now characterized as postindustrial through emphasis on technical and service jobs. Heavily industrialized, the Ohio Valley once epitomized what critics labeled the "Rust Belt." But, as we end the twentieth century, much economic adjustment has been made. Towns and cities have been downsized and much of the old industry is gone. Marginal farmland has been abandoned to forest regrowth, and the arduous task of reclaiming stripped and other despoiled land begun. It is a region worth thinking about positively once again.

Herein I seek to discover some of the basic characteristics of the Ohio Valley past which today set a template for the region yet emergent. I use as my mechanism the comparison of two travel accounts: one written at the very threshold of the American period of trans-Appalachian settlement, the other well over a century later when the early promise of the new west had reached maturity. Nicholas Cresswell's 1774 impressions are more appropriately forward-looking to signs of a new era opening. Reuben Gold Thwaites's 1894 impressions are more appropriately retrospective, seeking to understand both opportunities fulfilled and opportunities lost. I contrast the two to ask: What was seen and otherwise experienced in the Ohio Valley in the past? What do the images and experiences portend for an understanding of change today? What did changing landscapes mean to people in the past? What might they mean to us as we look to our future?

In 1774 a young Englishman of good family and bright prospects left his family's estate in the Peak District of England's Midlands to seek his fortune in North America. Circumstances contrived that he should cross the Appalachians and descend the Ohio. Nicholas Cresswell was not the first traveler to write about the new western country, but for insightful description of people and place few early writers excelled him. I place his trip among the better western adventures of the time; if his journal is not the stuff of great literature, then it is surely a most intriguing read for the details offered. Cresswell saw a wild place barely domesticated by a thin aboriginal population. But he also sensed the future, for already developers had arrived to build an urban framework upon which a commercialized agrarianism would transform the region's forests and prairies.

In 1894 an American college professor left his home at Madison, Wisconsin, for a summer's adventure on the Ohio. Reuben Gold Thwaites, a historian at the University of Wisconsin, floated with his family and an accompanying friend down the river to capture retrospectively the conditions that Cresswell and other travelers of the eighteenth century had known. Thwaites's career would be built largely around his republishing of the Ohio Valley's early travel writers. And to that literature he added a very personal view configured through his own journal. Thwaites's river was highly industrialized, especially in its upper reaches. Although Thwaites could identify locations where significant events had occurred, little of earlier contexts survived. The Corps of Engineers was beginning to control the river's flow and the land was substantially domesticated. Long gone were the Indian villages and early frontier towns. As the twentieth century loomed, the Ohio Valley had reached a state of maturity, and in many places even old age. Cities were already decayed in older riverfront precincts where the infrastructures of commerce and industry had grown obsolete. Thwaites's river was a place very different from Cresswell's, being separated as it was by 120 years. To play the experiences of the two adventurers off against one another is to offer a study of change.

NICHOLAS CRESSWELL'S OHIO VALLEY

Twenty-four-year-old Nicholas Cresswell sailed from Liverpool in April of 1774, arriving at Urbanna on Virginia's Rappahannock River in May. Making use of letters of introduction, he visited numerous families in and around Alexandria looking for investment or business opportunities and generally savoring a strange new world. After a brief illness attributed to the local climate, he took ship for Barbados in hopes of regaining his strength at sea. Recovered and fully acclimatized, he was back at Alexandria in October to resume his wanderings. Cresswell was much reduced in means by now; in order to pay tavern and other bills he had begun to borrow against the anticipated receipt of money from home. Although worn and threadbare, his clothes still bespoke the young English gentleman as he circulated among the better classes. He reported in his journal very formal and highly appropriate relationships, especially with female acquaintances. In April 1775, one year after his departure from home, he determined to pay his debts and, indeed, assume full responsibility for his support by acting the field agent for a consortium of investors in a land transaction beyond the Appalachians. Cresswell, who studiously kept his diary day to day, would enter the Ohio Valley not just as an observer, but as an active participant in its development.

"Crossed the Savage Mountain and through the Shades of Death," Cresswell wrote. "This is one of the most dismal places I ever saw. The lofty Pines obscure the Sun, and the thick Laurels are like a Hedge on each side, the Road is very narrow and full of large stones and bogs."[2] Generally, Cresswell followed the trajectory of Braddock's Trace toward the Forks of the Ohio at Fort Pitt. Braddock's defeat, the opening round of the French and Indian War twenty years earlier, had been the worst single catastrophe the British army had yet sustained in the field. The site of the debacle would be a major attraction to British vistors in America well into the nineteenth century. But now a new war was looming in aftermath of the eventual British victory over France and the Treaty of Paris in 1763. Disaffection with the British Crown and Parliament had spread widely among Americans, especially those on the frontier. On reaching Pittsburgh, Cresswell presented himself to the commandant at the fort. "It is a pentagonal form. Three of the Bastions and two of the curtains faced with brick, the rest picketed. Barracks for a considerable number of men, and there is the remains of a genteel house for the Governor, but now in ruins, as well as the Gardens which are beautifully situated on the Banks of the Allegany well planted with Apple and Peach trees."[3] Although European occupation of the site was relatively recent, these ruins spoke of history. Cresswell found Pittsburgh to contain some thirty houses, their inhabitants engaged mainly in the

Indian trade. The town was already the gateway to the West, the principal route being downriver.

Cresswell retraced his steps to Crawford's Station, southeast of Pittsburgh, where canoes could be constructed and provisions obtained more cheaply. There he also engaged a frontiersman to partner the coming adventure into the back country. This man, it was intended, would take a share of the anticipated land purchased in exchange for guiding Cresswell and his retainers, and for overseeing the logistics of camp. Although Cresswell exchanged his gentleman's garb for attire more suitable to a backwoods sojourn, he still expected to play the gentleman by contracting the difficult work to others. Down the Youghiogheny River to the Monongahela and on to the Ohio at Fort Pitt the party went, using two canoes "30 foot long and about 20 inches wide, made of Walnut trees, dug out something like a manger." The going at first was rough, for even in the high water of April they were obliged to push their canoes over numerous shoals. "Walnut and Cherry trees grow to an amazing size. I have seen several three foot diameter and 40 foot before they come to a limb," he noted.[4] Coal and limestone outcrops were frequently encountered. Game abounded.

From Pittsburgh they descended to Logstown, a deserted Indian town of the late war where the Indian allies of the French had headquartered. The country was empty. "Very few inhabitants, not a house to be seen in 40 miles, tho' the land is exceedingly rich, in general."[5] The river meandered between the bluffs presenting potential town sites first on the left and then the right, but not until the party reached the small garrison at Wheeling was anything townlike encountered. At Wheeling, Cresswell combined his party with that of one Captain George Rogers Clark. A few years later, Clark would head Virginia's Kentucky militia in its successful confrontation with the British at Vincennes. His victory at Fort Sackville was critical to the United States' claim to the trans-Appalachian West after the Revolution. "Lashed our canoes together and drifted all night," he wrote. The party stopped to climb the large Indian mound at present day Moundsville, West Virginia. "The great Grave is a round hill something like a sugar loaf about 300 feet in circumference at bottom, 100 feet high and about 60 feet diameter at top where it forms a sort of irregular basin." Cresswell, like most of the other journalists to descend the river in the eighteenth and nineteenth centuries, dealt statistically with the landscape in a straightforward, utilitarian way by constantly noting the sizes and quantities of things. Only with difficulty did most travelers wax romantic. "All these Hills appear to have been made by human art," Cresswell labored, "but by whom, in what age, or for what use I leave it for more able antiquarians to determine." Although this was a "new" country, the mound at Grave Creek spoke of a mysterious, distant past.[6]

The flotilla passed the mouth of the Muskingum and then the mouth of the Little Kanawha where a party coming upriver gave "very bad encouragement" saying that "the Indians are broke out again and killed four men on the Kentucky River." Spirits began to drop with the adventure taking on a new and ominous dimension. Moving down to the mouth of the Kanawha River, they found Fort Blair, recently built and garrisoned by about one hundred men. Continuing, they reached the Guiandot and then the Sandy beyond which the lands adjacent to the river were still unclaimed. They were, in Cresswell's words, "out of the inhabitants." On May 16 they passed the Scioto River. "Stopped to cook our breakfast on a small gravelly Island where we found plenty of Turtle eggs," he noted. That night they dined, as they often did, on wild turkey and several nights later they shot a buffalo "certain he would have weighed a thousand" pounds. Deer, elk, and bear were frequently seen along the river's banks as they drifted downriver reaching the Little Miami and then the Miami. "Shot at a Panther this afternoon, but missed him. Hot weather with Thunder," he reported. The party attempted in vain to find the "Elephant Bonelick" where the bones of prehistoric creatures were said to be strewn about the ground.[7]

Nineteen days and some 600 miles from Pittsburgh, the group began their ascent of the Kentucky River very fearful of Indians; "it was determined to keep two men on each side of the River as scouts. Cresswell found it disagreeable clambering over gullies and wading amongst the weeds as high as my head." Flocks of parakeets brightened the Kentucky's banks. "Saw several roads that crossed the River which they tell me are made by the Buffaloes going from one lick to another," he noted. The bison had engineered their traces between principal salt springs following the ridge lines and using the creeks that cut the steep bluffs of the Kentucky gorge. The group found that camping at such places facilitated movement inland away from the river. But a stampeding herd of bison could crash a camp carelessly placed in its path, and so it was that Cresswell's party lost the canoe containing most of the flour and other provisions. With rations drastically reduced the company began to eat buffalo meat regularly, and to quarrel. "Caught a large Catfish which measured six inches between the eyes. We supposed it would weigh 40 pounds," he wrote.[8]

They reconnoitered the territory with the intention of locating land claims. But over the ensuing days, as the Indian menace loomed larger than ever, numerous canoes came down the Kentucky bound for points east. A log crib was found stocked with corn and containing clothes and a gun left by people fleeing. When an indentured servant escaped taking the remaining provisions, dissension in the group climaxed. The end had come. Cresswell, for his part, threw in with a new group organizing to return. The Kentucky country, he convinced himself, was "badly watered and light timbered." He saw Kentucky as an infertile place. An infected foot added to his sense of misery, although by tone his journal keeps positive stride. But conditions had become most primitive and the level of discomfort great. "I believe there is but two pair of Breeches in the company, one belonging to Mr. Tilling and the other to myself. The rest wear breechclouts, leggings and hunting shirts, which have never been washed only by the rain since they were made."[9] Nicholas Cresswell missed the creature comforts of gentlemanly life.

But Cresswell remained ever-observant. He described the salt making experiments conducted at several of the salt licks or springs. He gave more vivid descriptions of the bison. At "Grinin's Lick" he wrote: "This is the largest Lick I ever saw. I suppose here is 50 acres of land trodden by Buffaloes, but there is not a blade of grass upon it. Incredible numbers come here to the Salt Springs." Earlier he and his companions had fired indiscriminantly into a herd of several hundred bison before they fled bellowing into the forest. At the lick, Cresswell bought a buckskin from which to fashion new breeches.[10]

Once the Ohio River was reached Cresswell's group, now consisting of "two Englishmen, two Irishmen, one Welshman, two Dutchmen [Germans], two Virginians, two Marylanders, one Swede, one African Negro, and a Mulatto," found the going difficult. His cryptic diary entry states: "Obliged to pole up the River. This is done with poles about 12 feet long, the men stand in the vessel, set the pole against the bottom of the River, and push themselves along. It is a laborious exercise." Again Cresswell's group sought and this time located the Big Bone

Lick where they camped for several days. "Found several bones of a prodigious size, I take them to be Elephants, for we found a part of a tusk, about two foot long, Ivory to all appearance. . . . All of us stripped and went into the pond to grabble for teeth and found several." It was at Big Bone Lick that the soles came off his shoes and Cresswell was forced to proceed barefoot.[11]

On June 20 the party encountered four Indian canoes. They prepared for battle expecting the worst, since only two of their twelve guns were fit for firing. "Tom O'Brien in the scuffle let his [gun] fall in the River and got her filled with water. He laid down in the bottom of the Canoe, begun to tell his beads and prayed and howled in Irish." But the Indians were friendly Delawares and, instead of fighting, trade ensued. At the mouth of the Kanawha members of Cresswell's second party also began to desert in order to trek overland to the "settlements." Morale was very low once again. He wrote: "Our provisions almost done, all our hooks and lines broken, all our feet so tender by standing continually wet that it is impossible for us to hunt, and the small quantity of provision we have is swarming with maggots."[12]

On July 11 Cresswell reached Wheeling and, himself, left the river walking east toward the Upper Monongahela Valley and Crawford's Station where his original clothes had been left. But he was not to resume a gentleman's guise. "These rascals," he wrote "have wore out all the clothes I left here, so that I am now reduced to three ragged shirts, two pair linen breeches in the same condition, a hunting shirt and jacket, with one pair of stockings." But Cresswell's indifferent dress, his whiskered and sunbaked features, and his changed demeanor fit him more successfully into frontier society. No longer the effete Englishman in appearance, he had found himself developing new sorts of relationships across a wide spectrum of people. "Last night Miss G. came. A fine blooming Irish Girl," he wrote. "The Flesh overcame the Spirit." However, Cresswell's decrepit appearance and shabby dress also alienated him from those who might have relieved his financial distress. Merchants refused to extend him credit or to honor drafts drawn on friends in the East.[13]

That clothes make the man is certainly a cliché, but an important one for understanding how the American frontier worked as social setting. Americans, generally lacking titles, used dress and demeanor as evidence of social worth. Clothes were important messages that said what an individual could do. Then as now, America was substantially a materialistic society, and, accordingly, what a person could do mattered much. When at long last Cresswell found employment it was as a trader to the Ohio Indians requiring him once more to leave settled country. "Mr. Anderson informs me that the Indians are not well pleased at anyone going into their Country dressed in a Hunting shirt. Got a Calico shirt made in the Indian fashion, trimmed up with Silver Brooches and Armplates so that I scarcely know myself."[14] This time Cresswell traveled by horse, helping to tend a string of pack animals. His group moved between Indian encampments toward the more permanent Indian towns along the Muskingum and Tuscawara Rivers in present day eastern Ohio. At New Schonbrunn, one of the Delaware Indian towns founded by Moravian missionaries, he found some sixty houses built of logs and covered with clapboards, the whole assemblage oriented to straight streets dominated by a large log meeting house. But most of the Indian settlements were eclectic assortments of crude log cabins, lean-tos, and wigwams. Cresswell emphasized the Moravian towns for their uniqueness, and the surprise of their civility. Also, they symbolized a new order emergent. Indians were coming increasingly under the influences of a commercial economy fostered by the fur trade.

Several Indian women had contracted to accompany the group, one teenaged girl attaching herself especially to Cresswell. "Squaws are very necessary," he wrote, "fetching our horses to the Camp and saddling them, making our fire at night and cooking our victuals, and every other thing they think will please us." Through Nancy, his companion, he was able to observe more closely the Indian's way of life. "Painted by my Squaw in the most elegant manner. Divested of all my clothes, except my Calico short breechclout, leggings, and Mockesons. A fire was made which we danced round with little order, whooping and hallooing in a most frightful manner."[15] He was but a novice at the diversion, but by endeavoring to act as his hosts did, he made for them considerable sport, thus ingratiating himself. On September 26, 1775, Cresswell was invited to attend an Indian council fire where chiefs of various Delaware, Shawnee, and other tribes met. War was brewing as rumors spread daily concerning open hostilities between American and the British forces around Boston.

In October, Cresswell returned to Pittsburgh, where he paid

off his debts, settled his accounts with his employer, and made his way quickly back to Alexandria. He would never return to the Ohio Valley. From Virginia he had hoped to sail home but found himself delayed with settling the affairs of the intended land speculation to which he had been party. Then the American Revolution began. Virginia was in political turmoil with a new state government replacing colonial authority. Always an outspoken royalist, Cresswell was accused of spying and came close to being jailed. Off he went to Philadelphia in August of 1776, hoping that Thomas Jefferson and other members of the Continental Congress would help him to leave. It would be July 1777 before he would take ship at New York, a city then under the control of British forces.

Nicholas Cresswell's recorded adventures illuminate the Ohio Valley at a critical time of transition. The region stood on the threshold of a new era indeed. A wilderness, so perceived by Europeans and Americans alike, was giving way to a new pastoral order symbolized by frontier stations and budding towns, and the quest for new farms had already taken settlers to the rich limestone soils of Kentucky. The Ohio Valley was rapidly emerging from its condition of assumed savagery toward one of civilization as was evident among the Indians of the Muskingum and the Tuscarawas. Unfortunately, the Revolutionary War in the West, which pitted the majority of the Indians as allies of the British against the Americans, would thwart that progress. The Moravian towns, for example, were destroyed. Conflict with the Indians would continue through the 1790s as the confederated tribes sought variously to establish the Ohio River as the frontier of white settlement. Indian war would loom in 1812, aided and abetted by the British once again. The result would be an end to the Indian presence in the Ohio Valley, save for a few very small remnant bands confined to reservations. The Ohio Valley would become an agrarian garden, but one tended exclusively by settlers largely European bred. To the south of the great river, where slavery flourished, a substantial African influence would be felt.

If Cresswell witnessed the shadowy beginnings of a new agrarian order, he saw more vividly the urban base upon which agriculture would thrive. Pittsburgh, by its situation, was destined to be a city, the region's lines of commerce already focusing there. Furs flowed east from Indian villages which themselves were town-like in function if not appearance. It would be the towns and cities that would outfit the migrants moving west by river or overland by trail and later by road. It would be in these same towns and cities that farm products would be marketed. Cresswell could not see the day when urban places would be linked by steamboat, canal, and railroad. But he did appreciate the power of the great river as economic integrator. To the Ohio and its major tributaries most of the region's major cities would be tied.

REUBEN GOLD THWAITES'S OHIO VALLEY

If Cresswell's view was primarily forward-looking at the start of a critical regional transition from wilderness to garden, then Reuben Gold Thwaites's view was primarily backward-looking in the thralls of still another unfolding era: that of burgeoning industrialism. In approximately a century, the Ohio Valley saw transition from pioneer farming in forest clearings dotted with log cabins to sophisticated commerce and manufacture in huge warehouses and factories. The Ohio River saw canoes and flatboats replaced by steamboats and then railroads whose tracks paralleled the river and leaped across its flood at intervals on bridges. The machine, indeed, had come to the garden, the agrarian and industrial impulses in the landscape standing often in awkward juxtaposition. If Cresswell could celebrate a future, then Thwaites could celebrate a past. When one was on the threshold of a new twentieth century, the changes that had come to the Ohio Valley over a relatively few generations seemed epic.

Thwaites's purpose in travel was the gathering of "local color" to inform his unfolding scholarship as a historian. He wrote: "The Ohio River was an important factor in the development of the West. I wished to know the great waterway intimately in its various phases,—to see with my own eyes what the borderers saw; in imagination, to redress the pioneer stage, and repeople it." His journal, published as *Afloat on the Ohio*, was dedicated to Frederick Jackson Turner, a colleague at Wisconsin.[16] Turner's just-published paper on the closing of the American frontier would excite a substantial following and influence the writing of American history for generations. American culture, society, and especially its body politic were seen to be molded through confrontation with wilderness isolation. Settlers were thrown on their own resources on the frontier.

The converting of the wilderness into a garden was seen by Turner as the formative impulse behind the distinctly American characteristics of independence and self-reliance. The 1890 Census suggested to Turner that the frontier had closed. What would happen to an American nation deprived of its formative frontier influences?

Thwaites's diary, written in a lucid style, clearly reflected the maturity that the Ohio Valley had achieved by the nineteenth century's closing. Whereas Cresswell exchanged travel companions frequently (and could not keep a partner and employees in company), Thwaites's party was of the most stable order. Traveling with him were his wife, their ten-year-old son, and a close friend, a medical doctor also from Madison. Their craft, a small fifteen-foot square sterned skiff, was shipped by railroad and arrived from Wisconsin by boxcar. The trip began on May 4, 1894, on the Monongahela near Charleroi, not far from Crawford's Station where much of Cresswell's activity had centered. They floated down to the site of Redstone Fort (the first Virginia settlement west of the mountains) thinking invigorating thoughts of frontier times. There Brownsville had grown, a grimy industrial place with belching smoke stacks. Immediately a romantic past came abruptly into juxtaposition with a utilitarian present; it would be a thousand-mile struggle to relate and reconcile the two. "To the student of Western history, Brownsville will always be a shrine—albeit a smoky, dusty shrine, with the smell of lubricators and the clang of hammers, and much talk thereabout of the glories of Mammon."[17]

Rarely were they out of range of a coal mine, foundry, or other industrial fixture, either active or abandoned. Workers' cottages, either unpainted or covered by the rust red used on barns and railroad bridges, clung to the valley wall at each coal tipple. Thwaites wrote: "Sometimes these huts, though in the mass dreary enough, are kept in neat repair; but often are they sadly out of elbows—pigs and children promiscuously at their doors, paneless sash stuffed with rags, unsightly litter strewn around, misery stamped on every feature of the homeless tenements."[18] Much of the promise of this western land so attractive to the pioneer-cum-developer already had dissolved in the face of mineral and other resource exhaustion. A mere century had left in many places a residual look of degradation.

Through the first of many navigation locks they made their way downriver. At McKeesport no camping place was to be found. "So far as we could see down the Monongahela, the air was thick with the smoke of glowing chimneys, and the pulsating whang of steel-making plants and rolling-mills made the air tremble." So up the Youghiogheny they rowed until a sylvan glade appeared. At Pittsburgh on a Sunday, with the lock closed, the men "shot" the dam while Mrs. Thwaites and the boy made their way with difficulty along a shore lined by docks and bordered by railroads. Then came the mighty Homestead Works where memories of the bloody strike of 1892 were fresh. But this day the river's shore was in a holiday mood: "nurses pushing baby carriages, self-absorbed lovers holding hands upon riverside benches, merry-makers rowing in skiffs or crossing the river in crowded ferries; the electric cars, following either side of the stream as far down as Pittsburg, crowded to suffocation with gayly-attired folk." Hundreds of steamboats lined the city's downtown waterfront. Elsewhere houseboats predominated and, tying up to one, Thwaites and his party left the river for a night's hotel stay. Here was a metropolis of some 600,000 people where 120 years earlier Cresswell found little more than a village.[19]

Of the Ohio below Pittsburgh, Thwaites wrote: "The railways upon either bank are built on neat terraces, and, far from marring the scene, agreeably give life to it; now and then, three such terraces are to be traced, one above the other, against the dark background of wood and field—the lower and upper devoted to rival railway lines, the central one to the common way."[20] The river towns greatly facilitated travel. The party carried little food, and, having little time for fishing and being little disposed to hunting, were dependent upon the grocery stores clustered around every landing. Towns focused on the river and the paralleling railroad. Not only could food be easily obtained, but also hotel rooms when inclement weather made camping less than practical. Down the river they went, Thwaites writing about locations significant in the past as well as describing landscapes encountered. Indeed, he was increasingly becoming absorbed in the then-contemporary scene. They floated past Ambridge, the site of Logstown and subsequently of Economy, the utopian community founded by the Harmonist Society. Strangely, Thwaites gave neither a mention.

The evidences of modern industry were no longer continuously in sight once they passed the Ohio boundary and East Liverpool. Stretches of greenery made the trip increasingly picturesque. "All about us lies a beautiful world of woodland," Thwaites wrote of their camp near New Cumberland on the

West Virginia bank. "The whistle of quails innumerable broke upon us in the twilight, succeeding to the calls of rose-breasted grosbeaks and a goodly company of daylight followers; in this darkening hour, the low, plaintive note of the whip-poor-will is heard on every hand, now and then interrupted by the hoarse bark of owls." It was the safe, gentle nature of songbirds, not the threatening, coarse nature of stampeding bison that Cresswell had known. It was the refined nature of the birdwatcher, not the Darwinian nature of the hunter and the hunted. Above all, a savage human enemy did not potentially lurk concealed along the river's bank. And everywhere wilder places merged with the garden. Thwaites continued: "There is a gentle tinkling of cowbells on the Ohio shore, and on both are human voices confused by distance."[21]

At intervals they were thrust back into urban worlds. At Steubenville and numerous other places sewer pipe and brick works, clay potteries, and iron and steel mills competed for riverfront supremacy. It was a highly degraded urban environment that came readily to view when such a place was approached from the river. Thwaites observed:

> But what interested us most of all was the appalling havoc which these clay and iron industries are making with the once beautiful banks of the river. Each of them has a large daily output of debris, which is dumped unmercifully upon the water's edge in heaps from fifty to a hundred feet high. Sometimes for nearly a mile in length, the natural bank is deep buried out of sight. . . . Fifty years hence, if these enterprises multiply at the present ratio, and continue their present methods, the Upper Ohio will roll between continuous banks of clay and iron offal, down to Wheeling and beyond.[22]

At Mingo Junction the party stopped to tour a steel works where the mill superintendent complained of the character of the work force which included many Hungarians, Serbs, and Croatians.

> They are willing to work for wages which from the American standard seem low, but to them almost fabulous; herd together in surprising promiscuity; maintain a low scale of clothing and diet, often to the ruin of health; and eventually return to Eastern Europe, where their savings constitute a little fortune upon which they can end their days in ease.

A very new world had matured on the Ohio, a world that Nicholas Cresswell certainly could not have guessed. It was a world where even Reuben Thwaites had difficulty, a world of an industrial America where exploited laborers were easily misunderstood. Thwaites, clearly reflecting his own status as an affluent, well-connected scholar enjoying the benefits of the upper middle class, wrote: "This sort of competition is fast degrading legitimate American labor. Its regulation ought not to be thought impossible."[23]

The Ohio River appeared to Thwaites little traveled. Although steamboats could be seen at many town landings, few were in commission and rarely did the party see more than two or three boats active in the course of a day. Railroads paralleled the river and it was from the freight and passenger trains that one obtained a sense of commercial movement. Thwaites mused: "The steamboat traffic may still further waste, until the river is no longer serviceable save as a continental drainage ditch; but, chiefly because of its railways, the Ohio Valley will continue to be the seat of an industrial population which shall wax fat upon the growth of the nation's needs."[24]

Down to Wheeling they floated. The city, seemingly anchored by its bridges, swept up the narrow terraces and lower bluff backed by "gaunt, treeless, gully washed hills of clay" which rose abruptly giving the place "a most forbidding appearance." Here again houseboats lined the waterfront: scows or "flats" of varying sizes upon which were built low-ceilinged cabins. There lived the families of fishermen, factory laborers, scavengers, drifters. It was not uncommon for families "to remain unmolested in one spot for years, with their pigs, chickens, and little garden patch about them, mayhap a swarm or two of bees, and a cow enjoying free pasturage along the weedy bank or on neighboring hills," Thwaites observed. At Wheeling, blacks in large numbers were seen along the riverbank for the first time.[25]

At Moundsville, the party located the great Indian mound down a "straggling street" in front of the big state penitentiary, "a solemn-looking pile of dark gray stone, with the feeble battlements and towers common to American prison architecture."[26] The mound was covered by a heavy growth of white oaks and had been penetrated by a vertical shaft and horizontal tunnel. Only recently the site had functioned as a beer garden, but was found by Thwaites to be a museum dedicated, it was claimed, to education.

Frequently the party stopped to converse with locals encountered along the river's banks. Mainly they were poor whites or "crackers" living on rented farms or squatting in houseboats—a kind of residual frontier flotsam that had been poorly absorbed into the evolving commercial economy. Poorly educated and impoverished, they still pursued a largely subsistence life based on barter just as in frontier times. And they were a provincial lot. "But I tell ye, sir, th' *I*talians and Hungarians is spoil'n' this yere country fur white men; 'n' I do'n' see no prospect for hits be'n' better till they get shoved out uv't!" one renter confided to Thwaites. This backwater culture was based on values counter to the work ethic thought to prevail in America. It was a life style based substantially on work avoidance. "This is clearly the lazy man's Paradise," Thwaites concluded. "I do not remember to have heard that the South Sea Islanders, in the ante-missionary days, had an easier time of it than this."[27]

Occasionally Thwaites sought to penetrate behind the scenes, to get inside cabins and other buildings seen otherwise only superficially in passing. By and large, most Americans expended little energy on overt public display. The country element along the river highly valued privacy. To enter a house was to see how people really lived. One opportunity came above Pomeroy on the Ohio shore as he ventured forth on one of his daily quests for fresh milk. "It was a large, square room, where I was so agreeably entertained," Thwaites wrote.

> The well-chinked logs are scrupulously whitewashed; the parental bed, with gay pillow shams, bought from a peddler, occupies one corner; a huge brick fireplace opens black and yawning, into the base of a great cobblestone chimney reared against the house without, after the fashion of the country; on pegs about, hang the best clothes of the family; while a sewing-machine, a deal table, a cheap little mirror, . . . a few unframed chromos, and a gaudy "Family Record" chart hung in an old looking-glass frame . . . complete the furnishings of the apartment.[28]

As the river's banks became less industrial and more pastoral, Thwaites's thoughts tended to focus back in time. He noted George Washington's travels on the river in search of land claims. On this stretch of river George Rogers Clark also was remembered, as were the flatboats that had been attacked and the would-be settlers to Kentucky who were carried off into Indian captivity. Thwaites had a copy of Samuel Cumings's *Western Pilot* and several diaries written by various early nineteenth century travelers on the river.[29] Passages would be read descriptive of the historical river and comparisons drawn. But Thwaites's eye always came back to the realities of the then-contemporary scene. It was as if the river would abide only short episodes of backward vision. At Sistersville in West Virginia the country was a "greasy neighborhood" of oil derricks, storage tanks, and refinery buildings. "An engine serves several wells,—the tumbling-rods, rudely boxed in, stretching off through the fields and over the hills to wherever needed," he noted. Before each well stood a standpipe, each with "a half bushel of natural-gas flame." Thwaites found it "a bewildering scene, with all these derricks thickly scattered around, engines noisily puffing, walking-beams forever rearing and plunging, the country cobwebbed with tumbling-rods and pipe lines, the shanties of the operatives . . . and the face of Nature so besmeared with the crude output of the wells that every twig and leaf is thick with grease."[30]

In the Long Reach below Sistersville the past intruded once again, not from the pages of a book but from a direct encounter with pastness in place. An inquiry for drinking water was made of two sisters at a dilapidated log house. The father allowed that he was "a pi'neer from way back." He owned his farm and farming was his life. But "jist yon ways," back of the house in the bluff face, there was a two-foot vein of coal, and he had struck a bank of fireclay that someday might be a "good thing for th' gals."[31] The smallest villages also spoke of the past with their handful of stores above the levee, the main streets filled with idlers who never seemed to have anything to do. At the mouth of the Muskingum at Marietta, Thwaites thought of the Moravian towns that once thrived to the north, Marietta itself seeming a bit like New England set down on the Ohio. Here the government of the Northwest Territory had been located through the 1790s, attracting Yankee traders and Yankee land speculators. Then down to Blennerhassett's Island near Belpre went the party, the place prominent in Aaron Burr's conspiracy of 1806–1807 to form in the West a new nation oriented to Spanish Louisiana.

The past was most easily recalled on the wilder stretches of the river which gave the sense of primeval nature. But these stretches were few and far between at mid-Valley, for nature long had been under assault. Terraces and bluff lines had been put to the plow, and industry had played the spoiler as it had upstream. The river had filled with silt from the fields and the refuse of the factories. A fisherman, some forty years on "this yere Ohio," called the fishing "never so poor." Thwaites wrote: "He thought the oil wells were tainting the water, and the fish wouldn't breed—and the iron slag, too, was spoiling the river, and he knew it."[32] Long gone were the days of large game animals. Vast quantities of driftwood in the river attested to an enormous waste of timber.

Thwaites and his party reached Point Pleasant at the mouth of the Kanawha and thought about the fort that had once stood there. Then down and over to Gallipolis where French Royalists had found themselves marooned, duped by promoters of the arborted Scioto Company land speculation. Then down past Huntington, Ashland, Ironton, Portsmouth, and then eventually Maysville, the jumping-off place for the interior of the Kentucky Blue Grass during the late eighteenth century. As they drifted on, evidences of Cincinnati began to accumulate along the river's banks. More and more of the hills were denuded of timber. Stone quarries and gravel pits grew in number. Farms were given more and more to market gardening, and farm houses were larger and more stylish. River traffic picked up. At length, a pall of coal smoke marked a final approach to the city. The shore downtown was lined with steamboats and the water offshore was crowded with craft large and small. Not wanting to risk trouble, Thwaites's skiff held to the quieter Kentucky shore off Newport and Covington and continued on its way leaving the city quickly behind. "Soon Cincinnati, shrouded in smoke, has disappeared around the bend, and we are in the fast-thinning suburbs—homes of beer-gardens and excursion barges, havens for freight-flats, and villas of low and high degree."[33]

Carefully they combed the Kentucky shore for Big Bone Creek, making frequent inquiries. Ascending the creek some two miles, they walked on, searching through the dense vegetation of former farm fields already reclaimed by forest. Finally a road was located, the people met in passing or dawdling on the porches of their cabins "yellow-skinned, hollow-cheeked folk, with lack-luster eyes." A strong sulfur odor announced the salt spring, but once located it presented nothing to see for their effort. Not only had the pioneer hunters come and gone, but so also had the collectors of fossils, the salt makers, and the operators of the spa that once promoted the briny water as healthful. Back on the river, they paddled down to Madison on the Indiana shore past Vevay, the once prosperous Swiss colony town. "The hills are steeper now . . . ; many of them, although stony, worked out, and almost worthless, are still, in patches, cultivated to the very top; but for the most part they are clothed in restful green."[34]

Unlike at Cincinnati, the Thwaites party did stop to tour Louisville, the third sizable river city encountered. But Thwaites's enthusiasm for the trip appeared to be waning: not because of any risky uncertainty (as had plagued Cresswell in Kentucky), but because of the monotony of repetition that had set in. The river's sights no longer brought the surprise of new discovery. The contemporary river held less and less mystery as geography. Once again, Thwaites's entries began to rely more on his sense of history and less on the contemporary scene. Although a day was spent in the city, Thwaites did not bother to describe any of the sites visited. Instead, he provided his readers with historical synopsis. Perhaps he was no longer keeping his diary so diligently. One senses that more and more of the text was written in the retrospection of a quiet Wisconsin study late in the summer when the diary was prepared for publication.

The contemporary landscape was emphasized only when novelities not yet described were encountered. And nothing was more novel than camping on Sand Island off Louisville under the great bridge.

> Far above our heads a great iron bridge crosses the Ohio . . . —a busy combination thoroughfare for steam and electric railways, for pedestrians and for vehicles. . . . The whirr of the trolley, the scream and rumble of locomotives, the rattle of wagons; and just above the island head, the burly roar of steamboats signalling the locks,—these are the sounds which are prevalent. Through all this hubbub, electric lamps are flashing, and just now a steamer's search-light swept our island shore, lingering for a moment upon the little camp.[35]

Below Louisville, towns were located primarily in the deep-cut notches in bluff lines where creeks reached the Ohio. Brandenburg on the Kentucky side was such a place: "sleepy, ill-paved, shambling."[36] Signs of human habitation were diminishing as the river and floodplain broadened. There were two lines of ever-separating willowed beach of sand or rock and, above the beaches, perpendicular walls of clay backed in the distance by wooded bluffs. Farm houses were now far afield and houseboats were seldom seen. A sense of isolation grew. Steamboats averaged only two or three per day. Ever the river's panorama opened before them revealing increasing rusticity.

At Cloverport, as at other towns, the river came temporarily back to life. At the wharfboat a steamer loaded, the black roustabouts "singing in a low pitch an old-time plantation melody" as they loaded on the freight. Below Troy the ranges of low hills disappeared leaving only the clay terraces near the river as backdrop. From here down to Cairo the view from the skiff was one of extreme sameness. The trip was now rapidly winding down. Owensboro offered some relief and Evansville "made a charming Turneresque study, as her steeples and factory chimneys developed through the mist." Then came Henderson, and thoughts of John James Audubon and his birds, and Mount Vernon with thoughts finally of the Harmonists (who had lived at nearby New Harmony before migrating back to Pennsylvania and Economy). Unimportant to Thwaites was Robert Owen, the Scottish industrialist and social reformer, who bought out the Harmonists' Indiana holdings to establish a short-lived utopian community of his own. Next came the mouth of the Wabash, low lying and without a town.[37]

They floated on to Shawneetown in Illinois and a remembrance of the salt making at nearby salines, the spires of churches and the tops of business buildings barely showing above the levee. At Cave-in-Rock, once the notorious haunt of river pirates, Thwaites noted river banks lined with cypress as well as giant sycamores, maples, and elms. Canebrakes too were prevalent. Since Louisville, railroads had been in little evidence and, accordingly, small steamboats were more frequently encountered. Finally, the mouth of the Cumberland was reached at Smithland and then the mouth of the Tennessee at Paducah. Passing Metropolis and the site of Fort Massac, Thwaites's thoughts settled again on George Rogers Clark, and the march made overland to Kaskaskia, Cahokia, and Vincennes. At long last, Thwaites and his party reached Cairo and the thousand-mile voyage was ended.

LESSONS FROM THE PAST

What should all of this mean to those of us interested in the Ohio Valley as a region? Certainly the two travelers, Cresswell and Thwaites, each from his own unique vantage point in time, experienced a place changing. Comparing their impressions gives us an outline view of that change. But we can also use their recorded impressions to sketch the nature of change itself. Indeed, Cresswell and Thwaites were, each in his own way, part of the process, especially Nicholas Cresswell who came as a land speculator turned Indian trader. But even Reuben Thwaites as a college professor turned tourist remotely impacted what the Ohio Valley was becoming through his writings.

Nicholas Cresswell was a part of, and therefore symbolic of, a long-ongoing process of Europeanization that by Thwaites's time had totally subdued North America. Europeans came to the continent to exploit its resources with dramatic repercussions for the native Indians. Whereas Indian society variously held the land and the other resources of the continent in common, the Europeans brought notions of private property keyed not to communal so much as to individual economic prerogatives. They made of nature commodities to be bought, sold, traded. The American Indian was incorporated into a vast commercial enterprise capitalized from and centered in Europe. Thus the New World was brought into a colonial relationship with the Old through the flow of such commodities as furs. Nicholas Cresswell came to participate as an agent of capital, first to speculate in land and then to engage in the exchange of furs.

Cresswell came as a mover and doer, a child of the empire. But the political climate was changing around him. England's overseas extension in North America, always solid economically, was strained politically. The Americans in their relative isolation (weeks by sea from the English seaports) had developed degrees of autonomy. Resentment of British authority had reached crisis proportions in Boston, Philadelphia, and other cities. Nowhere, however, was the sense of self-sufficiency more pronounced than on the frontier with its extreme isolation. Self-reliance and independence of action was necessitated in the back country. There a developed sense of individual self-worth was the very essence of survival. People judged others and were judged themselves on abilities demonstrated daily rather than on accidents of birth and upbringing alone. A new sense of personal destiny pervaded frontier ways where individuals seized opportunities and promoted self-interests relatively unfettered by community concerns. Cresswell felt more comfortable on the established seaboard, safer working in the old order of an America traditionally subservient to established British ways: an America always a colony. When the open hostilities of revolution put Britain and a new

United States at war, Cresswell's intentions focused immediately on a return to Derbyshire.

Cresswell was very uncomfortable, indeed, in the Ohio Valley. Undoubtedly the experience served him well later in life as a youthful adventure made increasingly golden in memory with each lapsing year. But only in Tidewater Virginia did he have America in stride. There society was stratified not unlike at home. He was secure using his letters of introduction to pass through the acquaintance and friendship nets of Virginia's well-to-do. In the Ohio Country, Cresswell's manners, and certainly his dress, initially set him apart from locals more suitably egalitarian in dress and behavior. Failed plans (failed partly for the insufficiency of plan and preparation and partly from bad luck) dramatically changed his circumstance, reducing him to poverty and throwing him totally onto the mercy of America's new democrats. He found himself not only in an alien physical environment of a wilderness country, but in an alien social environment of a crude frontier democracy. The lessons of altered demeanor were awkwardly but eventually learned, and a measured success obtained certainly in his sojourn as a trader.

Cresswell had come as a stranger to a new region and he had adapted to it in ways surprising even to himself. For example, had he not taken a temporary Indian wife? Such was the course for Indian girls among the region's tribes to contract seasonally with marriage partners. In the Indian world of domestic life, the female kept the camp, engaging in gathering and subsistence gardening, while the male was the hunter and protector. White traders were very attractive as partners for their ability to provide beyond the uncertainties of the hunt. Whites and Indians mingled freely beyond the more established American farming communities, at least during times of peace. Wilderness isolation invited symbiosis, for only in the freer atmosphere of the wild could whites get away fully from racial prejudice. That Cresswell chose the life of an English gentleman by returning to Edale insured that his diary would be elaborated in retrospection and finished in book form. However, it would be nearly a century and a half before the manuscript saw publication. The diary would be passed from generation to generation through the family until its contents loomed as simply too revealing of a lost era not to be published.

Cresswell's diary describes the beginnings of urbanization in the Ohio Valley. The river would serve as the main axis of regional development. Already Pittsburgh was established at the "forks" of the Monongahela and Allegheny Rivers as a jumping-off place for the West and principal actors in the drama of town planting were in the valley. Cresswell traveled with George Rogers Clark who, as part of his Revolutionary War exploits, established in 1778 the fort around which Louisville emerged. The Falls at Louisville were a hindrance to navigation and, as a "break of bulk" point, a site seemingly dictated by nature for city building. Cincinnati, on the great north bend of the Ohio, also emerged during the Revolutionary War. There settlers could easily leave the river for farms northward and westward in Ohio and Indiana. Located almost at the valley's center point, Cincinnati would become the region's chief metropolis. As Pittsburgh had already come to function in Cresswell's time, cities grew as entrepots through which farm and other commodities of the region were marketed. Manufacturing would quickly rise initially to process the region's farm output as well as other resources: pork packing, flour milling, iron manufacture, glass making, salt making.

Farming districts evolved by stages. In gross generalization, first came the pioneer hunters who pursued some subsistence farming. Often squatting without title to their land, they made the first improvements in a neighborhood by building rude cabins and beginning the forest clearing. As game became scarce, these people often trekked on to new grounds, staying in the vanguard of a constantly shifting frontier. Next came more serious agriculturalists who, with title to the lands they worked, actually broke the wilderness to a garden, many families staying over the generations in a given place, others moving on to better land always beckoning to the west. Finally came the more affluent farmers who bought already improved farms upon which to practice technologically sophisticated commercial farming. Slowly localities would evolve from barter and trade into a cash economy thoroughly oriented to the cities. Also operating on the frontier was the land speculator. This is what Cresswell had hoped to be. Speculators held often large tracts of land out of immediate development thus retarding temporarily an area's growth.

Basic differences would develop north and south of the Ohio River. In Kentucky's Bluegrass (but to a substantially lesser extent elsewhere in Kentucky and in what became West Virginia) the early pioneer classes would be subsumed by the big farmers sustained by the institution of slavery. South of the river a "metes and bounds" system of land survey, the tradition of using topographic landmarks to set property lines, resulted in a century of overlapping and otherwise conflicting land claims and much court litigation. The metes and bounds survey also produced an irregular landscape in the colonial pattern of Virginia. In the territory north and west of the Ohio River, a federal presence of a centrally administered public domain produced a very different landscape. Vast geometries were set down on the land, the township and range system of land survey as dictated by the Land Ordinance of 1785 being the most widespread. Townships six miles square were surveyed into mile-square sections which were in turn easily divisable into farms of 220, 180, 90, 60, or even 40 acres. Once roads were adjusted to the survey lines (where topography permitted) localities took on a squared-up look of classical regularity.

More importantly, federal land policies would tend to become more liberal over time allowing smaller purchase units, lower prices, and installment purchase. The poor but industrious farmer through the early decades of the nineteenth century would be able to go to the area north of the Ohio River, claim a farm, and pay for it over a number of years by working the land for profit. In the process still another kind of new democrat would evolve. From the Jeffersonian point of view, the ideal citizen's political interests in a democracy were rooted in the ownership of landed property.

In his journal, Reuben Thwaites took the measure of the river's north and south banks, comparing and contrasting what he saw in a search for significant differences. Above New Richmond, for example, he could conclude that the Ohio towns displayed "a greater degree of thrift" than those on the Kentucky bank.[38] Towns in that part of Ohio appeared to be more numerous, farms better tended, and farm houses of a better class than those across in Kentucky. But earlier he had not been able to see such differences. He wrote:

> Doubtless before the late civil war,—all the ante-bellum travelers agree in this,—when the blight of slavery was resting on Virginia and Kentucky, the south shore of the Ohio was as another country; but to-day, so far as we can ascertain from a surface view, the little villages on either side are equally dingy and woe-begone, and large Southern towns like Wheeling, Parkersburg, Point Pleasant, and Maysville are very nearly an offset to Steubenville, Marietta, Pomeroy, Ironton, and Portsmouth.[39]

The Ohio Valley as a wilder place gave way before the husbandry of a farmer class organized on an urban base of towns, some of which turned eventually into cities. Most of the towns and all of the cities, in turn, embraced industry: factories creeping out at the urban peripheries into the countryside. By the 1890s, both residual nature and the new garden that farmers had created would appear substantially ravaged by industry's heavy hand. The value of Thwaites's diary lies in the clear view he gives of this conflict. Thwaites was a knowledgeable historian looking back through the then-matured landscapes of industrialism toward simpler times. A region had been born, had been raised to the maturity of industrialization, and, in some aspects, literally had begun to die. Thwaites sought to see the lapsed era of regional birth, but his attention constantly was brought back to themes of industrial decay—not the decay of industry displacing traditional activities, but the decay of industrial refuse and despoliation that promised irreversible change in the valley's physical environmental base. In its maturity, the valley had been brought to slag heaps, abandoned mines and factories, and rundown worker housing.

Playing out in Thwaites's time were the processes of exploitation that Cresswell saw in their initial phases. It was a capitalistic engine of enterprise that sought profits for investors able and willing to speculate. Capital sought to exploit the valley's raw materials: its soil, timber, minerals, and even its people. As the land was settled and urban and rural fabrics of settlement were woven tightly, capital flowed increasingly into the manufacturing of products for export beyond the region. Regional enterprise hinged substantially on capital obtained from eastern cities or from Europe. The Ohio Valley's role in the one-world economy became increasingly sophisticated, but remained nonetheless colonial. Cycles of economic prosperity and depression were largely determined elsewhere. The big, expansive enterprises such as iron and steel production in Pittsburgh were controlled outright by distant owners. Giant firms defined most of the parameters under which small enterprises struggled in highly competitive markets, the big firms enjoying economies of scale that put small operations to disadvantage. The flow of capital in and out of business ventures had come by the late 1890s to create for the Ohio Valley a highly changeable regional economy charged with impermanence.

The built environment of America and, therefore, of the Ohio Valley always had been ephemeral. Everything in America seemed not only new, but constantly renewing. Capitalism, on a continent blessed with seemingly inexhaustible resources, had no pretenses to creating permanence in landscape. America was a land purpose-built to short-term business horizons. Investments in farms and factories were amortized quickly. Accordingly, America was a land marked by the extreme geographical mobility of its people. Americans invested, profited (or failed), and moved off to invest again in new endeavors elsewhere. This frontier mentality of constant new starts continued apace even after the virgin land of the frontier West had been claimed and developed. Frederick Jackson Turner was wrong. The frontier was not over. Its basic impulses had only been diverted from the development of rural land for farming to activities of more immediate urban focus.

The Ohio Valley, like the remainder of America, would witness constant cycles of investment and disinvestment as the fortunes of specific enterprises, neighborhoods, towns, and cities fluctuated. Disinvestment, under utilization, vacancy, abandonment, and outright degradation, would stand frequently juxtaposed with new investment, recent construction, remodeling, reuse, and replacement. Typically American, Ohio Valley landscapes were in a constant state of becoming either more or less than what they had once been. Although Americans might like to think otherwise, this change was rarely linear and not always in the direction of growth. Claims of progress might be used to justify change, but progress (however it was defined) was never guaranteed. After a century and a half of capitalistic enterprise, the valley was strewn with the ruins of failed dreams. They lined the river and were rarely out of view.

Indeed, by 1897, the Ohio River's margins represented something of an economic and social backwater, at least away from the cities. The intensity of the commercial farming frontier had swept westward and, with the coming of the railroads, the industrial establishment west of the Appalachians had begun to shift its locus north and west. Much industrial activity visible to Thwaites on the river was clearly obsolete. Steamboats were relatively few and their commerce meager. Small-town levees were relatively inactive and a river-oriented era was clearly ending. Widespread were the anachronistic vestiges of pioneering. Fishing, hunting, and various forms of scavenging persisted among the houseboat families who still lived largely by barter. Farm families on small tracts continued to live subsistence lives in pockets of humanity seemingly forgotten by time. There, forgotten Americans, stubbornly resisting change, were fighting a losing rearguard action with a modernizing world. But through them Thwaites was able to glimpse many of the same kinds of people that Cresswell had encountered at the beginning of the Ohio Valley's American settlement. Frequently, Thwaites met "genuine 'crackers' of the coarsest type—tall, lean, sallow, fishy-eyed, with tow-colored hair, an ungainly gait, barefooted, and in nondescript clothing all patches and tatters."[40]

As with Cresswell, Thwaites's way of dressing opened and closed social opportunities in his travels, endearing him to some and alienating him from others. His party comprised a strange outfit not usual to the river. Many of those encountered knew not what to make of a skiff loaded with pleasure seekers apparently needing nothing more than drinking water and fresh milk. The notion that they intended to travel nearly a thousand miles to the Mississippi met considerable skepticism on the upper river. "How fur down be yees goin'?" "Oh come, now! Don' be givin' us taffy! Say, hones' Injun, how far down air yew fellers goin', anyhow?" Locals could not easily place their intentions into local context. They were not merchants or canvassers. They were not fishing or hunting. They were not show people. "What 'n' tarnation air ye, anny way? Oh come now! No fellers is do'n th' river fur fun . . . !"[41]

The farmer class along the river stood in conspicuous contrast with the newest Americans attracted to the Ohio Valley's industrializing towns and cities. The "hyphenated" American had arrived from such places as Hungary, Italy, Poland, and Russia. Willing to take the very meanest positions as manual laborers, they seemed to stand in stark contrast with earlier immigrants from Germany and Ireland, who by the 1890s were well advanced in acculturation. The new people were a kind of factory flotsam. Traditional agrarian homogeneity seemed threatened by the new industrial heterogeneity. A comfortable rural provincialism seemed endangered by new ways city-based. Thwaites heard the bigotry expressed. He visited one mill where the new Americans worked. But, strangely, he did not visit the urban neighborhoods where the new towers of Roman Catholicism and Eastern Orthodoxy rose. Thwaites's retrospective view, focused as it was on a romanticized past of "history," could not see far into nor beyond the workplaces of the new social order. The often slovenly farms along the river could be idealized as vestiges of a yeoman farmer frontier, but mining camps and the factory neighborhoods of towns could only be denigrated for their lack of wealth and status.

Indeed, Thwaites tended to avoid the cities or at least to minimize his contact with them. Perhaps this reflected the vulnerabilities of having a wife and child in tow. City riverfronts were not really proper places in the 1890s for a cultured middle class family to idle away vacation time. It was past the menacing Homestead furnaces at Munhall outside Pittsburgh that the family rushed. Cincinnati, the region's economic capital, was bypassed too, so threatening did its waterfront loom with its alienating commerce. Only in Louisville, where a rustic campsite was available under the great bridge, was a city taken on and explored if only superficially. Was Thwaites acting out a basic American bias favoring the rural over the urban? To what extent did he represent a rural bias among the academic historians of his day?

Reuben Thwaites's career as a historian was based substantially on the editing and interpreting of early travel journals. Like Cresswell, he would return home to revise his diary as a manuscript. However, unlike Cresswell's opus, which was shared with but a few close family intimates, Thwaites's work saw immediate publication. The book informed his other work and, along with it, helped to define the Ohio Valley in the minds of a small readership of scholars. Thwaites was one of the last of the modern historians to treat the Ohio Valley as a distinctive region of importance. In the twentieth century other regional descriptors came to the fore to variously dissect the area and join its sundered parts to other regions, the river standing more as a divider between sections.

In Cresswell's day the Ohio River stood as the gateway to a new continent. The whole of interior North America lay potentially exposed to speculators, traders, and settlers. The river was the great highway to the future drawing in adventurers bent on exploiting the new country; the river was an integrator of region since the bulk of the early trans-Appalachian commerce moved along it. But, as the western frontier swept beyond the Ohio's drainage propelled by the new railroad technology, the valley, as region, loomed increasingly passé and provincial. The "West," the "Northwest," the "Interior Valley," and the "Mississippi Valley" were among the competing designations replacing it.

In the decades before the Civil War, a basic schism developed between "North" and "South" over slavery and related states' rights issues. And in most people's minds the Ohio River came to serve as a convenient boundary between the two sections west of the Appalachians to the Mississippi. After the Civil War, the former slave states certainly fit easily into such a regionalization with profound political, economic, and social ramifications that would last for generations. One could quibble as to whether the likes of Kentucky or West Virginia deserved full inclusion in the South, but such an issue did little to diminish the power of the South as a concept of place, and the Ohio River as a boundary. The idea of the Midwest, on the other hand, had its start in Nebraska and Kansas by way of describing the locations of those places in a north/south array of states and territories. The label and its application spread eastward to that focus of mid-continental railroad connectivity that was Chicago, and then to Chicago's hinterland across the likes of Indiana even as far east as Ohio.

Railroads played the biggest role in making the Ohio Valley an outdated geographical concept. They made the Ohio River substantially obsolete, although the Corps of Engineers would partially reverse that situation by upgrading the river for year-round barge traffic through the construction of more and larger dams and navigation locks. Before the trunk railroads, the Ohio River was indeed a regional organizer in an economic sense. Its cities were oriented to the river's banks. Urban energies cycled with the rise and fall of the river's annual flow. When the railroads paralleled the Ohio's banks and threw bridges across the current at strategic intervals, all of this changed rather abruptly. Cities became less river towns and more river crossing towns, important primarily in the connectivity of great railroad systems. Highways, of course, came in the twentieth century to more profoundly reinforce this reorientation away from the river.

LESSONS FOR THE FUTURE

Although one can learn much from reading the diaries of such travelers as Nicholas Cresswell and Reuben Thwaites, their recorded impressions are just that—impressions. What they described reflected highly personal beliefs about how their worlds functioned, and personal attitudes pro or con regarding the specifics of life so conceptualized. What they described reflected their objectives in travel rooted in life's overall intentionalities. Neither Cresswell or Thwaites came to live in the Ohio Valley, but both, each in his own way, sought to anchor a life there. Cresswell achieved a young man's ambition to adventure, risking quite literally life and fortune. The Ohio Valley more than fulfilled his need for excitement, and he would retire for the remainder of his life to quieter and more secure precincts. Thwaites sought to validate himself as historian by confronting firsthand the places where history central to his brand of scholarship once played out. He would become an outstanding spokesman for his adopted region, and its past.

Today's Ohio Valley, like every region, invites contemplation. What is this region to us as modern Americans? What benefits might we derive by contemplating its distinctiveness as place? Unfortunately, too few in modern America stop to ask such questions, for most Americans today take their surroundings—their geography—very much for granted. Geography is pushed to the background as some kind of naturally occurring given needing little contemplation. This lack of concern with places is a kind of deprivation. To be vague and uncertain of mind concerning the history of places, to not know what kinds of human satisfactions traditionally accrued place to place, and to be unable generally to read the symbolisms of human intentionality rooted in landscapes is to suffer a kind of ignorance, a blindness that substantially diminishes life. In ignorance people take what they get. Beached in the shallows of a popular mass culture and manipulated by the ephemeral tastes current to the commercial marketplace, Americans typically abide life in superficial stances vis-à-vis their surrounding geography. Although old travel diaries are highly selective in the information provided (and only with difficulty does the scholar extract from them a sense of reality as once might have been shared across a society at large), they do teach lessons about how to be in a place. They do instruct on how to sharpen regional consciousness.

Concern with both the past and the future is requisite to place knowing. Even Nicholas Cresswell came to the valley aware of and interested in its past. Dutifully he sought out the Indian mounds and the remains of mammoth and other beasts that spoke of a far distant past, indeed even a "prehistory." But he came as an agent of change, and the future implications of his actions were never far from his mind. He was aware that a very different future loomed and that he was very much a part of the change process. Although a historian, Reuben Thwaites also cultivated a future awareness. He noted the landmarks of modern industrialism and speculated about the despoiled environment, extrapolating forward as well as backward in time. He wrote from a consciousness that those processes of change, long dominant in the region, would continue and even accelerate. Both men thrust themselves into dialogues with the Ohio River by moving on its waters, their lives hinging on the fixing of places encountered in temporal perspective. Only then could places be fully experienced. Only then could one's being as an actor in a place be put in full context.

Cresswell's and Thwaites's rivers stand for us as metaphor. Rounding every bend, the river unfolded to their eyes, the vistas dissolving or, if you will, occluding behind. Vistas came in repeated cycles of seeing with variations on themes playing out over and over again. For Cresswell, the emphasis shifted from the evidences of advancing European civilization to that of isolated wilderness. For Thwaites, the emphasis shifted from the evidences of widespread industrialism to residual rusticity. So also has the region's history been patterned. Basic processes have worked and reworked the Ohio Valley over time in streams of human endeavor ever evolving and ever dissolving. Change over time has played out in landscape: the built environments of landscape ever emerging and ever occluding.

It would be easy to conclude that nothing stays the same and that things change. But that is only partially true. Things in the landscape may change considerably over time, but the underlying processes of change may be little altered if at all. In general, the legal infrastructure governing change in the Ohio Valley, as in the nation at large, has remained remarkably stable. It is an apparatus that sustains a capitalistic economy with emphasis on the prerogatives of private enterprise rooted in the ownership and manipulation of private property. America's political and economic systems encourage enterpreneurialism as risk taking turned on the exploitation not only of natural resources, but human resources as well. Political economic structures operate to perpetuate change. Change itself is the region's constant. But much of this change has been dictated from beyond the region, for the Ohio Valley remains substantially colonial to the control of economic centers elsewhere. It is a region in which localities have relatively little control over the capital, technology, market, management expertise, and other factors that fix competitive advantages and disadvantages.

Cresswell saw change as he looked forward from the perspective of a would-be capitalist attracted by the Ohio Valley's yet undeveloped resources. Thwaites, taking the backward glance, saw the proof of those expectations in landscapes of mature exploitation. And so it is that our generation will also excite and experience the results of change in a Valley constantly emerging and occluding. Landscapes change when new enterprises are launched and those surviving are brought variously to maturity. But most enterprises are ultimately abandoned as they falter in their command of capital, control of market, retention of management efficiency, or ability to innovate technologically, or as they face dwindling raw materials. For Thwaites the view was not only one of shifting industrial activity, but one of economic change even more profound. Two economies had operated from the earliest years of American settlement: the commercial economy with its international capitalistic engine and a barter economy still rooted substantially in subsistence living organized at the family and neighborhood levels. Today the latter is nearly gone. While it lasted, subsistence economy did bring definite stability to the valley, albeit of an exaggerated backwater kind.

Ohio Valley landscapes, as in America generally, have tended to the emphemeral. Structures have been lightly built even to the point of flimsiness. Amortized over thirty or forty years (and more recently upwards to ten) most buildings erected in the region have not been constructed to last over the long run. Traditionally, Americans, including those in the Ohio Valley, have not spent lavishly on maintenance and repair. Landscapes have not been maintained through constant repair, but rather are allowed to lapse into disrepair: overlapping accumulations of birth, maturity, and death characterize most places. Cresswell's view saw the clock of American settlement set for the first time west of the Appalachians. Thwaites's view was that of the same clock still ticking in remote places, but with a substantially run down mainspring. Save in the large cities and more prosperous towns, the mechanisms of economic growth had been retarded, offering apparent glimpses into past lifeways. In today's world, the mechanisms of landscape change continue to tick away, only now the ticking is vastly accelerated.

In the Ohio Valley, as in the nation at large, structures have tended to be set boldly into landscapes. Objects rear up out of the openness of surrounding space. The land itself has been struck off into grids of varying size from that of the township and range survey to that of smaller street grids in towns and cities. The objects of landscape array linearly from the paths of movement along roads and streets, and from along rivers. Only where topography has proven too varied has the orderliness of the road system bent into the curvilinear and the ad hoc of irregularity. Objects in the landscape, whether viewed from the river or from a street, tend to boldly contrast one with another in degrees of spatial isolation. America was an expansive place with abundant land allowing things to spread out often wastefully. Land uses under a "laissez-faire" economy (where the influences of government were minimalized) tended to be mixed rather than segregated by type. The valley has always been characterized by the sometime shocking and arcane juxtapositioning of unlike things, the negative spillover effects of which usually encourage instability.

In the configuring of space, Americans, including those of the Ohio Valley, have tended to emphasize the private over the public. The real character of America was sensed inside its houses, stores, and other buildings more so than on the public streets or, as in the case of the river, at the public levees. Public spaces tended toward base utilitarianism. Function dominated with little regard for the picturesque. Consequently, sentiment attached to the public landscape with difficulty, also hastening change. Enhanced functionality has always legitimized change, overwhelming aesthetic or other concerns conservatively rooted in the past. Public improvements have always implied increased utility (if not enhanced profitability for the vested private interests that stand to benefit): the future embraced and the past rejected in favor of enhanced functionality. Like the buildings that comprised it, landscapes of aggregated structures tended to a certain lightness of execution, a crispness of expression, and a character essentially ephemeral. The region's evolving landscape today may suffer different tastes in architectural styles, but the essential characteristics of impermanence remain.

What would Nicholas Cresswell and Reuben Thwaites think could they make their way through the Ohio Valley today? What would they think of the skyscrapers of metal and glass that soar from the centers of Pittsburgh, Cincinnati, Louisville, and other cities? What of the new freeways that now replace the railroads on city waterfronts? Or the new stadiums and convention centers nearby? The scale of the new symbols of progress might surprise, but the processes that produced them would not. What would they think of the vast steel mills now being torn apart for scrap? Even the once proud Homestead Works are being disassembled, and the Ohio River is now lined more than ever by dying factories and the remains of dead ones as the nation accelerates its postindustrial economic surge. What would they think of the continued farm abandonment? What of the widespread decline of small towns faced with rural depopulation? The scale of the change might surprise, but the processes that produced the change would not. The Ohio Valley continues its evolution apace as a quintessentially American place ever changing.

NOTES

1. John A. Jakle, *Images of the Ohio Valley: A Historical Geography of Travel, 1740 to 1860* (New York: Oxford University Press, 1977), 3–4.
2. Nicholas Cresswell, *The Journal of Nicholas Cresswell, 1774–1777*, edited by Samuel Thornely (New York: Dial, 1924), 62.
3. Ibid., 66.
4. Ibid., 68.
5. Ibid., 70.
6. Ibid., 71.
7. Ibid., 72–76.
8. Ibid., 77, 80.
9. Ibid., 82–84.
10. Ibid., 86.
11. Ibid., 87–90.
12. Ibid., 92, 94.
13. Ibid., 97, 100–101.
14. Ibid., 103.
15. Ibid., 113–14, 109.
16. Reuben Gold Thwaites, *Afloat on the Ohio: An Historical Pilgrimage of a Thousand Miles in a Skiff, from Redstone to Cairo* (Chicago: Way and Williams, 1897), xi.
17. Ibid., 5–6.
18. Ibid., 7.
19. Ibid., 13–14, 18, 21.
20. Ibid., 24.
21. Ibid., 37.
22. Ibid., 40–41.
23. Ibid., 44–45.
24. Ibid., 59.
25. Ibid., 52, 54, 59, 60.
26. Ibid., 64–65.
27. Ibid., 69.
28. Ibid., 122–23.

29. Samuel Cumings, *The Western Pilot.* Revised editions, 1829–54.
30. Thwaites, op. cit., 79.
31. Ibid., 80–81.
32. Ibid., 107.
33. Ibid., 183.
34. Ibid., 195, 208.
35. Ibid., 221–22.
36. Ibid., 224.
37. Ibid., 240–41, 256.
38. Ibid., 176.
39. Ibid., 157–58.
40. Ibid., 185.
41. Ibid., 33, 56.

Hubert G. H. Wilhelm

SETTLEMENT AND SELECTED LANDSCAPE IMPRINTS IN THE OHIO VALLEY

For the last twenty-seven years I have lived in Athens, a small university town on the Hocking River about twenty-five miles upstream from the Ohio. Southeastern Ohio is a beautiful part of the state, hilly and wooded and quite isolated. Few people still identify this region with the great events of the late 1700s when a young country, enamored with the idea of manifest destiny, began its thrust westward beyond the mountains and across the river which the Shawnee called Spay-lay-wi-theepi. Some two hundred years ago, the migrant streams of American settlers from the Northeast, East, and South came together in the hill country of southeastern and southern Ohio, fronting the great Ohio River. Their legacy of diverse customs, beliefs, and material traits remains an all-important geographical characteristic of the entire valley region.

Among the first to arrive were a group of Revolutionary War

officers from Massachusetts known as the Ohio Company of Associates, who in April of 1788 founded the first official settlement on the Ohio side of the river at its junction with the Muskingum. They called the settlement Marietta in honor of Queen Marie Antoinette of France and the support which that country had extended during the struggle for independence. Although New Englanders did not follow their leaders in large numbers into southeastern Ohio, the Associates were successful in effecting a settlement imprint. How else can one explain places with such classical names as Alexander, Troy, Syracuse, Carthage, and, yes, Athens, in a region that is part of Ohio's Appalachia and where one can also find Coon Hollow, Stinking Creek, Buzzard's Den, and Knockemstiff? The point, of course, is that those proper New Englanders who came down the Ohio River on flatboats were only a small part of the vast number of peoples with rather diverse backgrounds who converged on the river and the territory that became known as the Old Northwest.

As one travels the valley region of the Ohio River today, the evidence of the first effective, permanent settlement by non-native Americans remains clear to anyone who enjoys reading the landscape. An early German geographer, August Meitzen,[1] theorized that the first permanent occupants of an area will influence all subsequent occupants and therefore will have a lasting settlement effect. This idea by Meitzen, known as the *Altlandschaft*[2] theory of human settlement, is perhaps ideally illustrated in the United States. American culture derives its characteristics, both material and non-material, from English culture because the English were the first who effectively and permanently occupied large parts of this continent. While the Germans may have been more numerous, they came later and accommodated themselves to the earlier, dominant Anglo-Saxon influences.

The *Altlandschaft* concept is borne out in the Ohio Valley. For example, a traveler coming through Cincinnati on his way south who stops for breakfast in the Queen City may, just by chance, be served sliced tomatoes with his order of eggs and sausage.[3] This distinctly Southern custom was transferred, who knows when, north of the river and remains as one of many Southern settlement effects. Similarly, several Pennsylvania type barns have survived in Adams County, Ohio, and just outside of the Ohio River Valley proper. These structures indicate the settlement in the early 1800s of a small group of migrants from Pennsylvania.[4] Because of its size and distinctive overhang or forebay which extends by several feet over the banked first floor, this barn is unlike most of the other barns in the area and easily recognized. The legacy of contrasting traditional settlement influences throughout the Ohio River Valley is everywhere. Collectively, they are visible proof of the attraction which the river and the valley held for the American settler. In a way, the Ohio valley region must be viewed like the lower end of an enormous funnel which pulled all comers toward a common routeway into the interior.

THE SOUTHERN SETTLEMENT FRONTIER

The settlement assault on the Ohio River Valley and adjacent lands was spearheaded from the Kentucky territory of Virginia. Years before similar cessions on the north side of the river, the Indians had relinquished their hold on the land. The map showing the advance of the settlement frontier (Fig. 1) reveals quite dramatically the population bulge pressing forward through the Kentucky country. In a recent study, two cultural geographers, Terry Jordan and Matti Kaups, suggest that the pronounced westward thrust by Americans, especially in Kentucky and Tennessee, was an adaptive response to settlement by America's backwoods culture.[5] Its adherents were a mingled lot, composed of English, German, Scots-Irish, and others, who developed their peculiar ways, including ephemeral land use practices and settlement mobility, in the hills of the Appalachian region. The latter was influential in affecting the migration of these folk toward the southwest along the longitudinal valleys of the Appalachian Ridge and Valley area. From there they pushed westward through one or another of the infrequent gaps in the mountains, eventually arriving in the rolling country of the Nashville and Bluegrass basins.

By the 1760s, "long hunters" or groups of rifle men, searching for game, new routes, and settlement sites or "stations," were active throughout much of Kentucky. They came by way of the Cumberland Gap, which had been discovered by Dr. Thomas Walker and his party of explorers in April 1750. The Cumberland Gap is one of those sites that is part of the geographical consciousness of most Americans. Not everyone would be able to pinpoint it, but most know that it is a place in the Appalachians through which the hordes of frontier folk

Figure 1

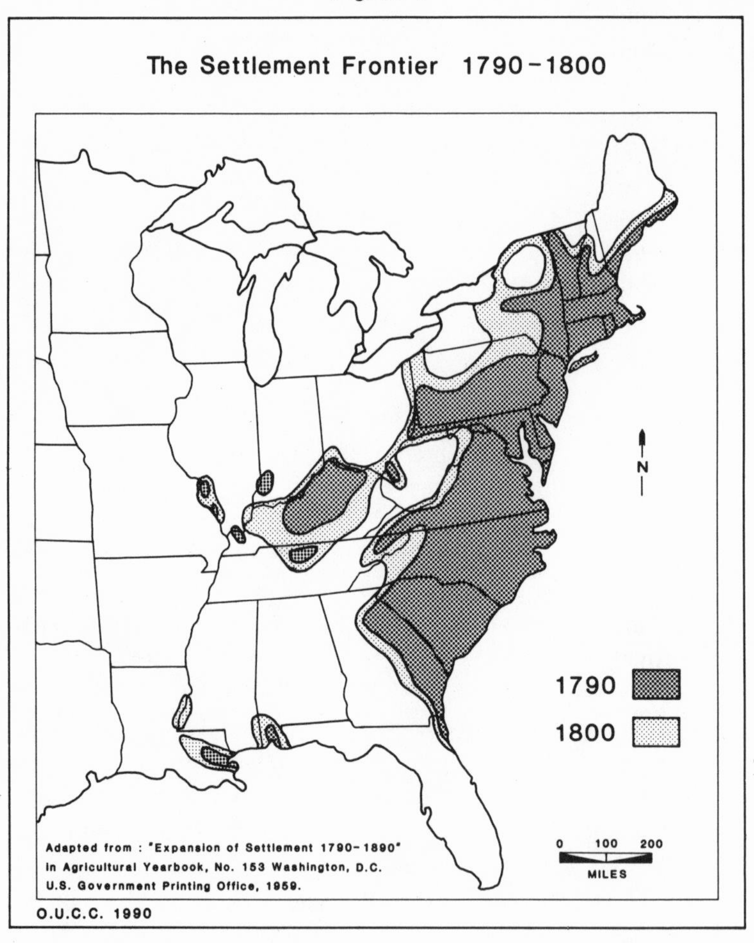

passed on their way to better lands on the other side of the mountains. In 1775 Judge Richard Henderson, who was interested in speculative land ventures in the Blue Grass country, hired Daniel Boone to cut a road from the Gap to the Kentucky River. This was the beginning of the famed Wilderness Road which in due time included branches terminating on the Ohio River at Louisville, Covington (opposite Cincinnati), and Maysville, Kentucky. Boonesboro, at the intersection of the Wilderness Road and the Kentucky River, became one of the earliest settlements of Kentucky. Similarly, the road triggered the founding of Harrodsburg, Frankfort, and Lexington. By the late 1700s, the road was made passable for wagons. The numbers of migrants swelled and literally thousands would pass through the Gap within a week or less, all headed for those beckoning interior lands probably purchased from speculators somewhere in the East. These were the settlers who would take the place of the earlier backwoods peoples who formed a rather tenuous advance guard.

In Allen W. Eckert's superb novel *The Frontiersmen*, which centers on the struggle for control of the Ohio Country, Captain Thomas Bullit, leader of a surveying party in northern Kentucky, arranges to meet with the great Shawnee chief Black Fish. Eckert's biographical sketch of that meeting illustrates well the population pressure from south of the river. The date is May 18, 1773, and Captain Bullit addresses Black Fish:

> Now we come from Virginia to settle that country on the other side of the river, as low down as the falls. We only want this country to settle and cultivate the soil. There will be no objection to your hunting and trapping in it, as heretofore. I hope you will live with us in friendship.

Black Fish's response is representative of his people's fading power in the face of ever greater settlement pressures by the new Americans:

> We are not pleased to know you plan to settle in the Can-tuc-kee lands and we cannot stop you, but since the Shemanese [Whites] are determined to settle south of the Spay-lay-wi-theepi [Ohio River], they must be aware that they are not to disturb us in our hunting. . . . We desire you will be strong in discharging your promises towards us as we are determined to be strong in advising our young men to be kind, friendly and peaceable towards you."[6]

A few years after that supposed conversation, the Shawnee's sacred "Middle Ground" or hunting domain, located in central Kentucky, had been taken over by the settlers from Virginia who could hardly bide their time to push the frontier north of the river. On April 24, 1779, settlers selected the first lots at a place where the Ohio River plunges across its most prominent falls. By December of the same year the first cabins had been built and Louisville had become a geographic fact.[7] Just a few years later, in 1788, Marietta and Cincinnati were established on the northern bank of the river. All of these new river towns were sought out by settlers who were headed for the interior. Cincinnati, because of its location at the northern apex of the huge bend in the river, became the favored jumping-off point for the mass of settlers moving on into western Ohio or the Indiana country.

That settlement advance began in earnest with the legal support of a major Indian land cession. In 1794, the combined Indian tribes were defeated at the Battle of Fallen Timbers, near present-day Toledo, Ohio, by "Mad" Anthony Wayne's American Legion troops and Kentucky Volunteers. This military victory led to the signing of the Treaty of Greenville in 1795 which opened most of Ohio and a small segment of southeastern Indiana to white settlement. Additional land cessions, completed between 1803 and 1819, removed the majority of native American land claims from Ohio westward through Illinois and the westernmost part of Kentucky. Of special significance to the settlement of southern Indiana were the treaties of Fort Wayne, Vincennes, and Grouseland concluded between 1803 and 1805.[8] Vincennes, which had been an island of European settlement on the lower Wabash River since the early 1700s, became a focal point for both territorial and political control of the Indiana country. In fact, it survived as the territorial capital until 1813 when Corydon, a few miles to the north of the river, took over that position.

Equally important were earlier decisions by the Congress of the United States to implement federal survey and land sales in all of the Northwest Territory (U.S. Land Ordinance, 1785), and facilitate, in an area where slavery was prohibited, the establishment of government, education, and religion (Northwest Ordinance, 1787). Thus the stage was set for one of history's greatest human migrations, settlement, and subsequent regional development deep in the interior of the American landmass. The central actor in this unprecedented "geographic happening" was the Ohio River, together with its valley and tributary valleys both north and south. By that crucial date of 1795, Kentucky counted a population of 220,000, while the other side of the river was a virtual population vacuum. This situation is basic to an understanding of the distribution of American settlement and cultural groups which followed.

THE OHIO RIVER AS REGIONAL BOUNDARY

The Northwest Ordinance of 1787 assured that the Ohio River would become a distinct demarcation line by prohibiting the extension of slavery north of the river. Of course, that decision greatly influenced cross-river migration, encouraging those who sought land to support individual families rather than the development of large scale, commercial agriculture. But in the Kentucky territory backwoods and planter systems of agricultural land use clashed. By the late 1700s, the planter economy of Kentucky had evolved around the production of tobacco and hemp, with considerable emphasis on corn, wheat, and rye production and cattle raising.[9] These were not the kind of plantations common to the coastal areas of Virginia and the Carolinas. Another difference was in the number of slaves owned—on the average between two and ten.[10] Nevertheless, a stratified class structure based on race with the African American on the bottom survived in Kentucky, while individual freedoms became identified with areas north of the river. There, the absence of slavery helped function as a pull factor for both blacks and whites from the South and many heeded it, spreading northward across the Ohio River.

Of course, a very direct geographical influence to cross-river settlement from Virginia and Kentucky existed in the VMD, the Virginia Military District of Ohio (Fig. 2). Here, between the Scioto and Little Miami rivers, Virginia retained title to a small segment of its earlier, very extensive claim to trans-Appalachian areas of the public domain. Much of the land in the VMD was ideal for agriculture and was disposed of as military land warrants. But even without that designated area for Southern settlement to the north of the river, the migration by both Virginians and Kentuckians into Ohio, Indiana, and Illinois became pronounced and helps to explain the cross-river diffusion of Southern material traits and customs.

Figure 3 shows the relative distribution of Southern settlers in Ohio. The influence of the VMD on the distribution of these settlers is obvious. Southerners, however, did not confine themselves to the District alone, but spread over much of southern Ohio, Indiana, and Illinois. A recent article by Gregory S. Rose, a geographer, argues that the National Road is a more likely dividing line between North and South than is the Ohio River.[11] His map (Fig. 4) of Northern and Southern Nativity Dominance depicts quite dramatically the overwhelming prominence of Southern settlers in all three states. In fact, one possible meaning of Indiana's nickname, "Hoosiers," is people from the high country or highlands. Since there is little real "high country" in Indiana, it may well refer to the Appalachians or the Upland South where so many of Indiana's early settlers have their roots.[12]

Figure 2

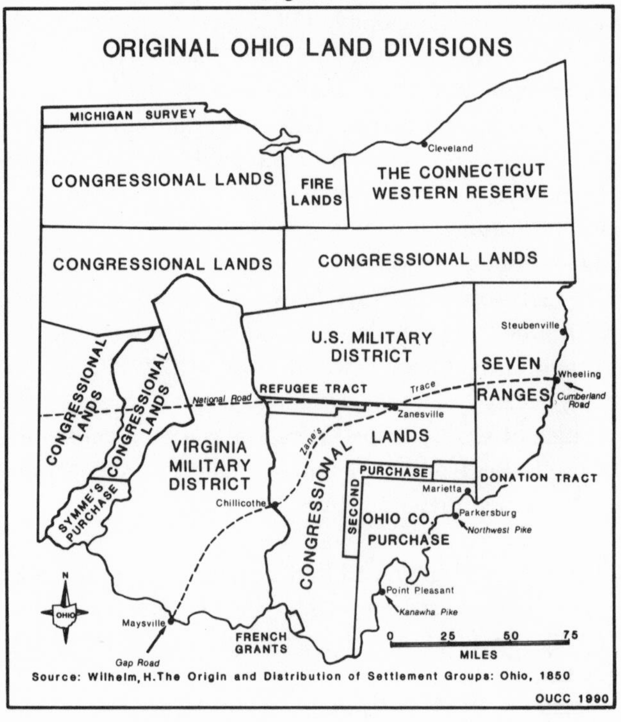

Because the National Road roughly divides Ohio, Indiana, and Illinois into level and hilly terrain areas, it was influential in dividing Northern and Southern settlement groups. The similarity in terrain north and south of the river and continuity of contact with the Ohio River by way of its northern tributaries were considerations when Southern settlers decided to make the move into the area of the Northwest Territory. While the majority of the settlers entering Ohio from the South were from Virginia, those entering Indiana came largely out of Kentucky.[13] The explanation probably lies in the earlier opening of Ohio for settlement, the relative proximity of Virginia to Ohio, and the prevailing southeast to northwest direction of stream valleys, such as the Kanawha, Big Sandy, and Licking valleys, which acted as migration routes. The location in Ohio of the Virginia Military District has to be counted as a major factor, attracting large number of Virginians who settled in the Ohio country. By 1850, 83,300 of 102,671 or 81 percent of Southern-born residents in Ohio were from Virginia.[14]

Geographers in general have placed the regional boundary

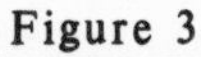

Figure 3

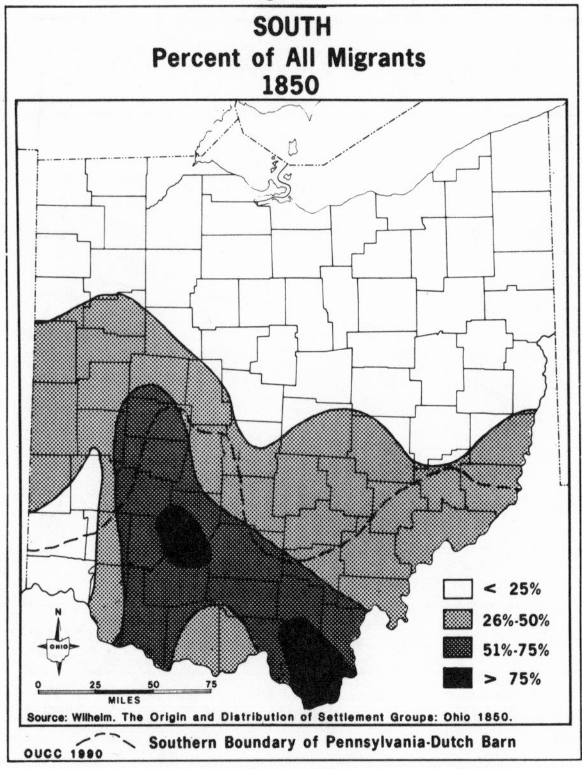

between North and South slightly to the north of the Ohio River. Figure 5 shows three such boundaries adapted from well-known regional texts on Anglo America.[15] Because geographical boundaries are in reality transition zones, the location of a boundary becomes an individualistic and somewhat subjective exercise. One can be sure, however, that each interpreter of regional geographic characteristics would not lack in arguments in support of the specific location of a regional boundary. So, although the three boundaries between North and South show relatively close accordance, they also vary sufficiently to reflect individual interpretation. It is interesting to note that all three boundaries are located north of the river in Illinois and Indiana, while they are more or less parallel with it between Ohio, Kentucky, and West Virginia. An explanation is that the proponents of these boundaries considered not only cultural-traditional factors but contemporary regional development as well. When viewed in that context, the western portion of the Ohio River Valley and adjacent areas are predominantly

Figure 4

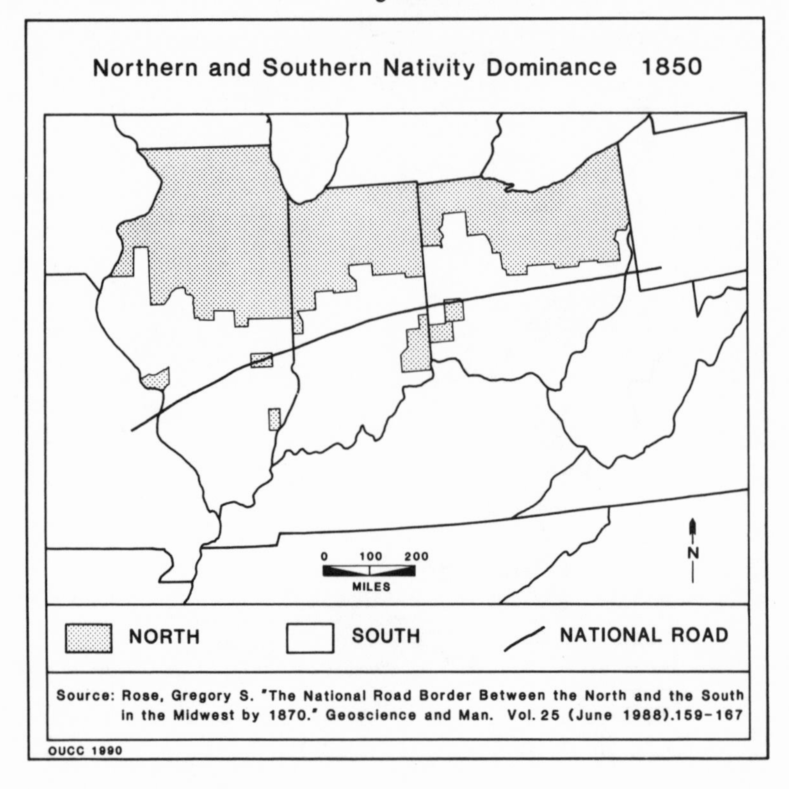

rural-agricultural, while toward the east the valley is much more dominated by the industrial activities of America's manufacturing belt or "Rust Belt." This pattern becomes especially evident as one moves upvalley from Portsmouth, Ohio, where electric power, chemical, and metal fabricating plants vie for valley location and access to Ohio River water.

The foundations for industrial development in the Upper Ohio Valley were laid during the early 1800s around a trinity of mineral resources: iron ore, salt, and coal. Centered on Ironton and Portsmouth in Ohio, and Ashland in Kentucky, one of the country's early industrial empires flourished. Known as the Hanging Rock Iron Region after the pronounced rock ledge next to the Ohio River, its center was the town of Ironton. From Kentucky northward into Ohio, some sixty-five cold blast charcoal furnaces turned out pig iron for foundries in Cincinnati, Columbus, Pittsburgh, and a score of other places where the iron was converted into farm tools, household items such as kettles and stoves, fences, and parts used in the manufacture of

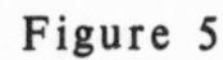

Figure 5

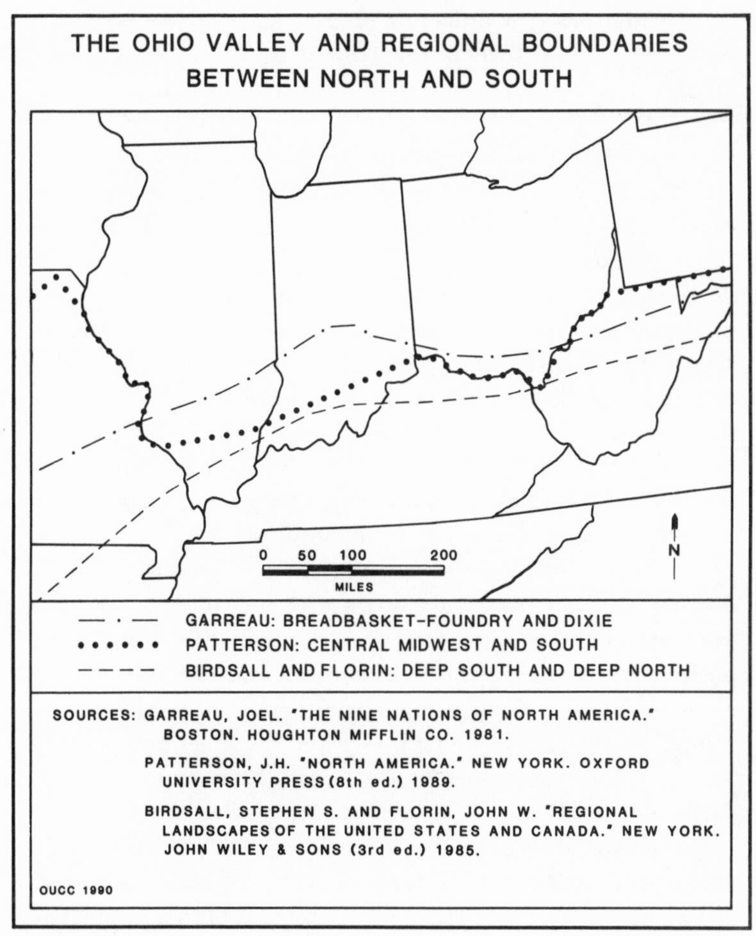

river boats, railroad cars and engines, and bridges. Before the Hanging Rock region's economic decline (its last furnace in Jackson, Ohio, was shut down in 1916), it furnished much of the ordnance used by the North during the Civil War.[16]

The manufacture of pig iron in the Ohio Valley was important to the viability of the major urban centers in the valley region. The infant industries of these towns relied heavily on this raw material whose shipment was eased by river transport. The charcoal-furnace settlements, however, were short-lived and, as a result, their legacy in the Ohio Valley is not very strong.

More important to the success of early trans-Appalachian settlements, including the ephemeral furnace towns, was the occurrence of salt licks. The present-day concentration of chemical industries in the Ohio and adjacent Kanawha valleys reflects the early manufacture of salt and related products. Frederick Jackson Turner[17] theorized that the availability of salt on the frontier, especially in Kentucky, Ohio, and Virginia (present-day West Virginia), was the single most important factor contributing to the success of frontier settlements, their growth, and westward expansion. John Jakle[18] has provided an excellent summary of the historical geography of salt occurrence, manufacture, and trade in the Ohio Valley region. His detailed maps showing the inter-relationship of salt licks, towns or stations, and trade routes leave little doubt about the significance of salt to regional development in the early West. The availability of cheap salt, together with corn-fed hogs from the southern counties of Ohio's Virginia Military District and the German settlement in the Miami River Basin turned Cincinnati into the nation's first major meat packing center. Of the city's two nicknames, Porkopolis is probably as well known as Queen City. Procter and Gamble, one of Cincinnati's best known industries, evolved from the historical combination of salt and pork bellies. Jakle, describing early Cincinnati, writes, "meat packing attracted the most attention. The slaughterhouses were located . . . along Mill Creek which was nicknamed 'Bloody Run' for the color of its water . . . when slaughtering was done. . . . Swine prowled the streets, barrels of pork lined the quays, and cartloads of their carcasses filled the city."[19]

In contrast to iron ore and salt, which lost their Ohio Valley importance by the early 1900s to more favorable resources in other parts of the country, coal continues as both a settlement attraction and legacy. The latter is well represented by Appalachia, which is both a region and a concept. As a regional name, Appalachia has an early and somewhat nebulous origin, taking its name from the "Apalachee Indians who lived in what is now northern Florida."[20] By the early 1800s, it was the accepted term for the country's eastern mountain system whose subdivisions from east to west include the Piedmont, Blue Ridge, Ridge and Valley, and Allegheny and Cumberland plateaus. The federal planning region of Appalachia was first delimited by the federal government in 1965 as that area where specific socioeconomic indicators lagged behind the rest of the country. In Kentucky, Ohio, Pennsylvania, and West Virginia, the designated area of Appalachia coincides relatively well with the Allegheny and Cumberland plateaus and therefore incorporates a large segment of the Ohio Valley. Here, but especially in eastern Kentucky and southern West Virginia, settlements have been marked by "the sequence of heady booms and heart-breaking busts in the cycling of coal demand and production."[21] Most of these settlements lie outside the immediate area of the Ohio Valley. The river, however, has been the important link in the transport of coal. Over one half of its total tonnage is coal, which moves both up and downriver.[22] Much of the downriver traffic of coal is destined for the Tennessee Valley and its numerous coal-fired utility plants. In his well-known book *Night Comes to the Cumberlands: A Biography of a Depressed Area*, Harry Caudill[23] considered the use of strip mined Appalachian coal to fire TVA utility plants as a major contributor to the economic decline of Kentucky's Cumberland Plateau. Along with coal and various other bulky products hauled by barges on its surface, the river today must also carry a large load of sediment, the byproduct of changes in mining technology from underground to surface or strip mining.

In 1780, Virginia, and its western appendage of Kentucky, had an estimated population of 538,004 or over 200,000 more than Pennsylvania, the next largest state.[24] Population pressure from the south combined with the pull of inexpensive and free lands north of the Ohio River extended Southern settlement influences into parts of this country which are considered to be Midwest rather than South. It is not my intention, however, to foster an impression that Southerners with their particular values and material traits overwhelmed the northern valley region. Instead, it should be kept in mind that the river as the singularly important routeway into the interior affected the convergence of settlers from all the country's diverse areas as well as from overseas. Therefore, the valley region, especially north of the river, should be recognized as one of considerable cultural diversity and mixing. It was a different sort of region than the more uniformly patterned settlement areas that border it toward the north and the south. Both the numbers of settlers and their varying backgrounds contributed to a general regional vitality which was expressed in the growth of roads and agricultural activity, towns, commerce, and manufacturing.

By the 1830s, canals began to accentuate the linkage of the river northward to the Great Lakes, especially Lake Erie. Travelers in the valley increasingly sought out the states north of the river where development was concentrated and the construction of the first railroad in Ohio between Sandusky on Lake Erie and Cincinnati in 1846 further enhanced movement between the river and the lake. Goods from the valley region continued their traditional flow downriver by steamboat to New Orleans and from there by oceangoing boats to the East Coast. But the lakes were beginning to take their toll on the transport patterns between the interior and the East. By the 1840s, shipping capacity on the Great Lakes had increased nearly fourfold and competition between river, overland, and lake carriers was severe.[25] The spread of the railroads throughout the interior and the advantages of lake transport to reach Eastern markets by way of Buffalo and the Mohawk and Hudson valleys greatly affected Ohio River traffic. Exacerbating this decline of river travel and transport was a general economic stagnation of the valley region brought on by regional variations in economic development and the concomitant social and political contrasts between North and South. It was as if an entire area had been pricked by the proverbial poisonous thorn and had dropped into a prolonged period of slumber. Jakle ends his excellent historical geography, *Images of the Ohio Valley*, with some appropriate comments about the people of the area and their regional allegiances:

> Few people living in the Ohio Valley today share a sense of identity predicated on the region's past. Middle Westerners look north to the new lake cities and the farms of the corn and dairy belts for a sense of past landscape, and Southerners look more to the coastal cities and plantations of the Deep South. The authentic landscape heritage of the Ohio Valley has been little appreciated.[26]

Since the 1860s, when river transport yielded to rail traffic and New Orleans gave up its premier position as outlet for Midwestern products to Chicago and other Great Lakes ports, the Ohio River has made a remarkable comeback. The Civil War and its aftermath certainly blocked any early recovery. In fact, real change did not come until relatively recent times, coincident with the increasing importance of the country's Southern states. The economic interconnection involving Ohio River transport between the TVA states and the northern Appalachian coal fields has already been mentioned. More important yet to the interior are the Gulf states and their resources of sulfur, natural gas, and petroleum, as well as the Caribbean and continental South American regions because of bauxite resources. Conversely, the Southern states because of population increases and greater emphasis on livestock production in their agriculture are dependent on the Midwest for grain shipments. All of these and other products move in some form or another across the navigable water lanes of the Mississippi, Missouri, and Ohio rivers. Yet, while the river is again flexing its muscles as a deliverer of goods and products, the valley region as a whole, the Cincinnati-Louisville urban areas notwithstanding, benefits more from its scenic, rural, and isolated character than from any of the developments directly related to the river. One need only check the distribution of national and state forest and park lands in the Ohio Valley region to gain an understanding of both the physical and human geography of that area. The national forests of Illinois, Indiana, and Ohio are all located in the hillier, southern parts of these three states, and immediately adjacent to the Ohio River. Here, outmigration and land abandonment have been endemic. As a result, competition for land favors public ownership. Of course, it can also be argued that the land in these parts is better off in public ownership, which assures tree growth and protection against the ravages of water runoff and erosion.

PLACES, PATTERNS, AND FORMS IN THE VALLEY REGION

As a cultural geographer and landscape enthusiast, I have often experienced the joy of locating a house, barn, or other structure that represents the early settlement legacy in the valley. In our contemporary society where change is equated with progress, the survival of these rare examples of traditional architecture is tangible evidence of the dramatic events that swept across the Ohio Valley region in the late 1700s and early 1800s. They give us a better sense of place.

Economic stagnation in the valley region halted the further growth of many a river town. Portsmouth, at the confluence of the Scioto with the Ohio River, was envisioned to rival Pittsburgh some day in both size and function. And why not? Portsmouth's location was most auspicious—at the junction of two major rivers, near the iron furnaces of the Hanging Rock region, and, most important, at the southern end of the Ohio-Erie Canal which linked the town with Cleveland. But all of these geographical advantages were for naught when the economic gradient of the country became increasingly east-west oriented and goods were carried on rails rather than water. Portsmouth grew rapidly during its first decades, reaching over ten thousand in population in 1870. Then its growth leveled off, coincident with the decline of river commerce. But the city revived as a rail transfer point for coal on the Norfolk and Western and several other lines and as a steel manufacturing town. It reached its maximum population of 42,560 in 1930, but has experienced only decline since then.[27] The 1980 Census recorded a population of 25,943, the lowest since 1910, symptomatic of the continuing economic problems in the valley.[28] Portsmouth's future is not particularly encouraging. Coal traffic is down and the steel mill closed its doors a number of years ago. Efforts by the city to build on its historical importance as a river and canal town and manufacturing center have had some success, especially as they relate to the downtown preservation and restoration activity. Portsmouth, however, was a "company" town, and "big" houses that would attract visitors are fewer in number than in other towns with a slightly different past.

Such a valley town is Madison, Indiana. The town developed at a huge northward loop in the river, and is strategically located on the northern apex of the loop, before the river turns abruptly southward and heads for Louisville. This site formed the ideal "break in transportation" for travelers, settlers, and goods between the river and the newly acquired lands in the Indiana territory. The earliest settlement of the site occurred in 1806, and "after the land sales in May, 1808, and the sale of lots in Madison in 1811, the town and the country commenced filling up pretty rapidly with settlers."[29] Madison prospered as a transfer point and commercial center, and in 1827 added an educational institution, Hanover College, to its variety of early river town functions. Furniture making was an important local manufacturing activity. By 1836, one could travel from Madison to Indianapolis on Indiana's earliest railroad—the first railroad, in fact, in the Northwest Territory.[30] Built to link with the river, not to compete, it illustrates settlement progress and development of areas north of the river.

But again the favorable interrelationship of river and railroad proved temporary. By 1850, Madison entered its period of economic stagnation and dormancy. Surprisingly, this was a blessing in disguise. Without the opportunity for further growth, Madison was literally caught in a time warp from which it did not break out until after World War II. Because few could afford to make changes in the town, Madison retained the architectural characteristics of its antebellum "golden years." Local residents came to appreciate the great houses of the past and with the help of architects, historians, preservationists, and local volunteers launched an ambitious preservation and restoration program. In 1960, Historic Madison was incorporated; since then it has served as a national model for the historic preservation movement. It is encouraging to visit Madison and realize that preservation and restoration can become a community-wide project, extending across all social and economic levels. A standard of appearance and aesthetics links the mansions on Main Street with the shotgun houses along back alleys.[31]

As Virginians and, later, Kentuckians poured across the river into the new lands of Ohio, Indiana, and Illinois, they were joined by Easterners, especially Pennsylvania migrants and, of course, New Englanders. Recent immigrants, most of them from Germany and Ireland, added to the downriver diversity of its early occupants. The Ohio country, in particular, became the testing ground for a number of different settlement groups. The map of Ohio's land subdivisions (Fig. 2) is a patchwork of congressional, private, and company holdings. As might be expected, several of these front onto the Ohio River.

The different settlement groups that converged on the Ohio Valley occupied the new country according to their particular regional traditions. New Englanders were town builders, relied heavily on cattle and sheep, and attended Congregational churches. Settlers from the East were either Lutherans or Presbyterians, depending on whether they were of German or Scots-Irish background. They raised wheat and practiced crop rotation, and many spoke Pennsylvania-Dutch, a German dialect still heard in southern Ohio today. During field work in 1969 in Fairfield County, Ohio, I was asked by an elderly farmer after entering his house "to make the door to." This, as some readers will recognize, is a literal translation of the German "mach die Tür zu" and was a phrase common among Pennsylvania-Dutch settlers. Southerners introduced tobacco cultivation to Ohio and the fattening of cattle and hogs on corn. Some attended new kinds of fundamentalist churches.

Many of the German and Irish immigrants arriving in the early 1800s came as laborers or took up crafts and small business occupations in the rapidly growing river towns. Places like Marietta, Pomeroy, Ironton, and Portsmouth retain in family names, religious practices, brick construction, and conservative voting habits their strong German settlement influence.[32] Cincinnati, of course, became a virtual "German" town, functioning both as a terminus for German immigrants and as a way station to the rich agricultural areas of western Ohio or southeastern Indiana. Cincinnati's attraction has often been attributed to its similarity to the Rhine Valley of Germany. Most likely, however, the impetus was provided by an early German settler, Martin Baumann, who came to Cincinnati in 1795 and rose to become one of its prominent businessmen. Baumann actively recruited German craftsmen and laborers for his wide-ranging commercial and industrial activities which included a fleet of river boats, a foundry, and Cincinnati's first sugar refinery.[33] In 1900, Cincinnati's Germans numbered 133,000, nearly one half of the city's total population.[34]

LAND DIVISION

Unquestionably, the most prominent settlement imprint in the valley relates to the varying approaches to land subdivision and survey. With the exception of its farthest western part, Kentucky was laid out according to Virginia practices and laws, in metes and bounds fashion. Individuals after obtaining a warrant for a certain amount of land could select their tract wherever they wished, then use topographic features to help set boundaries. It was a system ideally adapted to the sparsely settled frontier and the individualism of its settlers. Simon Kenton, the famous wilderness scout and hero of Allan Eckert's *The Frontiersmen*, learned very early in his adventures about the benefits of "tomahawk improvements." Merely by using a tomahawk to blaze a number of reference trees and driving a few stakes to ensure legality of the delimited area, one could become proprietor of a thousand acres or more. Kenton, needless to say, was very interested in this method of laying claim to land "and in an unusually short time . . . had become a rather good surveyor."[35]

Of course, "tomahawk improvements" were an ideal way of lining one's own pockets, and land speculation went hand in hand with the metes and bounds system. Additional settlement characteristics were the irregular pattern of property boundaries and the variations in size and land value of claims. The former reflects the individual choice in laying down a boundary, while the latter are representative of when a claim was made and the kind of land that was available. The first-comers, naturally, had the opportunity to chose the most desirable land, usually fertile valley areas fronting on a river. Because land was cheap and frontier agriculture necessitated large acreages, sizable properties were selected. Jordan and Kaups suggest 300 to 350 acres per capita as the minimum amount of land needed on the Kentucky frontier, or approximately 2,000 acres for a typical family.[36] This need for large individual holdings is borne out by the action of the Kentucky land court in 1779, allowing squatters to claim 400 acres as their preemption right plus an additional 1,000 acres if improvements had been made.[37] In 1779, improvement of land meant that it had been cleared of trees.

Similarly, Virginia was quite generous in its allocation of military bounties. In fact, "to soldiers of equal rank, Virginia gave nearly ten times as much land as did Congress."[38] This Southern attitude regarding settlement size ranges north of the Ohio River into the Virginia Military District (VMD) of Ohio (Fig. 2), and a small area in southern Indiana next to the Falls of the Ohio. For example, a soldier with less than three years of service could get 100 acres, while a major general's military warrant was good for 15,000 acres.[39] To this day, the VMD in Ohio includes some of the state's largest farms. Madison County, in the heart of the District, has an average farm size of 364 acres, or 167 acres more than the average for the state.[40] The Southern settlement legacy is repeated in numerous other ways, including the survival of rural black settlements, land use practices, town patterns, building types, religious affiliation, and linguistic elements, especially place names. In 1850, a time when Ohio rapidly moved toward industrialization and urbanization, nearly one-half of all the state's black population lived in the rural counties of the VMD.[41] Many of these had entered Ohio as free laborers along with former plantation owners or were simply attracted to the area because of the availability of work. Today, the descendants of these early black settlers continue to live in the area, especially in some of the towns, as for example Chillicothe, Circleville, and Washington Courthouse.

Southern land use centered around tobacco, corn, and livestock. The VMD became renowned as an area of corn production. In fact, the Corn Belt of the Midwest probably had its start in the counties of Ohio's VMD where the trinity of Midwestern agriculture—corn, cattle, and hogs—was well established by the mid 1800s. Cattle were grazed on the open range and fattened on unhusked corn in feedlots.[42] This practice, which developed in the East, had been diffused into the interior of Kentucky, where agriculture was based on corn, wheat, and rye, "and cattle were fattened in open feed lots during the winter."[43] From Virginia and Kentucky, the feedlot cattle fattening process came into Ohio and other Midwestern states. Hogs, as the traditional meat animal of the South, were a natural byproduct of this system, functioning as scavengers for leftover corn in the feedlots. This agricultural system remains extant in the VMD and is particularly noticeable in Fayette, Clinton, and Highland counties.

The raising of tobacco, which in Ohio is often recognized as a truly Southern transplant, did not really come into its own until the Civil War. With Kentucky tobacco production cut off, it became well established in the Ohio river counties ranging from Clermont to Gallia, with Brown and Adams counties most important. The emphasis is on white burley, which is raised primarily for chewing tobacco. Brown County remains an important producer today.[44] In retrospect, without the important function of the river as a political and economic boundary, tobacco production in southern Ohio might never have become a regionally significant cash crop. Ripley, a river town in Brown County, Ohio, continues to function as a tobacco market and each year celebrates its Tobacco Festival.

The settlement contrasts between the VMD and adjacent congressional areas are particularly well shown in the different cadastral systems. The metes and bounds survey, as a typical Southern imprint in the VMD, has already been described. However, most of the Ohio Valley land was eventually surveyed, subdivided, and sold based on the federal Land Ordinance of 1785. The implementation of that system began next to the Ohio River and its intersection with the Pennsylvania Line. From there this survey, often referred to as the American Rectangular Land Survey or Township and Range Survey, was laid down over most of this country and Canada. It had a most extraordinary landscape-shaping effect as properties, field and fencelines, and roads were aligned with the straight survey lines of north-south and east-west directions. The road pattern of Salt Creek Township (Fig. 9) in the congressional survey area east of the Scioto River contrasts sharply from that of Deer Creek Township west of the river and in the metes and bounds survey of the VMD (Fig. 9). This rectangular system was less well known to settlers from the East and South. It replaced the freedom of an individual claim with the strictures of the government deciding how the land shall be patterned, how and where the land should be allocated for settlement, and in what acreages and costs.

The Old Seven Ranges of Ohio (Fig. 2) became the first area ever surveyed under the stipulations of the Land Ordinance of 1785, and remain as an example of the trials and tribulations encountered before the survey reached its final form. For example, the section numbering began in the southeastern part of a township, proceeding northward to Section 6 and then skipping back to the southernmost column of sections for No. 7. The last section (No. 36) was therefore located in the northwestern corner of a township, or contrary to the familiar numbering direction from northeast corner to southeast corner. Needless to say, these aberrations in the survey continue to confound people who are unfamiliar with it.

Several other defects in the early survey characterize land division in Ohio's valley region. For example, in the beginning of the survey there was no compensation for meridional convergence. As a result, odd-shaped section lines are common in southern Ohio. These reveal the problems surveyors faced as they attempted to affix a straight-line survey to a curving earth. This defect was eventually corrected when a series of east-west baselines was established and corresponding adjustments of uniform size townships and sections to less land were made. Accomplished by eliminating a column of townships at each succeeding baseline, they resulted in the characteristic ninety-degree kink in north-south running section or township roads. Many a young country boy learned about this peculiarity of the American settlement landscape the hard way. A continuous straight stretch of section road was ideal for nighttime weekend drag racing. Disaster, however, awaited anyone who forgot about the survey offsets. The lucky ones ended up with a bruised ego and loads of soil and cornstalks underneath the bumper and hood.

The implementation of the rectangular survey was strongly influenced by the government's wish for efficient and organized sales of land. In the Land Ordinance of 1785 Congress not only set down the spatial details of the survey but also decreed the minimum purchase area at a minimum price per acre. By multiplying minimum area times minimum price one arrives at the "threshold price" of settlement. Land offices were established to assure the orderly process of land sales within the surveyed areas. Settlers who followed the first surveying crew into the Seven Ranges could arrange their land purchase through an office in Pittsburgh. The first land offices in the Ohio country were located in Steubenville and Marietta and were conducting business by 1800.[45]

If the government had anticipated a rush on land in the Seven Ranges, it was in for a surprise. There were few takers; the story goes that land could not even be given away to Hessian soldiers. The problem was the very high "threshold price." In 1785, Congress, hoping to make money quickly and keep undesirables out, set 640 acres or one entire section as the minimum purchase area and two dollars per acre as the minimum price. As it turned out, few frontier folk could afford a "threshold price" of $1,250. Instead, land speculation flourished, something that the federal government tried to discourage. As a result, Congress over a number of years adjusted the requirements for minimum area and minimum price. In 1832, it set the final and lowest quantities at 40 acres and $1.25 per acre or a "threshold price" of $50.[46] These different and often changing approaches by the federal government to land sales had an impact on Ohio's settlement landscape in terms of farm size and land use. For instance, hog farming, which is typical in southwestern Ohio, does not require enormous acreages because it is labor intensive. The decrease in "threshold price" allowed for smaller farm sizes ideally suited to the traditional hogs-corn combination of Southern farmers.

TOWN PLANS

In contrast to the pervasive irregularity of properties, fields, fencerows, and roads in the VMD, towns were platted in regular, grid pattern fashion. The Southern estate-type farming that characterizes much of the VMD had little need for towns; those that do exist have gained some size because of their function as county seats, marketing, and small manufacturing centers. They were laid out in rectangular blocks with a block or part of one set aside for the location of the courthouse (Fig. 6a). Southerners as well as settlers from the Middle Atlantic states appear to have relied on a similar model when it came to town platting. The Philadelphia Plan with its central square cut out of the adjoining blocks (Fig. 6b) "was regularly adopted in the early cities of southeastern Pennsylvania and occurs at least occasionally in all parts of the United States."[47] The diffusion of that plan southward was assured as excess populations from southeastern Pennsylvania moved up the Shenandoah Valley and into the adjoining Blue Ridge and the rolling Piedmont country of Virginia and the Carolinas.

Upon further westward diffusion, the original plan was modified and occurs quite frequently as a simple block square or "Shelbyville Square," so named after Shelbyville, Tennessee.[48] This version, which was further simplified by location of the courthouse at the intersection of the two principal central streets, occurs quite often in the VMD and is in contrast to the town plats in areas settled primarily by Pennsylvanians. Chillicothe, Hillsboro, and Wilmington, the county seats of Ross, Highland, and Clinton counties, respectively—all of them located in the VMD—were laid out in that fashion. Only in Wilmington does the courthouse actually occupy the central portion of the square next to the intersection of Main and South streets (Fig. 6a). Of course, the regularity of the grid pattern town in the VMD ends at the town's margins. In the countryside, road location was influenced, though not controlled, by metes and bounds survey. As a result, highways, especially county and township roads, were located with physical site advantage rather than survey line control in mind. This contributed to a much greater frequency of right-of-way conflicts with private property owners, but assured proper terrain location of roads and shortest distance between places. One of the best summaries of the influence of contrasting survey systems on the settlement landscape is found in *Original Survey and Land Subdivision* by Norman J. W. Thrower,[49] a comparative study of metes and bounds and congressional surveys in Ohio. In support of the above discussion, Thrower points out that in his study area in the VMD only 8 percent of road mileage corresponded with survey lines. In contrast, 77 percent of all public roads followed survey or township and section lines in the congressional survey area.[50]

Unlike the Southerners, settlers who entered the Ohio Valley from the East, especially Pennsylvania, adhered more strictly to the Philadelphia Plan in laying out their towns. Cambridge, Lancaster, and Somerset were all platted around the characteristic "diamond square" whose corners extend into the adjoining blocks (Fig. 6b). The county courthouse and other public

Figure 6

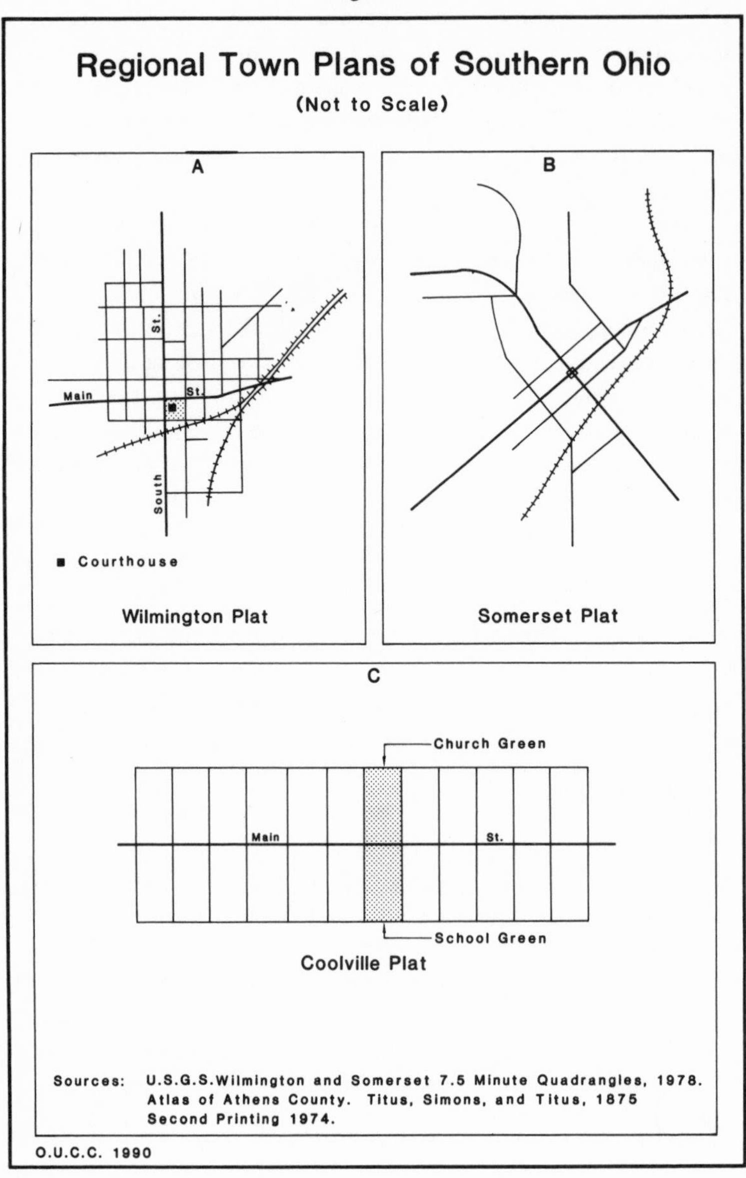

structures are usually located in one or the other of the four corners rather than in the center of the square.

A third type of town in the valley relates to New England settlement. Earlier in this chapter, the founding of Marietta by a group of New Englanders was mentioned. The Ohio Company of Associates, as they called themselves, had purchased over a million acres from Congress in southeastern Ohio (Fig. 2), and planned to use that region as the base from which to extend their federalist notions of political grandeur over the remainder of the Northwest Territory. Their vision came to naught, however, when Southern Democrats usurped power and established Chillicothe rather than Marietta as the first capital of Ohio. Nonetheless, New Englanders did leave their "calling card" on the landscape. They named places and laid out the land to create centrally located, compact settlements. The large number of small towns in the New England settlement area is indicative of their intention to have settlers live in communities. Even the farmers lived in town, going out each day to work in their fields or outlots.

Coolville (Fig. 6c), founded in 1813 in Athens County, is a typical New England street village. It was platted around three streets and a large central green where churches, burial ground, and schools were located. House lots fronted each of the three streets; outlots or fieldlots were allocated outside the village. Outlot Street survives to this day as one of the small roads leading from the village into the surrounding area. Both Marietta and Athens were similarly platted, with sizable commons areas in addition to the public greens or parade grounds. The location of Ohio University in Athens speaks to the New Englanders' need for higher education and respect for public areas. The university might never have been located where it is had Pennsylvanians or Southerners established the community.

These towns, with their classical names, laid out around greens, divided into house and outlots, even sometimes providing a university setting, were all part of a vision to establish in the hills of southeastern Ohio a society patterned after those of New England. In contrast to the negative image of Ohio's Appalachia, which relates to the boom and bust nature of coal mining, New Englanders spoke in rather glowing terms about their purchase area in the West. Manasseh Cutler, the leader of the Associates, gave the following account: "This country may from a proper knowledge be affirmed to be the most healthy, the most commodious, and the most fertile spot on earth, known to European people . . . A paradise of pleasure opening in the wild . . . and the garden of the universe."[51] Can this be real or is it only the promoter speaking? George Washington, a close friend of Cutler, does affirm the notion of southeastern Ohio as an ideal settlement area. In a letter written in 1788, Washington comments: "If I was a young man, just preparing to begin the world, or if in advanced life and had a family to make provision for, I know of no country where I should rather fix my habitation than in some part of the region."[52]

The auspicious beginnings of New England settlement in the Ohio Valley did not last. The Associates ended their function as a settlement organization in January 1796, not quite eight years after the founding of Marietta.[53] The land would eventually be sold to settlers from Pennsylvania and Virginia who entered the region after floating down the Ohio on flatboats or crossing directly from Virginia into southeastern Ohio. Two early roads, the Northwest Pike and the Kanawha Pike, reached the Ohio River directly opposite the New England purchase area. These folk carried their own "cultural baggage," and in time made their own imprint on the landscape of the region while also accommodating themselves to the earlier New England settlement influences.

FOLK BUILDINGS

How do specific cultural trait elements, related to particular regional American populations, correlate with the pattern of settlement? To answer this question, let us examine the material trait boundaries for three traditional artifacts: the Pennsylvania barn, the Southern barn, and the log cabin (Fig. 7).

The distribution of the Pennsylvania barn (Fig. 8) relates primarily to the westward migration of settlers from Pennsylvania. It is an ideal diagnostic form, and can be used to delimit Midland settlement characteristics from Southern ones. The southern extent of that barn type, based on the work by Robert Ensminger,[54] coincides very well with ideal terrain and soil conditions for intensive grain and livestock farming. Pennsylvania settlers preferred these conditions and stayed outside the hillier and poorer lands in the more southerly parts of Illinois, Indiana, and Ohio. Conversely, Allen Noble's[55] boundary of Southern type barns aligns itself almost perfectly with that by Ensminger and reflects the cross-river settlement from Kentucky, Virginia, and other Southern states.

Similarly, the northern boundary of log construction[56] serves to indicate the Southern settlement influence. Although migrants from the East or Midland section certainly were carriers of that building tradition, its foremost practitioners were the

Figure 7

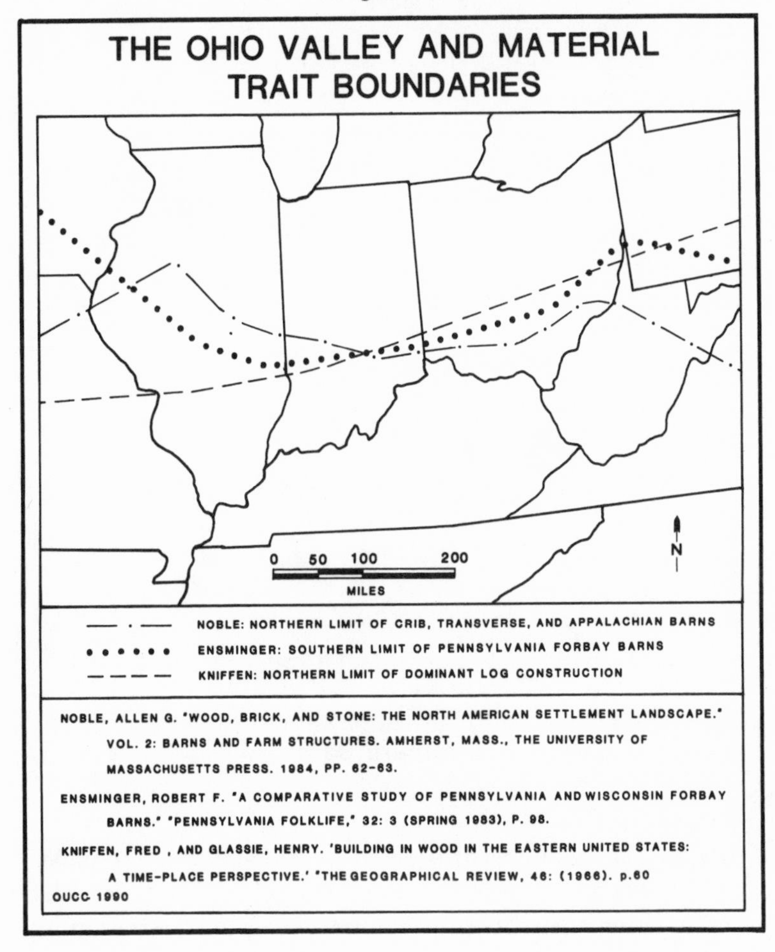

backwoods folk who entered the Ohio Valley region by way of the Upland South and the trans-Appalachian areas of Tennessee and Kentucky. Terry Jordan's work on the origins of American log construction has shown its close relationship to Swedish and Finnish practices of the Delaware Valley region and the diffusion of these practices with the backwoods pioneers into the central and southern Appalachians.[57] From there, the American log cabin, rather than house, was carried into the interior as the frontier dwelling of choice.

Traditional structures of all kinds, especially houses and barns, are certainly one of the most ideal settlement indicators. The valley area of Ohio, along with similar regions in Indiana and Illinois, was occupied according to time-honored

Figure 8

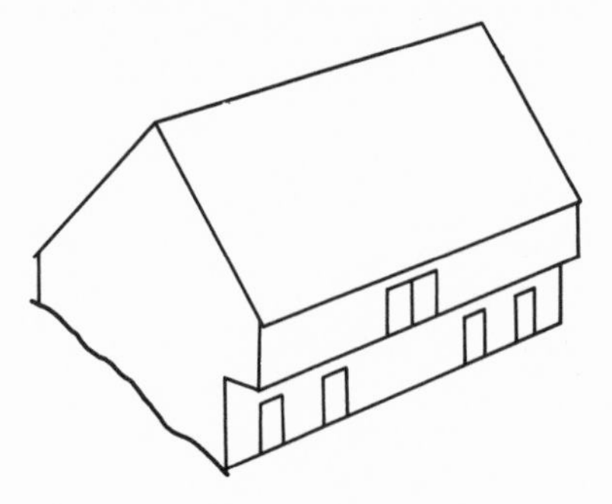

Pennsylvania Barn

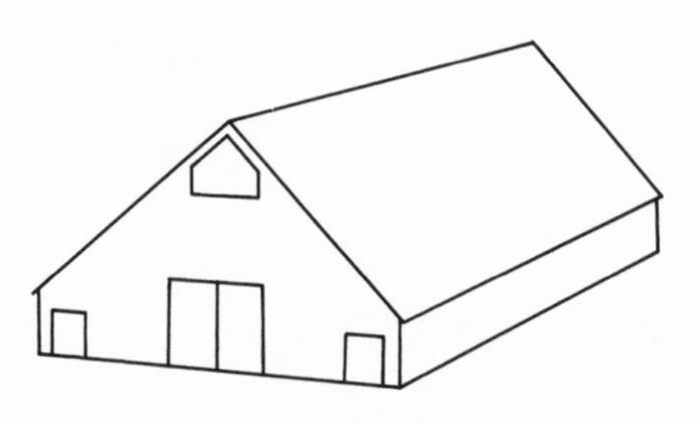

Southern Barn

practices, including what types of houses and barns to build and how to build them. As the country began to industrialize and isolation was reduced by improvements in transportation and communication, traditional structures in much of the Midwest were replaced by standard type tract houses and outbuildings. But in the Ohio Valley, along the southern and eastern margins of America's Midwest, diversity in settlement forms still survives.

Nowhere is this more true than along the Scioto River in south central Ohio, which constitutes the border between the VMD and Congress lands (Fig. 2). There Southern and Eastern migrant populations converged. Although some overlapping between these different settlement groups occurred, it is minor, and the Scioto River has remained a distinct cultural boundary. This spatial variation becomes quite evident when one considers specific settlement forms. Figure 9 shows the distribution of barn types in two townships of Pickaway County, which straddles the Scioto River. In the VMD, Southern barn types prevail, while to the east of the river, in Salt Creek Township, Pennsylvania bank barns are typical. Settlers from Pennsylvania followed Ohio's first interior road, Zane's Trace (Fig. 2), into the southern parts of the state, acquiring land primarily in the congressional land districts. These settlers introduced into Ohio one of the state's characteristic rural structures, the Pennsylvania, Switzer, or Forebay barn (Fig. 8), noted for its size, banked lower floor, and overhanging second story—in Ohio often called the "overshoot"—which gives the barn its characteristic appearance. This barn ideally fit the grain-livestock agriculture of the Pennsylvania folk.

The Southern barn (Fig. 8) is immediately noticeable as one crosses the Scioto River and enters the Virginia settlement area. Its development probably relates to earlier forms in the southern Appalachians and in all likelihood was influenced by Appalachian log-building techniques. The barn was well adapted to Southern-type agriculture in which corn was the single most important grain. Frequently the barn's central drive is flanked by corn cribs. It is topped by a huge hayloft, easily identified from the large opening on the main gable side of the barn and the projecting hayhood. Cattle and horses were usually kept in the side sheds next to the main unit of the barn. The large number of these barns in the VMD supports the cross-river settlement from Virginia and Kentucky. Similarly, this barn was diffused along with Southern settlers into Indiana and Illinois.[58] In fact, it ranges beyond the most direct areas of Southern settlement and becomes the typical "horse barn" of the Midwest and parts of the Great Plains. The southern boundary of the Pennsylvania Barn in Ohio (Fig. 3) is deflected northward as it passes through the VMD, indicating the strength of the Southern settlement effect.

Log cabins, houses, and cribs are among the truest folk settlement forms surviving in the valley region. Jordan makes a clear distinction between cabins and log houses. The former represent the initial, backwoods phase of settlement; they consisted of a single room and small loft, with logs laid clear to the ridge pole, and the roof covered with clapboards. If necessary, this single room structure could easily be taken down and rebuilt at a new location. The Lincoln homesteads, first in Kentucky, then in southern Indiana, and finally in central Illinois, illustrate both the migration of Southerners to the north of the Ohio River and the diffusion of an Upland South material culture trait. New Salem, located near the Sangamon River in

Figure 9

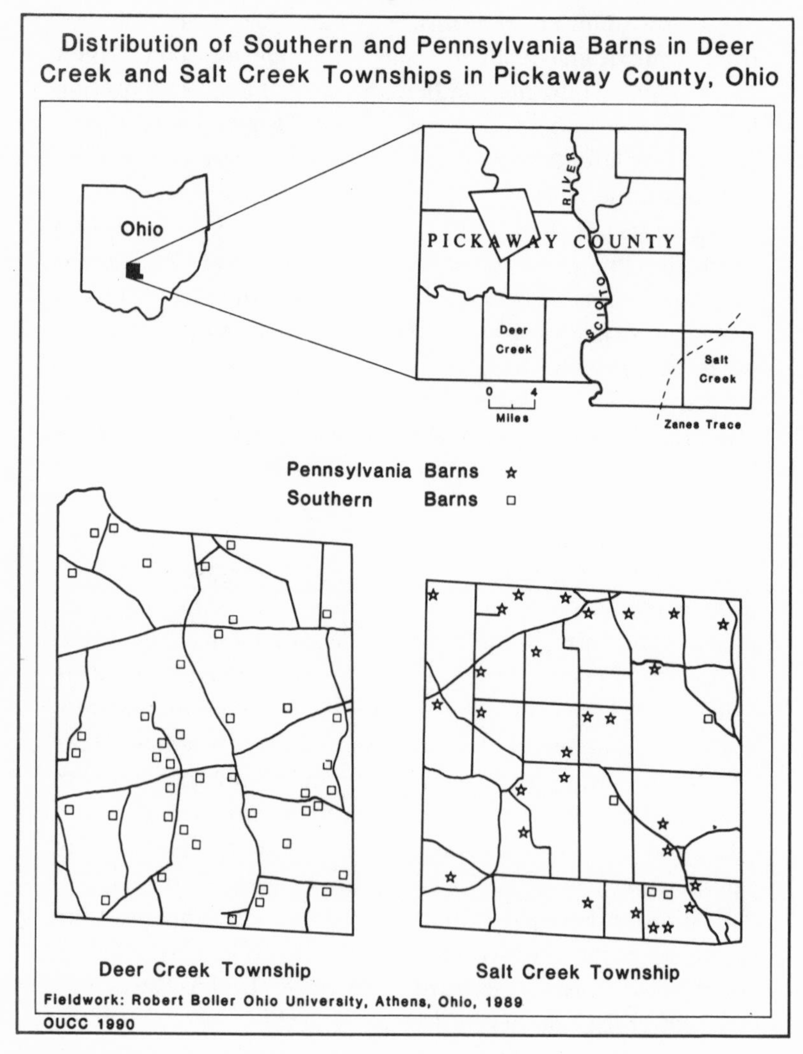

Illinois and the final destination of the Lincoln family, consisted of log structures that differed very little from those earlier ones in Kentucky and Indiana. Few of these earliest frontier cabins have survived.[59] However, many of the substantial log structures of the secondary or permanent settlement phase remain extant and many continue to be occupied. Southeastern Ohio experienced a resurgence in log building during the 1930s with the aid of the WPA. Today, the region is in its third log building phase, with emphasis on log kit houses. The story of Ohio log construction has been well told in *The Archi-*

tecture of Migration: Log Construction in the Ohio Country, 1750–1850 by Donald A. Hutslar.[60]

One of the common log buildings in the valley region was the "saddlebag" house. It consists of two cabins built onto a central chimney. Those that remain have undergone the usual changes or additions which turn a log structure into a house, including front porch, rear lean-to, some sort of wall covering, and a metal roof. The old sandstone chimney is often the only clue to the original structure hidden under all the contemporary bric-a-brac. The saddlebag is probably an ancestral form related to a house that is widely distributed in the VMD and came into Ohio most likely with the Southern fieldhands who often accompanied the large property owners. The house had a wide distribution in the Eastern Tidewater area and was carried from there westward.[61] It became the typical sharecropper house of the Deep South. In Kentucky, as elsewhere, it was often called a tenant house.[62] In the valley region of Ohio, this small house is evidence of the Southern settlement imprint.

Another building type can be used to show the influence of contrasting settlement groups as they converged in the Ohio Valley. The American I-house originated somewhere in the East and became the standard rural dwelling of the 1800s.[63] In the collective psyche of its builders, it stood for success and status. For those readers not familiar with the I-house, it is a two story house, one room deep, consisting of four rooms, two down and two up. More often than not, it has an L or T addition in the back that houses the kitchen. Its name is taken from the first letter of Indiana, Illinois, and Iowa, where this kind of house is quite characteristic.[64] It was built by both Easterners and Southerners, but with the usual differences that come about as peoples and their artifacts diverged spatially and over time. In the valley region of Ohio and states westward, it is possible to differentiate between Eastern and Southern (or Virginia) I-houses. The Eastern or Pennsylvania I-house has a steeply pitched gabled roof, single central chimney or paired gable end chimneys, single or double doors, and either balanced or unbalanced window placement. In contrast, the Southern or Virginia I-house might have a lesser roof pitch, small central roof dormer, paired chimneys on the roof ridge or exterior ones, double porch, and central doors both up and down. Some are slightly raised off the ground, a typical Southern building trait. These diagnostic form elements are, of course, not always repeated, but together constitute a type that is unquestionably Southern. Montell and Morse in their book *Kentucky Folk Architecture*[65] describe and illustrate a number of Southern I-houses, the same as those found north of the river. I recall my confusion during my early days of field work in southern Ohio when I located many houses with a door on the second floor leading into nowhere. Only later did I learn about Southern settlement and I-houses in the Ohio Valley. Obviously porches, and especially double porches, are difficult to maintain and are the first thing to go. Such vernacularization of structures makes reading the common things in the landscape both fascinating and perplexing.

Among the common local houses with roots in New England was the Saltbox. The earliest Saltboxes were built in the late 1700s in areas settled by New Englanders, especially from Massachusetts and Connecticut, where the house was popular in the 1600s.[66] Virginians who settled in southeastern Ohio may have perpetuated this type of house because their background includes houses with rear lean-to additions, forming the characteristic "saltbox" shape. The Saltbox remained a popular type until the early 1900s when it was often used as a company house in the coal mining towns of the region.[67]

As much as the settlement landscape of Ohio's valley region reflects the downriver migration of Northeastern, Eastern, and Southern settlers and their traditions, there are several architectural artifacts in the valley which relate to upriver diffusion. Among these is the "shotgun" house which is characteristic of the townscapes of both large and small river towns. The "shotgun" is a one-story, three-room, gable-front house whose origins may be in distant West Africa.[68] It was a popular house in New Orleans, especially among Blacks. It persisted as a popular type during the period of rapid growth of river communities along the Mississippi and Ohio rivers in the first half of the nineteenth century. It survived changing fashions because as a house of poorer folk it was not replaced by new types. In southeastern Ohio, the "shotgun" was taken from its geographic context of river towns and was used as a company house in some mining districts.

The "Creole" house is another Deep South structure that can be found along the river in Ohio. It is a one and a half story house notable for its large end gable roof that projects over an integral front porch. This integrated type of porch is the most diagnostic element of the "Creole" house. Several are located in Pomeroy, Ohio, a river town between Marietta and Portsmouth.

Finally there remains the question of the pyramid-roof houses which are a ubiquitous type in the valley. They are especially common in the coal mining areas. Specifically known as a Southern Pyramidal, this house ranges "from an elemental one-floor box to extreme forms with a veritable haystack of interlocking pyramids, facets, and dormers."[69] It is particularly widespread throughout the southeastern part of the United States and most likely reached our region with the development of the railroads and the onset of coal mining. In fact, it became the most common company house in southeastern Ohio. As a vernacular house type, it deserves much closer scrutiny than it has received so far.

CONCLUSION

On a map showing cords of wood sold in the United States in 1840, we can see a solid dark line of heavy sales from Pennsylvania down the Ohio and Mississippi valleys to New Orleans.[70] The map serves as an ideal indication of population density and regional development and is symbolic of the singular attraction of these two waterways as settlers spilled across the Appalachians. It also supports the analogy made at the beginning of the chapter, that the Ohio River functioned like a huge funnel, pulling the migrants from their original settlement areas in the Northeast, East, and South toward a common direction into the interior. Translated into settlement landscape terms, it meant that the Ohio Valley became home to all kinds of peoples and backgrounds. Although mixing and acculturation did occur, there was usually sufficient isolation and separation of settlement groups to ensure the survival of traditional practices. This explains the diversity in the settlement landscape and, at times, the strange juxtaposition of dissimilar settlement forms as, for example, a farmstead with a Southern I-house and a Pennsylvania barn.

Two American regional settlement groups were numerically most important in the valley region, those from the South and those from the Middle Atlantic. The latter group consisted primarily of settlers from Pennsylvania, while Virginians and Kentuckians comprised the Southern "flock." Although these two groups followed geographically contrasting migration routes, both had common linkages in the culture-trait complex of southeastern Pennsylvania and the Delaware Valley. For example, the Southern backwoods folk, just like the settlers from Pennsylvania, adhered to log construction methods and building I-houses, practices that were rooted in the Middle Atlantic region. Of course, time and cultural divergence or separation from the parent culture altered old ways and produced new ones. When the two migration streams converged in the Ohio Valley, contrasts rather than similarities were typical.

A case in point is religion. Large numbers of Pennsylvania settlers were members of the Evangelical United Brethren Church (EUB). Historically, this church represents the German language branch of the Methodist Church. Before their merger with the Methodist Church, EUB churches were a helpful guide to Pennsylvania settlement in southern Ohio.[71] Conversely, Southerners who came into Ohio during the early 1800s brought with them The Disciples of Christ Church, a denomination that dates from the revival movement on the frontier of Virginia and Kentucky and has been used as an indicator of "Border South" settlement to the north of the Ohio River.[72]

The Ohio River, rather than forming a regional boundary, bisects an area that is situated between South and Midwest. For a variety of reasons, Southerners assumed settlement and landscape-shaping control over much of the northern valley region. Their imprint is perfect in the Virginia Military District of Ohio, and is strong in Indiana and Illinois and beyond the urban-industrial corridor of the Upper Ohio Valley. European immigrants seeking work were a significant population component in the Upper Valley. They were less important downriver, especially outside the principal urban centers of Cincinnati and Louisville.

It matters little which term—Upper South, Border South, or Ohio Valley—is used to identify this region. It is a different place because of the character of its settlement landscape which still includes many of the traditional settlement forms introduced from the South, East, and Northeast. The hilly nature of the region, the shift of the country from river to rail transportation, and the legacy of the Civil War imposed a certain isolation on the area. This isolation, as much as anything, has contributed to the distinctiveness of the Valley: a place that is neither South, Midwest, or East, but rather a region all its own where such words as corn pone, Johnny cake, and smearcase may not yet be considered archaic.

NOTES

1. August Meitzen, *Das Deutsche Volk in Seinen Volkstümlichen Formen* (Berlin: Verlag von Dietrich Reimer, 1882).

2. The term *Altlandschaft* was coined by the German geographer Otto Schlüter. See Otto Schlüter, *Die Siedlungsräume Mitteleuropas in Frühgeschichtlicher Zeit, 1. Teil, Einführung in die Altlandschaftsforschung*, Forschungen zur Deutschen Landeskunde (Remagen: Verlag des Amtes für Landeskunde, 1952).

3. Milton B. Newton, "Sliced Tomatoes for Breakfast," *Pioneer America*, 9:1 (July 1977):11.

4. Hubert G. H. Wilhelm, *The Origin and Distribution of Settlement Groups: Ohio 1850* (Athens, Ohio: Cutler Printing, 1982), 46.

5. Terry G. Jordan and Matti Kaups, *The American Backwoods Frontier: An Ethnic and Ecological Interpretation* (Baltimore: Johns Hopkins University Press, 1989), 1–37.

6. Allen W. Eckert, *The Frontiersmen: A Narrative* (Boston: Little, Brown, and Co., 1967; reissued in paperback by Bantam Books, Inc., 1970), 73–74.

7. Ralph Brown, *The Historical Geography of the United States* (New York: Harcourt, Brace and Co., 1948), 242.

8. Ibid., 237–38.

9. Robert D. Mitchell, "The Formation of Early American Cultural Regions: An Interpretation," in *European Settlement and Development in North America: Essays on Geographical Change in Honour and Memory of Andrew Hill Clark*, James R. Gibson, ed. (Toronto: University of Toronto Press, 1978), 83–84.

10. Ibid.

11. Gregory S. Rose, "The National Road Border between the North and the South by 1870," *Geoscience and Man*, 25 (1988):159–67.

12. Raven I. McDavid, Jr., and Virginia McDavid, " 'Cracker' and 'Hoosier.' " *Names*, 21:3 (1973):161–67.

13. Gregory S. Rose, "The Southern Origins of Ohio and Indiana's Pioneers," paper presented at combined meetings of ELDAAG and SEDAAG, Charleston, West Virginia, November 1989. Cited with permission of the author.

14. Wilhelm, *The Origin and Distribution of Settlement Groups: Ohio 1850*, 57–88.

15. Figure 5 is based on maps from the following three regional texts: Stephen S. Birdsall and John W. Florin, *Regional Landscapes of the United States*, 3rd ed. (New York: John Wiley and Sons, 1985), 18; Joel Garreau, *The Nine Nations of North America*, 8th ed. (Boston: Houghton Mifflin Co., 1981), unnumbered map section; and J. H. Patterson, *North America*, 8th ed. (New York: Oxford University Press, 1989), 204.

16. Wilbur Stout, "The Charcoal Iron Industry of the Hanging Rock Iron District: Its Influence on the Early Development of the Ohio Valley." *Ohio Archaeological and Historical Quarterly*, 42 (1933):72–104.

17. Frederick J. Turner, *The Frontier in American History*, (New York: Henry Holt and Co., 1962), 18.

18. John A. Jakle, "Salt on the Ohio Valley Frontier, 1770–1820," *Annals of the Association of American Geographers*, 59:4 (1969):687–709.

19. John A. Jakle, *Images of the Ohio Valley* (New York: Oxford University Press, 1977), 152.

20. David S. Walls, "On the Naming of Appalachia," in *An Appalachian Symposium*, J. W. Williamson, ed. (Boone, N.C.: Appalachian State University Press, 1977), 56–76.

21. Karl B. Raitz and Richard Ulack, *Appalachia: A Regional Geography* (Boulder, Colo.: Westview Press, 1984), 217.

22. Ibid., 324.

23. Harry Caudill, *Night Comes to the Cumberlands: A Biography of a Depressed Area* (Boston: Little, Brown and Co., 1962), 305–24.

24. James T. Lemon, "Colonial America in the Eighteenth Century," in *North America: The Historical Geography of a Changing Continent*, Robert D. Mitchell and Paul A. Groves, eds. (Totowa, N.J.: Rowman and Littlefield, Publishers, 1987), 122.

25. David H. Mould, "Canals and Railroads in the Hocking Valley Region of Ohio, 1825–1875," Ph.D. dissertation, Ohio University, Athens, Ohio: 1989, 142.

26. Jakle, *Images of the Ohio Valley*, 163.

27. Cynthia Williams, ed., *Ohio Almanac, 1971* (Lorain, Ohio: Lorain Journal Co., 1971).

28. State of Ohio, *Ohio Population Report: Twentieth Federal Census* (Columbus, Ohio: Compiled by the Office of the Secretary of State, 1980).

29. Frances K. Eisan, *River Village: Gateway to the West* (Wabash, Ind.: Milliner Printing Co., 1976), 12 (the author quotes an article written by Col. John Vawter, April 13, 1850).

30. Ibid., 25.

31. The town's architectural gems are given appropriate recognition in John T. Windle, *The Early Architecture of Madison, Indiana* (Indianapolis: Indiana Historical Society, 1986).

32. Hubert G. H. Wilhelm, "The Route West: German Immigration in Ohio before 1850," in *French and Germans in the Mississippi Valley: Landscape and Cultural Traditions*, Michael Roark, ed. (Cape Girardeau, Mo.: Center for Regional History and Cultural Heritage, Southeast Missouri State University, 1988), 209–28.

33. Carl Wittke, "The Germans of Cincinnati." *Bulletin of the Historical and Philosophical Society of Ohio*, 20 (1962):3–14.

34. Albert B. Faust, *The German Element in the United States*, vol. 1 (New York: Houghton Mifflin Co., 1909), 426.

35. Eckert, *The Frontiersmen: A Narrative*, 77.

36. Jordan and Kaups, *The American Backwoods Frontier: An Ethnic and Ecological Interpretation*, 123.

37. John F. Hart, *The Look of the Land* (Englewood Cliffs, N.J.: Prentice Hall, Inc., 1975), 55.

38. C. E. Sherman, *Original Ohio Land Subdivisions*, vol. 3 of the Final Report, Ohio Cooperative Topographic Survey (Columbus, Ohio: 1925, reprinted by Ohio Department of Natural Resources, Division of Geological Survey, 1974), 20.

39. Ibid.

40. U.S. Department of Commerce, *1987 Census of Agriculture*, vol. 1, Geographic Area Studies, Part 35, Ohio (Washington, D.C.: U.S. Government Printing Office, 1987).

41. Wilhelm, *The Origin and Distribution of Settlement Groups: Ohio 1850*, 30–31.

42. David A. Simmons (preparer), "The Virginia Military District: A

Historic Context," in *Ohio Comprehensive Preservation Plan* (Columbus: Ohio Historic Preservation Office, 1987), 14.

43. Mitchell, "The Formation of Early American Cultural Regions: An Interpretation," 84.

44. Simmons, "The Virginia Military District: A Historic Context," 15.

45. Thomas A. Burke, *Ohio Lands: A Short History* (Columbus, Ohio: Auditor of State, 1987).

46. Hart, *The Look of the Land*, 60. Also see Benjamin H. Hibbard, *A History of the Public Land Policies* (New York: Macmillan Co., 1924; reprinted, Madison: University of Wisconsin Press, 1965), 32–55.

47. Edward T. Price, "The Central Courthouse Square in the American County Seat." *Geographical Review*, 58 (1968):39.

48. Ibid., 44.

49. Norman J. W. Thrower, *Original Survey and Land Subdivisions*, no. 4, Monograph Series, Association of American Geographers (Chicago: Rand McNally and Co., 1966), 5.

50. Ibid., 95.

51. P. Lee Phillips, *The First Map and Description of Ohio 1787 by Manasseh Cutler* (Washington, D.C.: W. H. Laudermilk and Co., 1918), 18.

52. H. Z. Williams, *History of Washington County, 1788–1881* (H. Z. Williams and Sons, Publishers, 1881; reprinted, Knightstown, Ind.: Bookmark, 1976), 49.

53. Hubert G. H. Wilhelm, "New England in Southeastern Ohio." *Pioneer America Society Transactions*, 2 (1979):13–30.

54. Robert F. Ensminger, "A Comparative Study of Pennsylvania and Wisconsin Forebay Barns," *Pennsylvania Folklife*, 32:3 (Spring 1983):98.

55. Allen G. Noble, *Wood, Brick and Stone: The North American Settlement Landscape*, vol. 1, Houses, vol. 2, Barns and Farm Structures (Amherst: University of Massachusetts Press, 1984), 62–63.

56. Fred B. Kniffen and Henry Glassie, "Building in Wood in the Eastern United States: A Time-Place Perspective," *Geographical Review*, 54:1 (1966):40–66.

57. Terry G. Jordan, "A Reappraisal of Fenno-Scandinavian Antecedents for Midland American Log Construction," *Geographical Review*, 73 (1983):58–94.

58. Robert W. Bastian, "Indiana Folk Architecture: A Lower Midwestern Index." *Pioneer America*, 9 (1977):115–36.

59. Jordan, "A Reappraisal of Fenno-Scandinavian Antecedents for Midland American Log Construction," 58–94; and Jordan and Kaups, *The American Backwoods Frontier: An Ethnic and Ecological Interpretation*, 135–78.

60. Donald A. Hutslar, *The Architecture of Migration: Log Construction in the Ohio Country, 1750–1850* (Athens: Ohio University Press, 1986).

61. Henry Glassie, *Patterns in the Material Folk Culture of the Eastern United States* (Philadelphia: University of Pennsylvania Press, 1968), 102.

62. Lynwood W. Montell and Michael L. Morse, *Kentucky Folk Architecture* (Lexington: University Press of Kentucky, 1976).

63. For information on the I-house see Fred B. Kniffen, "Louisiana House Types," *Annals of the Association of American Geographers*, 26 (1936):179–93; Fred B. Kniffen, "Folk Housing: Key to Diffusion," *Annals of the Association of American Geographers*, 55 (1965):549–77; Henry Glassie, *Folk Housing in Middle Virginia* (Knoxville: University

of Tennessee Press, 1975); Allen G. Noble, *Wood, Brick and Stone: The North American Settlement Landscape*, vol. 1, Houses (Amherst: University of Massachusetts Press, 1984).

64. Kniffen, "Louisiana House Types," 165.

65. Montell and Morse, *Kentucky Folk Architecture*, 26.

66. Gail M. Gillespie, "Pre- and Post-Industrial Saltbox Houses as Features of Local Evolution in Athens County, Ohio," M.A. thesis, Ohio University, Athens, Ohio, 5–10 and 95.

67. Ibid., 91.

68. John Michael Vlach, "The Shotgun House: An African Agricultural Legacy," (Part 1), *Pioneer America*, 8:1 (1976):47–56.

69. Peirce F. Lewis, "Common Houses, Cultural Spoor," *Landscape*, 19 (1975):20.

70. Michael Williams, "Clearing of United States Forests: Pivotal Years, 1810–1860," *Journal of Historical Geography*, 8:1 (1982):12–28.

71. Hubert G. H. Wilhelm. "Southeastern Ohio as a Settlement Region: An Historical Geographical Interpretation." *Proceedings of the Pioneer America Society*, 1 (1972):96–129.

72. Bruce Bigelow, "The Disciples of Christ in Antebellum Indiana: Geographical Indicator of the Border South." *Journal of Cultural Geography*, 7 (1986):49–58.

Michael Allen

THE OHIO RIVER: ARTERY OF MOVEMENT

In 1852, Ohio boatman Joseph Hough reminisced about his forty-six-year career as flatboatman on the Ohio and Mississippi rivers. He noted that many dramatic changes had taken place: "Now Steam Boats of the first class are plying to and from every point on the Ohio and Mississippi rivers; railroad cars, stage coaches, and private carriages are constantly in requisition to convey you from almost every point in the country." Hough was amazed that these "great changes . . . have taken place in forty-six years!" Could Joseph Hough have observed modern Ohio River traffic, he would no doubt have expressed even greater wonderment at the degree of change. Modern port cities, locks and dams, and diesel-powered towboats would seem inconceivable to an early nineteenth century riverman.[1]

As an artery of movement, the Ohio River has witnessed a long and continuing progression of river craft and rivermen. The early Indian canoemen were succeeded by European explorers who were themselves succeeded by a burgeoning non-steam river commerce of flatboats, keelboats, and lumber and log rafts. With the launching of the *New Orleans* in 1811, the "Steamboat Age" on the Ohio began. While the railroads supplanted the steamers following the Civil War, river commerce later reemerged and has endured by means of the snub-nosed, diesel towboat until the present day. The recent return to the Ohio River of "sternwheelers" like the *Delta Queen* and the *Mississippi Queen* serves as a dramatic epilogue to the long history of the Ohio as an artery of movement.[2]

The original Ohio boatmen were Native Americans, paddling their sleek, wooden canoes up and down its waters. These craft could move entire tribes from one locale to another, and served in time of war to facilitate quick movement and surprise attack. A cruder Indian boat—the "bull boat"—was constructed from branches and mud shaped to form a sort of bowl. Goods as well as people could float downstream in these craft, and a sort of embryonic commercial life developed. When the early English and French explorers arrived on the scene, they adapted the Indian craft to their needs. So too did the white fur traders. By the middle of the 1700s, a full-fledged riverboat commerce was imminent. This was the dawn of the so-called Keelboat Age on the western waters.

The keelboat was a sleek, prowed, upstream craft, averaging about sixty feet in length and eight feet in width. When boatmen referred to the keel as a "low-draft" vessel, they meant that keelboats could run in shallow water. Equipped with sails and rigging, a keelboat resembled a miniature sailing vessel or a small ocean-going frigate. However, keels were dependent upon much more than their sails for propulsion up the swift currents of the Ohio and Mississippi. They often had to be rowed, poled, or hand-winched upstream by the herculean efforts of their crews. While a downstream trip from Louisville to New Orleans might take as little as three weeks, the upstream return might very well take three or four months.

Obviously, these sorts of hardships did not make for a major role for keelboating in early river commerce. Contrary to popular belief, the flatboat, not the keel, was the mainstay of early American riverboating. Yet the keelboats provided valuable service for a brief stint in the late 1700s and early 1800s, carrying furs, lead, salt, and whiskey downstream, and coffee, sugar, and trade goods north to the Ohio Valley.

What sort of men were engaged in this trade? It is difficult to say with great certainty, for these illiterate frontiersmen left very little evidence for historians to ponder. Another problem in describing keelboatmen is that such an aura of heroic legend has grown up around them. To later generations, keelboatmen became folk heroes in every sense of the word. Indeed, keelboatmen were said to possess such muscular prowess and boisterous ways that they must be "half horse, half alligator."

There is no better example of the distortions inherent in this folk hero-worship than the figure of Mike Fink, the "King of the Keelboatmen." Mike Fink, the original "half horse, half alligator" boatman, was a real person. Born near Fort Pitt (modern-day Pittsburgh, Pennsylvania) around 1770, he took to the woods at an early age as a hunter, scout, and Indian fighter. He made his first keelboat trip down the Ohio in his early twenties, using Pittsburgh and then Wheeling as his home ports. From then until his violent shooting death in the Montana country in 1823, we know very little about the real Mike Fink, for the myth makers and journalists have intermingled fact with fiction to the point that the truth has been almost entirely lost.

The mythical Mike Fink so captured the imaginations of nineteenth century Americans that he became a folk hero of the same stature as Davy Crockett and Daniel Boone. Scores of stories were written about him in nineteenth century newspapers, journals, almanacs, and novels. His abilities as a marksman are almost always a feature of the stories. So too are his racist beliefs, which nineteenth century Americans found highly amusing. In one tale Mike shoots off an Indian's scalplock and becomes the object of his hatred and revenge. In another he shoots off a "Darkey's Heel" at a hundred yards, so, as Mike explained it, "he kin wear a decent boot!"

The most famous of Mike Fink's shooting feats, however, is his practice (supposedly true) of shooting a whiskey cup off a friend's head and then having the cup shot off his own. In this way the two boatmen show their friendship and trust in one another as well as their skill with a rifle. Mike's death in Montana was reconstructed by journalists to revolve around this "shooting of the cup."

Drinking and fighting were also specialties, and in many tales Mike's main accomplishment seems to have been getting himself roaring drunk and then starting a brawl. Fink boasted that he could "out-run, out-hop, out-jump, throw down, drag out, and lick any man in the country." In Emerson Bennet's novel *Mike Fink, a Legend of the Ohio*, Mike bragged:

> Hooray for me you scapegoats! I'm a land-screamer—I'm a water-dog—I'm a snapping turtle—I can lick five times my own weight in wild cats. I can use up Injens by the cord. I can swallow niggers whole, raw, or cooked. I can out-run, out-dance, out-jump, out-dive, out-drink, out-holler, and out-lick any white thing in the shape o' human that's ever put foot within two thousand miles of the big Massassip.[3]

But while the Mike Fink stories are action-packed, they do not tell us much about the real keelboatmen. To discover this, one should peruse the diary of William Adams, a keelboatman contemporary of Mike Fink. Adams's description of his crew's voyage upstream from the Lower Mississippi and then up the Ohio to the mouth of the Cumberland River makes for agonizing reading. Adams and his crewmates spent each day from sunup to sunset rowing, pushing, poling, and pulling their keelboat up the winding western rivers. On one particularly grueling day the men "cursed" one another because they made so little progress. When they finally made camp, they were within sight of their "last place of encampment." Adams's crewmates drank a great deal and got into fights just like Mike Fink and his crew, but somehow this story loses the romance one usually attributes to the exploits of hard-living "half horse, half alligator" boatmen. The traits that seem so attractive in folklore lose their attraction in reality. William Adams's memoir depicts keelboating as it actually was: an extremely taxing mode of labor engaged in by a rough and crude group of pioneer rivermen.[4]

The heyday of the keelboat was short-lived. The introduction of steamboats to the western rivers in 1811 put the keels on the road to extinction; shippers naturally switched to this more expeditious and economical mode of upstream travel. But it is noteworthy that the steamboat did not drive one non-mechanized rivercraft out of business. Flatboats continued to ply the artery of movement in huge numbers throughout the first half of the nineteenth century.[5]

Back in the days before steam power, the produce of the American frontier—pork, flour, corn, animal skins, fruit, vegetables, and whiskey—was shipped up and down the Ohio and Mississippi rivers on thousands of flatboats. Although the upstream-bound keelboats were replaced by steamboats, flatboats endured well into the nineteenth century as a prime means of downstream travel.

Many flatboats were not strictly commercial craft. For instance, Colonel Aaron Burr commanded a flatboat "flotilla" in the ill-fated 1806–1807 expedition that led to his trial (and acquittal) for treason. No one knows exactly what the former vice-president was up to, but it probably had something to do with an invasion of Spanish territory. (Looking back on his flatboating days, Burr often commented that he was simply ahead of his time—Sam Houston and David Crockett were lionized for their Texas exploits thirty years later.) There is an interesting footnote to the Burr story, however: His flatboats were constructed on the Cumberland River by none other than Andrew Jackson, a Burr associate who was himself a former keelboat entrepreneur.

More common than military craft were the "emigrant flatboats." Frontier emigrants bound for Ohio Valley climes often loaded all their worldly belongings onto a flat at Pittsburgh, bought a copy of Zadok Cramer's *Western Navigator* to guide them, and pushed off hopefully into *la belle rivière*. If they were lucky, they arrived at their destination in one piece. Senator Henry Clay often boasted of his family's early nineteenth century flatboat trek to Kentucky. Like tens of thousands of pioneers during the "Great Migration," the Clays sailed downstream from western Pennsylvania, headed for the promising Bluegrass State. At peak navigation season, these emigrant flats appeared everywhere on the Ohio. Men, women, children, dogs, pigs, cattle, and horses all traveled together and must have made quite a picture.

Flatboats were flat-bottomed (hence the name), box-shaped craft averaging fifty feet in length and twelve feet in width. Boatmen navigated by means of a huge stern oar and three smaller oars, one each on the port, starboard, and bow. Once a flatboat reached its destination it was dismantled and sold for lumber. Many sidewalks and shanties in the deep South (and even an occasional church, to the misfortune of the congregationists' sense of smell!) were built of this waterlogged timber. Having dispensed with their cargo and craft, the flatboat's crew had to somehow return home. Many walked hundreds of miles home on the Natchez Trace (an important trail running between Natchez, Mississippi, and Nashville, Tennessee) or rode horseback.

But a long walk home over the Natchez Trace was not the only hardship endured by the early flatboatmen. They worked in the freezing Ohio Valley winters and the sweltering summers. They slept out in the open on furs, and battled hordes of insects. They ate plain meals which in the early days consisted almost exclusively of salt pork, beans, coffee, and whiskey. While it is true that flatboatmen enjoyed periods of leisure, when they worked they worked very hard. Flatboatmen battled navigation hazards like ice, fog, snags, sandbars, caving-in banks, rapids, falls, and eddies. When a boat ran aground, the crew often had to spend hours in ice-cold water pushing it back into the current.

And if all that was not burdensome enough, there were dangerous men about. During the 1780s and 1790s, Ohio River flatboatmen fell prey to warring Ohio Valley tribes like the Shawnee and Miami. There are many recorded instances of boatmen killed by these hostile tribes. One common tactic used by Indians was to lure flatboatmen ashore by pretending to be stranded white settlers. Then they would attack the unsuspecting boatmen. John Fitch, later a pioneer in steamboat technology, was captured by Delaware Indians in such an incident in the 1780s. The Indians killed one of Fitch's men, then marched the remaining flatboatmen northward and turned them over to British soldiers who eventually set them free. Other boatmen were less fortunate. However, Anthony Wayne's defeat of the major Ohio Valley tribes (which led to the Treaty of Greenville in 1795) meant that boatmen no longer faced the Indian threat.

But early flatboatmen feared dangerous white men as well. River pirates threatened early Ohio boatmen who neared Cave-in-Rock, the Natchez Trace, and other dreaded locales. One must note, though, that historians studying river piracy have learned to weigh their evidence with a grain or two of salt. River pirates did haunt the Ohio, but their exploits have been exaggerated in bloody folktales and local legends to such an extent that it is extremely difficult to discern the truth.

Samuel Mason, the most celebrated pirate of Cave-in-Rock, probably never even practiced his brutal trade on the lower Ohio River. The only documented accounts of this Revolutionary War veteran-turned-outlaw indicate that he pillaged much further south, on the Natchez Trace. Mason was captured in Spanish territory in 1803, but he soon killed his captors and was never seen again. Local legends say that vigilantes in turn captured him, cut off his head, and stuck it on a pointed stick on the Natchez Trace.

Actually, this tale of "Mason's Head" is a spin-off of an equally grisly folktale about the Kentucky outlaws Micajah and

Wiley Harpe—or "Big Harpe" and "Little Harpe," as they were known in the late eighteenth century Ohio Valley. The Harpe brothers supposedly were headquartered at Cave-in-Rock for a time, and stories have Wiley Harpe joining Mason after Micajah's capture and decapitation.

Many of these tales are undocumented. All that historians know for sure is that the Harpes committed several bloody murders in Kentucky during the late 1700s. Thus all the hair-raising tales of the Harpes and Mason (and their supposed partners in crime Camilla the Pirate, Colonel Plug, and the infamous rogue "Nine Eyes") on the Ohio River may be just that—"tales." But one does not have to search too far to find less dramatic but verifiable accounts of river pirates on the lower Ohio and Mississippi rivers.

Ohio flatboatman Joseph Hough remembered that during the early 1800s "bands of robbers were yet much dreaded by merchant navigators of those rivers." Pirates John Turner and James Colbert attacked and stole from Spanish keelboat crews south of St. Louis in the late 1700s.

The most famous Ohio River flatboatman to fall victim to pirates was none other than Abraham Lincoln. Lincoln made two 1820s flatboat trips south, one from "Old Sangamon Town" in his newly adopted state of Illinois. Legend depicts Abe Lincoln viewing a New Orleans slave auction and vowing to "hit it hard" if he ever got the chance. In fact, his southern experiences were more frightening than inspiring. Bound for New Orleans with a flatboat load of produce in 1828, Lincoln and Allen Gentry secured their boat to the Louisiana shore one night and fell fast asleep. They were soon roused, however, by a gang of black toughs "with intent to kill and rob them." Lincoln and his crewmate chased away the thieves, but only after a nasty fight.[6]

Yet Lincoln's run-in with river pirates in 1828 happened to fall at the end of a lawless era. As time passed and civilization slowly advanced throughout the Ohio and Mississippi valleys, river piracy became less and less a problem. Vigilance committees, militia, and police departments arose to apprehend criminals and throw them in jail. The once wild stretches of the Ohio River became civilized places where law and order prevailed and commerce flourished.

Still, it is plain to see that flatboating, especially during the early years, was a very difficult and, at times, dangerous business. What sort of men would work under these conditions?

Were they the rough and rowdy crew of "Alligator Horses" that some storytellers like to imagine, or were they merely "slave labor"—overworked and underpaid?

Surprisingly, historians have experienced great difficulty in learning about real flatboatmen. Because very few early boatmen could or would write, they left few diaries and letters for us to study. During the past years, however, some of this kind of evidence has surfaced, and we can now make some generalizations. The average flatboatman was a white Ohio Valley male, of English or Celtic ancestry, and averaging twenty-eight years of age. Of course, there are exceptions to this rule. Black boatmen, slave and free, worked the Ohio River during antebellum years, and so too did Franco-Americans. There were a few women, American Indians, French, and German and Scandinavian-descended flatboatmen. But after considering the exceptions the generalizations still apply.

A few examples prove this point. John G. Stuart, a Kentuckian who made a flatboat trip to New Orleans in 1806, was simply a young man looking to see the world and experience a few adventures. Joseph Hough, a merchant from Miami, Ohio, was an entrepreneur who personally navigated dozens of his own flatboats loaded with produce to the South. Like many other flatboat merchants of the 1800s, he was "builder, owner, captain, and for most of the way down the rivers, also the pilot" of his own boats.

William P. Dole, a Wabash River merchant and flatboatman, was elected to the Indiana state legislature and eventually became a congressman and United States Indian Commissioner. Ceylon Lincoln and Simon Sherman were Wisconsin teenagers who piloted the western rivers, and George Forman was a Canadian lad who left home at seventeen to become a flatboatman, raftsman, and steamboatman on the Ohio, Illinois, and Mississippi rivers from 1849 to 1851.

The heyday of flatboating was the 1840s, over thirty years after the introduction of the steamboat on western rivers. Why did the flats survive steamer competition while the keelboats languished? This is a difficult question, but much of the answer lies in the fact that Jacksonian America saw such an economic boom that there was plenty of opportunity for flatboatmen even after the steamers took the lion's share. Flatboats were cheap to build and operate, and so almost anyone could take a chance and try to "make a go of it." Moreover, the steamboats brought federally subsidized river improvements (dredging and clearing of snags) which made life easier for flatboatmen and even lowered their insurance rates. Finally, one should note that steamboats gave flatboatmen one thing that the pre-steam rivermen needed so badly—a cheap and expeditious passage home. Flatboatmen during the Steamboat Age became "commuters"—forgoing the rough Natchez Trace foot route for a three-dollar passage home on the deck of a steamer. From 1811 until the Civil War, flats and steamers flourished in this symbiotic relationship.

The 1846–47 season proved to be the golden zenith of Ohio River flatboat commerce. The increasing efficiency of steamboats combined with a new competitor—the railroads—to slowly blunt the flatboatmen's competitive edge. Their trade declined gradually thereafter. The Civil War and the coming of the railroads severely reduced the economic importance of flatboating. Yet thousands of flatboatmen continued to sail the Ohio and its tributaries well into the 1890s.

One final note about flatboats is vital to understanding modern river commerce. The shape of these craft closely resembles the shape of modern steel towboat barges. This is no coincidence. As flatboating declined, many steamboatmen began to buy up old flats and lash them alongside their steamers to increase their cargo capacity. Steamboatmen soon learned that a number of flats, sans crew, could be lashed together and "towed" (actually "pushed" is the correct term, but boatmen have historically refused to use it and cling tenaciously to the misnomer) expeditiously from one river port to another. This practice of pushing flats began sometime before the Civil War and was common during the postbellum years. The process evolved gradually into our modern system of pushing barges up and down the Ohio. Thus the old wooden flatboat is a nineteenth century ancestor of the twentieth century's steel "towboat barge."[7]

Before assessing the role of steamboating on the artery of movement, one more non-steam mode of transport warrants our attention: the lumber and log raft. Rafting began in the early nineteenth century, when the advance of civilization westward grew so great as to create a constant demand for saw logs and sawed lumber. On the Ohio, Monongahela, and Allegheny rivers, rafts plied in increasing numbers during the Jacksonian era. This trade flourished and endured, in one form or another, well into the twentieth century. Indeed, on tributaries such as the Cumberland, raftsmen were moving timber in the 1920s in a fashion strikingly reminiscent of their nineteenth century ancestors.

The western rivers raftsmen were immortalized by Mark Twain in a projected chapter of *Huckleberry Finn* that first appeared in *Life on the Mississippi*. In this sketch Huck Finn secretly boarded a lumber raft and observed the raftsmen—"a mighty rough-looking lot"—drinking, dancing, and spinning yarns. One raftsman named Ed talked a good deal about how "the muddy Mississippi water was wholesomer to drink than the clear water of the Ohio." It seems that Ohio water was sorely deficient in mud, which raftsmen should keep "stirred up" and drink profusely. But the capper of the piece was when Huck viewed a battle between raftsmen, preceded by the most eloquent of alligator horse boasts:

> Whoo—oop! I'm a child of sin, *don't* let me get a start! . . . I scratch my head with lightning and purr myself to sleep with the thunder! When I'm cold, I bile the Gulf of Mexico and bathe in it; when I'm hot I fan myself with an equinoctial storm; When I'm thirsty I reach up and suck a cloud dry like a sponge; when I range the earth hungry, famine follows in my tracks! Whoo-oop![8]

Of course, Twain's fanciful sketch does not tell us much about actual timber rafting. Ohio River timber rafts were often huge rectangular affairs 300 feet in length and 50 feet in width, composed of logs or sawed lumber. Raftsmen built rafts in a manner similar to the modern barge tow—many different pieces were attached together to form the finished rectangular product. If raftsmen were moving logs, they would gather groups of them together in the river (branding them first for identification) in rectangular units called "stringers" or "cribs." Hickory saplings were pegged and strapped across the logs in the stringer to secure the small units. Then several stringers were fastened tightly together (again using hickory withe and wooden pegs) to form the finished raft, or "drift" as it was sometimes called. (Raftsmen referred to Monongahela or Cumberland drifts, designating the raft's point of departure.) They built lumber rafts much as they did log rafts, strapping hundreds of sawed planks together with hickory withe and wooden pegs and then combining stringers into drifts. As the nineteenth century progressed, raftsmen substituted metal "chain dogs" for pegs, but only after warning their sawyer customers of potential hazard.

Weather permitting, raftsmen could build a drift in three or four days. Navigation proved tricky, with as many as ten to fifteen oarsmen standing a single shift on a large raft. They steered with long (eighteen to twenty feet) oars stationed around the perimeter of the craft. Rocks, rapids, bends, and shoals all presented hazards. Most raftsmen sailed in high water to avoid running aground, but that entailed winter work in the freezing Ohio Valley. During peak season, rivertown residents observed the long drifts: "All day long, one after another the rafts come round the bend."

Who were the raftsmen? Judging from firsthand accounts, many were young farmers and teenaged boys looking for a few extra dollars to supplement their incomes. Since rafting was often a winter pursuit, a farmer could afford to take a month away from his idle farm to earn enough to make the next land payment or perhaps add a few head of cattle or pigs to his herd. Some farmers turned entrepreneur and logged their own timber and rafted it to the nearest sawmill. And then, of course, there was a class of professional raft pilots who earned their living exclusively through plying these cumbersome craft downstream. Evidently their skills were in great demand.

When off duty, raftsmen slept in a rude shanty built toward the center of the drift. They cooked over an open sandpit firebox. Bacon, beans, coffee, whiskey, and an occasional rabbit, deer, or squirrel were the customary fare. On the Upper Cumberland River in the late nineteenth century, common hands earned eight to fifteen dollars for a trip to Nashville. A pilot earned more, depending upon his skills. Arriving at their destination, raftsmen pocketed their wages, quaffed some drinks, saw the sights, and returned home on the next upstream-bound steamboat.

Henry Baxter, a well-educated Pennsylvanian who rafted lumber on the Ohio River in 1844, left a hefty diary of his daily activities. Baxter would sail his small raft into a river port and stay there several days, selling lumber to local builders and businessmen. When business began to wane, he gathered his crew together, launched the raft into the southbound current, and set up shop in the next likely location. He spent an entire season in this fashion, taking time to see the sights in Cincinnati (including performances by a Shakespearean troupe and the world-famous magician Alexander Hermann) and to read a number of novels and scores of newspapers and magazines. Interestingly, Baxter was a devout Democrat who spent a good deal of his time arguing politics with anyone who would oblige him. He adored James K. Polk and vilified the Kentucky Whig Henry Clay. For someone doing much of his business in Kentucky, this was probably not a very fruitful endeavor.

George Forman worked on lumber and log rafts as well as steamers and flatboats during the late 1840s and early 1850s. He remembered rafting as a pleasant occupation except when the raft ran aground and burst asunder. Forman spent two weeks one winter "going up the River gathering up the cribs of our raft. Many places we would work up to our necks in the ice cold water . . . and sleep on shore on the ground with our feet to a log fire and no cover over us."[9]

Tales of discomfort could easily turn to tragedy. Lynwood Montell, in *Don't Go Up Kettle Creek*, records the story of John Cummings, a Wolf River raftsman who came upon a stranded raft in the dead of winter. There were two men on board, one of them dead from exposure:

> We went to them. One of them was dead, and the other was just barely breathing. We got him out first. Went back and got the other one. . . . [The other rescuers] had a covered wagon and a big fire; had bed blankets and everything. . . . There's one old man there. He said, "I've brought a quart of moonshine whiskey." They just jerked the buttons off the freezing man's clothes and stripped him off. The old man went to bathing him in that whiskey. Had it milk warm, and he was a-breathing pretty good when we took the dead one out. They was from East Port, Tennessee. I forget their names. I was about seventeen. They'd hit what they call a towhead [sand bar] in there and they couldn't see that night. Anyhow, it got up on them and their raft stuck there.[10]

Rafting endured well into the twentieth century, but in most of the Ohio Valley it became mechanized. Steamboats began to tow lumber and log rafts, but unlike barge tows, rafts traveled in the steamer's wake. This practice was common on tributaries and stretches of river without locks and dams, for river improvements proved disastrous to the cumbersome log and lumber tows. With the proliferation of sawmills closer to the timber supply, the rafting business began to wane. Railroads and logging trucks completed the cycle of mechanization, and log and lumber rafting grew less and less important to transport on the artery of movement.[11]

Until 1811, Ohio rivermen worked in what must have been a serene and quiet world. The silence was broken only occasionally by the splash of an oar, the drone of insects, or perhaps the stirrings of a village the boatmen passed along their way. But the 1811 voyage of the steamboat *New Orleans* put an end to that silent world of the pre-steam riverboatmen. When Nicholas J. Roosevelt successfully sailed this wood-fired, sidewheel-driven craft down the Ohio and Mississippi, the "Steamboat Age" on western rivers had begun.

Flatboatmen were initially stunned at the sight and sound of these steam-belching monsters. Most expressed extreme misgivings. Joseph Hough noted that in 1816 pioneer steamboatman Henry Miller Shreve was considered "insane," and Hough refused to ride a steamer home to Ohio, choosing instead to travel by horse! Yet by the 1820s steamers were plying the Ohio and Mississippi in increasing numbers and many former skeptics had themselves become steamboat pilots. Moreover, the steamers brought in their wake federally subsidized river improvements such as dredging and the clearing of snags. The once silent Ohio River echoed with the sounds of the Industrial Revolution.

Early Ohio and Mississippi steamers set important trends in design and locomotion. Understanding well the potential importance of steam-driven, low draft vessels on western rivers, steamboatmen developed sternwheeled (as opposed to sidewheeled) boats with a shallow (two to three feet) draft. This new design also incorporated a more powerful and efficient boiler and engine combination. By the 1820s these boats served as prototypes for future Ohio River steam vessels.

Modern romantic images of Ohio River steamers tend toward the magnificent, but the workaday steamboat was a small (approximately 300 tons), practical craft, with few fancy trappings. The average lifespan of a boat in this rigorous trade was about five years. Peak shipping time was during high water—late fall (immediately following harvest) and early spring. Then the Ohio was dotted with steamers carrying flour, pork, whiskey, tobacco, and cotton. Interestingly, one of the most important varieties of freight was the human variety: European immigrants, frontier farmers, returning flatboatmen, businessmen, and others all flocked aboard the steamboats during the antebellum years.

Once aboard, a typical passenger did not reside in the splendid steamboat cabins pictured in so many movies and television shows. True, there were first class accommodations, and those who could afford them rode the steamboat in style. Most could not, and rode "deck passage" on the lower level. There they found a berth among the cargo and fared as best they could. Steamboat deckhand John Habermehl remembered the deck room as "an open comfortless place . . . All bleak and bare, no stool, no table, no utensils of any kind, aside from a few dim lanterns, a long sheet iron stove [for cooking and heating] and bunks on the side, which reminds one of a horse stable."[12]

An Ohio River steamer carried a crew of twelve, including a captain, pilot, engineer, mate, and deck crew. Like non-steam crews, these men varied in age according to their rank and occupation. The common hands included farm boys and city urchins and an increasing number of Irish and German immigrants. Free blacks worked aboard steamers, and so too did slaves. Black or white, decking on a steamboat was a hard way to make a living. No wonder one steamboat deckhand, in a pessimistic moment, summed up his experiences by saying:

> I had not saved a cent. It was impossible to work long enough to earn anything. No one could stand the work of over one trip, it was so hard, working night and day. It was the want of sleep prevented it. After every trip there was a necessary rest and it took all the earnings to pay for the board. Then again, it was sometimes hard to get work, and to be "hard up" or "dead broke" was the common lot of most Boatmen. It was a fearful life, living from hand to mouth, and with less comfort than the brutes.[13]

Steamboat racing has always proven a fascinating and romantic subject for historians of the artery of movement. This stems from an old river tradition most articulately described by Mark Twain in *Life on the Mississippi*. Twain wrote at some length of the "vast importance" and "consuming excitement" of an impending steamboat race: "Politics and weather were dropped, and people talked only of the coming race."[14]

Twain seems unaware of the fact that steamboat racing was very dangerous and often had tragic consequences: "Racing was royal fun," he insisted. "The public always had an idea that racing was dangerous; whereas the opposite was the case."[15] Most authorities disagree. Historian Daniel Boorstin points to a rash of steamboat accidents that occurred during the mid-nineteenth century, most of them a direct result of boiler explosions during riverboat races. From 1825 to 1850 there were at least 150 major steamboat engine explosions on Western rivers, killing over 1,400 people. Nearly 30 percent of all steamboats built before 1850 were lost to accidents, mainly explosions.

Why? Boorstin contends that steamboat racing and accidents were a manifestation of a nation of people in a hurry. The "technology of haste" led to the development of the dangerously high-pressure steam engines used on the Ohio and Mississippi rivers. The daredevil captains who piloted these steamships always pushed their engines to the limit, often beyond. One such pilot bragged; "I tell you stranger, it takes a man to ride one of these half alligator boats, head on a snag, high pressure, valve soddered down, 600 souls on board and in danger of going to the devil!"[16]

The combination of braggart steamboat captains and foolhardy passengers led inevitably to disaster. Steamboat pilots meeting in Cincinnati in 1838 declared that the passengers shared as much blame for the rash of engine explosions as the river pilots themselves. Restless gold-rushers, land-rushers, speculators, hasty immigrants, and merchants often urged their riverboat captains to "go on the fastest" and praised and patronized those who did. Seemingly everyone in America was in a hurry to get somewhere—to find that pot of gold at the end of the rainbow. They enthusiastically embraced the Industrial Revolution (and the steamboats it produced) as a sure means of getting them to wherever it was they were bound. But these Americans could never go fast enough. As the astute travel writer Baron von Gerstner observed:

> The Americans are, as is known, the most enterprising people in the world, who justly say of themselves, "We always go ahead." The Democrats here never like to remain one behind another: on the contrary, each wants to get ahead of the rest. When two steamboats happen to get alongside each other, the passengers will encourage the captains to run a race which the latter agree to. The boilers intended for a pressure of only 100 pounds per square inch are, by accelerated generation of steam, exposed to a pressure of 150 and even 200 pounds, and this goes sometimes so far, that the trials end with an explosion . . . the races are the causes of most of the explosions, and yet they are constantly taking place. The life of an American is, indeed, only a constant racing, and why should he fear it on board the steamboats?[17]

Ohio River towns boomed during the Steamboat Age. "The invention of the steamboat was intended for us," observed the editor of the *Cincinnati Gazette*, adding, "the puny rivers of the East are only as creeks or convenient waters on which experiments can be made for our advantage." By 1830, over 400 steamboats were navigating the western rivers. Travel time upstream from New Orleans to Cincinnati was cut from approximately three months (by keelboat) to a seemingly miraculous three weeks. Louisville's town fathers had joined with developers to build a lock bypassing the Great Falls, the only remaining bottleneck on *la belle rivière*. And Louisville, Pittsburgh, Cincinnati, and Jeffersonville, Indiana, fostered a number of shipbuilding enterprises.

From 1811 until approximately 1830, steamboat commerce increased dramatically and profits soared. The relatively inexpensive pricetag on a new steamship combined with available bank credit to attract hundreds of Jacksonian entrepreneurs. Entry into this market was surprisingly widespread: unlike the railroad industry, steamboating never saw the rise of a monopolistic elite to dominate the trade. This was rough and tumble capitalism at its best and worst. The downside appeared after 1830, when the intense competition began to take its toll. Supply overtook demand, and then profits plummeted in the Panic of 1837. The trade stabilized in the 1840s and 1850s, but no one ever again enjoyed the bounties of the 1811–1830 seasons. Ironically, at the same time that steamers were beginning to run the flatboats out of business, the railroads were poised to significantly cripple all modes of river commerce.

In 1829 Americans laid their first rails on the east coast, and pointed them south and west. By the 1850s all of the major Ohio River ports boasted direct rail connections with all major markets. The steamboat's days were numbered. Of course, the proud steamboatmen would not admit this, and it would be a half century before they accepted their defeat. The decades of the 1860s, 1870s, and 1880s saw this important drama acted out in the Ohio Valley.

Statistics show a gradual shift in almost every market (coal is an important exception) from river to rail transport. In Cincinnati and Louisville, during the 1880s, railroads took the majority of tobacco, pork, and corn shipments. For example, eighty-five percent of all leaf tobacco imported to or exported from Louisville in 1885 was carried via rail. The once invincible steamboatmen were losing the battle for markets, for reasons that are not difficult to discern. Steamers were bound to the river, its seasons of navigation, and its fickle ways. Because of this, steamers were at times slow and unreliable. Railroads, on the contrary, were speedy and reliable, and offered direct, year-round service not only to port cities but to towns and villages hundreds of miles from a navigable stream. No wonder merchants took their business from the river port to the train depot.

However, steamboats did not entirely disappear. On a few portions of the Ohio and its tributaries where rail service was poor or nonexistent, steamboats continued to ply well into the twentieth century. On the Upper Cumberland River of Kentucky and Tennessee, for instance, poor roads and the late arrival of the railroads created a limited but stable market for steamers during the first two decades of the twentieth century. Elsewhere river commerce continued, but lost its vibrance and competitive edge. Riverboatmen pondered their fate and searched for an answer to their problems. What they needed was a new kind of boat, one so powerful and efficient that it could compete with the railroad engine despite the handicaps posed by being river-bound.[18]

The answer to the rivermen's dilemma would ultimately be the towboat. As noted, steamboats had been towing barges since before the Civil War. The technique showed promise, but steamboatmen needed new technology and river improvements in order to compete on a year-round basis with railroads. During the late nineteenth and early twentieth centuries, the combination of federally subsidized river improvements and a new, radically engineered riverboat once again gave rivermen a competitive edge on the artery of movement.

One of the unheralded pioneers of modern towboat navigation was a Briton turned West Virginian named Charles Ward. By 1903 Ward had modified the latest in European marine technology for Ohio River conditions. His boat, the *James Rumsey*, was powered by an improved steam engine and boasted a water-tube boiler, multiple-expansion engine, and screw propeller (as opposed to paddlewheel) propulsion. The result was, quite simply, much more power. In a March 7, 1903, "pushing" duel with the mighty sternwheeler *D. T. Lane*, the *James Rumsey* pushed the hapless *Lane* up and downstream with ease. Ohio Valley newspapers lauded the "superiority of this class of vessels" and proclaimed that the "construction of river boats has been revolutionized." Barge towing would never be the same.

But what of the old problem of seasonal navigation? How could even the new steamboats compete when they were still constrained by low water? Congress came to the rescue soon after Ward's breakthrough when, in 1910, politicians jumped on the "nine foot" bandwagon. Since the 1880s there had existed a movement to deepen the Ohio's channel to insure year-round navigation via federally funded locks and dams. The Army Engineers built its first such facility, Davis Island Lock and Dam, below Pittsburgh in 1885, and by 1900 two other projects had begun. The 1910 law provided for eventual construction of the fifty-four locks and dams necessary to provide a year-round, nine-foot-deep channel on the Ohio River.

During and after World War I, the federal government regulated and subsidized inland transport along with other key industries. The Army Corps of Engineers completed the Ohio River project in 1929. In the meantime, towboat technology took one final step into modernity with the replacement of steam engines by diesel-powered internal combustion engines. In 1931, the snub-nosed, twin-screw, diesel-powered towboat *Herbert Hoover* served as prototype for the towboats of the modern western rivers.

World War II spurred yet another jump in river commerce and federal involvement in that commerce. Congress agreed in 1954 to replace the Ohio River locks and dams with nineteen modern "high-lift" structures. The new 1,200–foot lock chambers were designed to hold tows of seventeen barges, thus cutting down a good deal of traffic congestion on the Ohio. The coal boom of the 1970s proved lucrative to towboat operators; unfortunately, business in the 1980s and 1990s has declined considerably. With established towboat companies going out of business and union jobs on the decline, Ohio towboatmen are looking to the future with great concern.

To the trained economist, river commerce makes perfect sense for an age of economic transition. In times of increasing fuel and transportation costs, Ohio River towboats offer one of the most efficient and economical modes of transportation available. Modern towboats vary in size, from 600 to 700–horsepower harbor boats in Pittsburgh to the 10,500–horsepower monsters that can easily push two dozen coal barges on the Lower Ohio. In addition to coal and petroleum products (gasoline, oil, and asphalt), chemicals like ammonia account for more and more river tonnage.

Crew size varies. While a small 1,800 horsepower towboat might carry a crew of six, the large boats carry as many as thirteen—two pilots, two engineers, a cook, first and second mate, and six deckhands. They work long, twelve-hour days in sequences of six hours on, six off. Thus no one ever gets more than five or six hours' sleep at a single time. Many boatmen work thirty days and then take fifteen days off; others are on a forty-twenty schedule, and a few work thirty-thirty. As crew members come and go, the boat rarely stops its movement up and down the river, from loading to unloading point and back again.

One pilot serves as captain, and is paid accordingly. He works the six A.M. to noon and six P.M. to midnight shifts. In addition to steering the craft, he handles many administrative chores. The captain (referred to sometimes by the crew as "Skipper" or "Cap") reports to the home office twice daily on the shortwave radio, computes the payroll, coordinates crew rotation, and keeps track of expenditures for food, minor repairs, and other incidentals. He handles crew relations and enforces the ban on alcohol and drugs aboard all towboats. He deals with all port officials and, if necessary, the U.S. Coast Guard. His co-pilot, on the other hand, does little more than steer the boat on his watch (noon to six P.M. and midnight to six A.M.) and take care of minor administrative duties that arise when he is on watch. He is a pilot, not an administrator, and is paid less than the captain.

The engineer ranks next in the crew hierarchy. On a large boat (for example a 10,500–horsepower craft), a chief engineer is assisted by a second engineer or oiler. They stand watches that parallel the captain and pilot. The chief engineer (the men call him "Chief") is responsible for care of the two boat engines, performing routine maintenance and, when in drydock, supervising major engine repairs. In addition, the Chief is often the ship's handyman, watching over electrical and plumbing systems, the air conditioning plant, the washer and dryer, and even the cook's refrigerator. The second engineer cleans the engine room thoroughly, helps with oil and filter changes, minor tuneups, and anything else the Chief needs him for. The two engineers are truly "Jacks-of-all trades."

The first mate and second mate also stand opposite watches, and each is in charge of his respective deck crew. Their main job, of course, is to supervise the deckhands when they "make tow"—connecting the steel barges tightly together with steel wires so that the tow can be safely pushed up and down the river. If a tow is especially large, sometimes the deck crew that is supposed to be sleeping will be called out for "overtime," and all hands will work round the clock until the tow is complete. A good mate knows all the tricks of connecting barges and arranging them in a fashion to expedite travel. Of course, making tow is not the only chore of the mates and deckhands. They check and tighten the tow four times daily while en route, mend lines and rigging, clean the toilets ("heads") and pilots' quarters, wash the linen, unload the grocery boat, wash ("souge") the boat, and chip and paint during good weather. The mates make sure the deckhands are busy at something all of the time.

Last, but certainly not least, is the cook. The cook is paid less than the captain, pilot, and engineers, but more than the mates and deckhands. Some would argue that, with the exception of the captain, the cook is the most important person on the boat. Food is very important to rivermen, and an old river expression is, "the more you eat, the more [money] you make." The cook serves as the entire galley department, ordering the groceries and planning the meals, cooking and serving the meals, and even washing the dishes afterwards. A typical towboat dinner, served at noon, consists of roast pork, mashed potatoes and gravy, green beans with bacon, Great Northern beans, biscuits, relishes, and pecan pie and ice cream for dessert. The crew wolfs this fare down quickly, and six hours later is ready for more!

Yet the cook does more than just prepare food, and there are other reasons for the importance of the job. The galley provides the focus for most "social life" on board; there men watch television, swap tales, smoke, and play cards as well as drink iced tea and sodas and eat their meals. As chief of the galley, the cook's job is to make it a home away from home, with a clean table and ash trays, snacks, crushed ice, sodas, a full coffee pot, and an inviting atmosphere for recreation. In many ways the cook is the boat's "social director." A good cook makes for a good towboat, rivermen say. And a good cook can make all the difference in the world to towboatmen who find themselves spending Thanksgiving Day or Christmas en route, or at an oil dock in the industrial district of an Ohio River port city.

All kinds of men and women (many cooks are female) are drawn to towboat life. Let us look at an actual towboat on the western rivers—the *Mamma Lere*—and examine its roster: "W. T.," the old pilot from Maysville, Kentucky, has worked on the river since 1947. "Fleety" Hodges, the cook, is seventy years old, but prefers towboat cooking to drawing her social security check. Andy Robitschek is a deckhand who grew up in Kenya with his missionary parents. (Andy is also a professional saddle-bronc rider in the Arkansas-Oklahoma-Texas rodeo circuit and a sometime junior majoring in Journalism at Murray State University in Kentucky.) The oil tankerman is an ex-Marine and Vietnam vet who keeps (illegally) a loaded .32 caliber automatic pistol in his dresser drawer. Captain Dave Miller discusses philosophy, and sings and plays folk, country, rock, and blues on his acoustic guitar. There are all kinds on the Ohio River—young, long-haired youth working alongside rednecks and "good ole boys." Obviously, they share something in common—a desire to leave "the bank" (as they disparagingly refer to the rest of the world) and go to work on the river.

Why would a person want to leave a life on the bank to work on a towboat for thirty to forty days at a time? In a thirty-year career, a riverman spends ten years at home and twenty on the boat! The work is hard, often frustrating, in the Ohio Valley's sweltering summers and freezing winters. Nor is the pay always good. An average Ohio River Union deckhand in 1990 probably makes $75 for a twelve-hour day, and non-union hands make less. On the other hand, mates, cooks, and engineers make up to $125 per day, and pilots command a wage of approximately $175. Then too, the company furnishes room and meals. A towboatman who does not drink or gamble (both illegal but common on towboats) incurs no expenses whatsoever during his trip. Thus a man who earns $3,000 per month can save a great deal of money, even if he has a family at home and only works seven or eight months a year. In this way river work can be a means of improving one's station in life, especially for those with a high school education or less.

But other less economic motivations compel men to take up a life of towboating. Many professional towboatmen are loners. They enjoy leaving the hustle and bustle of life on the bank for thirty to forty days at a time. They also enjoy the status and prestige that river rats enjoy in their hometowns. As Mate Jimmy Dale Berryhill said: "Now you tell someone that you're a mechanic, a clerk, a plumber, or a druggist, and they'll just look at you. That's nothin' special. But you tell someone that you're a *towboatman* . . . Well, that's got a ring to it." Despite the long hours and hard work, the romance is still there. Perhaps this fact is best shown in the tales and yarns that comprise the folklore of the Ohio River towboatmen.

Dave Miller, who began his career out of Jeffersonville, Indiana, for American Commercial Barge Lines, knows the river and its folklore well. He can show you where boats have sunk after failing to pass treacherous stretches of river, and bridges that have claimed the lives of entire towboat crews. "Once in 1903," he says, a steamer "rounded a bend south of Vicksburg and was never heard from again." Andy Robitschek claims that "Charlie," the ghost of an old black cook who got drunk and drowned in the river, continues to haunt the towboat *Ole Miss*: "Why ol' Charlie turns on lights, and sometimes you can hear him running up and down stairs and slamming doors in the galley!" Charles is also responsible for several "cold spots." "Ghosts *always* leave cold spots," Andy explains, in a style reminiscent of Tom Sawyer himself.

Bud Brooks, the first mate on the towboat *Mamma Lere*, will point out "Freedom Point"—a place where, in the early 1800s, a black slave swam the entire width of the river in order to escape his master. Bud also spins yarns about "killer catfish." "Those catfish are sometimes four to five feet long, and weigh up to 200 pounds!" he claims. "And I know for a fact that one of 'em ate two skindivers up by the Marietta-Parkersburg bridge last summer!" But the classic Ohio River story involves a crew of river rats hitting the bank and, like their ancestor Mike Fink, getting into a drunken brawl. According to Captain Dave Miller, one West Virginia tavern-owner had good reason to regret evicting an entire crew of drunken towboatmen from his dockside bar. "Those boys sure got their revenge," he remembers. "They went back to their boat, tied a couple of lines to that tavern's dock, and pulled the bar, customers and all, right into the Ohio River!"[19]

Obviously, the folklore of the Ohio creates a strong bond between those who choose to spend their lives on the river. And this mythology forms a strong connection between the towboatmen and those eighteenth and nineteenth century rivermen who preceded them. Just as the stories of Mike Fink and the "alligator horse" appealed to nineteenth century Americans, modern Americans look with a bit of envy at the southbound Ohio River tows, and wish that they too might be towboatmen and make that trip down *la belle rivière*. The modern towboatman is thus an actual and a mythological descendant of the flatboatmen, keelboatmen, raftsmen, and steamboatmen who preceded him on the artery of movement.[20]

There is an epilogue to this story of the artery of movement. In a way, Ohio riverboating has come nearly full circle, for the 1970s saw the return of the "sternwheeler" to the river. True, the luxurious *Delta Queen* and *Mississippi Queen* fire their boilers with diesel oil, not wood or coal as in the Steamboat Age. Then too, an old steamboatman would feel awfully strange on a boat that boasted whirlpool baths, saunas, gymnasiums, and movie theatres! Yet, to the untrained eye, the sight of these huge pleasure craft conveys an image of nineteenth century steamboating, and Americans (including a former president) have flocked on board. A proposed Illinois state law to legalize gambling on its waterways opens up a number of possibilities. Perhaps we will return to the days of the old steamboat card rooms and riverboat gamblers.

Whatever the fate of the modern sternwheelers, towboating will no doubt continue until its technology is improved or superseded by yet another marine technology. There will always be riverboating on the Ohio. The Indian canoes, flatboats, keelboats, rafts, steamboats, and towboats have all made their way down *la belle rivière* in a two century procession. More boats will follow. The Ohio serves as a magnet not only for an economy, but for a culture. A real riverman—and many men and women have worked the Ohio for thirty or forty years—can sit in the wheelhouse or on a milk crate on the stern of the boat and stare at those lush, forested banks for hours on end. Most of them do. The Ohio Valley comprises a large part of the boatman's life, just as it comprises a large part of the economic and cultural life of the nation of which the boatman is a part.

Mark Twain once wrote of his riverboating days: "If I have seemed to love my subject, it is no surprising thing, for I have loved the profession far, far better than any I have followed since."[21] Ohio Valley rivermen and their countrymen on land feel much the same way. They are drawn, irresistibly, to the artery of movement.

NOTES

1. "A Brief Account of Mr. Hough's Life Written by Himself in 1852." *Bulletin of the Cincinnati Historical Society*, 14 (October 1966), 312.

2. For a general introduction to the literature of riverboating, see my "Historical Works on Early American Riverboatmen," *Bookman's Weekly*, 78 (November 24, 1986), 2141–43.

3. Emerson Bennett, *Mike Fink, a Legend of the Ohio* (1852; repr. Upper Saddle River, N.J.: 1970), 28.

4. William Adams, "Journal of the Barge Lovely Nan, Lewis West, Master, July 9, 1807–November 20, 1807" (MS in Ohio Historical Society, Columbus). Quotations are from entries of July 14 and September 11.

5. For keelboating see Michael Allen, *Western Rivermen, 1763–1861: Ohio and Mississippi Boatmen and the Myth of the Alligator Horse* (Baton Rouge: 1990); Michael Allen, "Sired by a Hurricane: Mike Fink, Western Boatmen, and the Myth of the Alligator Horse," *Arizona and the West*, 27 (Autumn 1985), 237–52; Leland D. Baldwin, *The Keelboat Age on Western Waters* (Pittsburgh: 1941).

6. Abraham Lincoln, "Short Autobiography," in John G. Nicolay and John Hay, eds., *Complete Works of Abraham Lincoln* (12 vols.; New York: 1905), vol. 6, 28–30.

7. For flatboating see Allen, *Western Rivermen, 1763–1861*; Baldwin, *Keelboat Age*; Michael Allen, "The Riverman as Jacksonian Man," *Western Historical Quarterly* (Fall 1990).

8. Mark Twain, *Life on the Mississippi* (1874; repr. New York: 1986), 54, 56.

9. George Forman, "Biographical Sketch of the Life and Ancestry of Geo. Forman of Stratford-Ontario, Canada, written in 1875 and 1883 by Himself," E. Luella Galliver, ed. (typescript in Western History Research Center, University of Wyoming, Laramie).

10. Lynwood Montell, *Don't Go Up Kettle Creek: Verbal Legacy of the Upper Cumberland* (Knoxville: 1983), 106.

11. For rafting see Henry Baxter, "Rafting on the Allegheny and Ohio, 1844," *Pennsylvania Magazine of History and Biography*, 51 (1927), 27–78, 143–71, 207–43; Michael Allen, ed., "Reminiscences of a Common Boatman, 1849–1851," *Gateway Heritage, Quarterly Journal of the Missouri Historical Society*, 5 (Fall 1984), 36–49; Montell, *Don't Go Up Kettle Creek*; Thomas R. Cox, "Transition in the Woods: Log Drives, Raftsmen, and the Emergence of Modern Lumbering in Pennsylvania," *Pennsylvania Magazine of History and Biography*, 104 (July 1980), 345–64.

12. John Habermehl, *Life on the Western Rivers* (Pittsburgh: 1901), 30, 55–56.

13. Forman, "Biographical Sketch."

14. Twain, *Life on the Mississippi*, 139.

15. Ibid.

16. Daniel Boorstin, *The Americans: The National Experience* (New York: 1965), 101.

17. Ibid., 98–99.

18. For steamboating see Louis C. Hunter, *Steamboats on the Western Rivers: An Economic and Technological History* (Cambridge, Mass.: 1949); Eric F. Haites, James Mak, and Gary M. Walton, *Western River Transportation* (Baltimore: 1975); Allen, "Reminiscences of a Common Boatman"; Boorstin, *The Americans*.

19. All of the above quotations from towboatmen are based on interviews conducted by the author and published in "Life on the Mississippi—Towboat-Style," *The Lookout*, 74 (June-July 1982), 13–16.

20. For towboating see Hunter, *Steamboats on Western Rivers*; George P. Parkinson, Jr., and Brooks F. McCabe, Jr., "Charles Ward and the *James Rumsey*: Regional Innovation in Steam Technology on the Western Rivers," *West Virginia History*, 39 (January-April 1978), 143–80;

Michael C. Robinson, *History of Navigation in the Ohio River Basin* (Washington, D.C.: 1983); Allen, "Life on the Mississippi—Towboat Style."

21. Twain, *Life on the Mississippi*, 122.

Darrel E. Bigham

RIVER OF OPPORTUNITY: ECONOMIC CONSEQUENCES OF THE OHIO

Fernand Braudel observed that "the history of a people is inseparable from the country it inhabits . . . [A] country is a storehouse of dormant energies whose seeds have been planted by nature, but whose use depends on man."[1] From the earliest times, man's work on and along American rivers tapped their enormous power. Many, like the Susquehanna, offered more scenic than economic value. Others, like the Missouri, influenced development up and down their banks over long periods of time. Yet few rose to the regional and national consequence of the Ohio.

This chapter will focus on the Ohio River Valley, a segment of the 700–mile Ohio River basin which flows 981 miles and descends from a 710–foot elevation at its origins in Pittsburgh to its mouth at Cairo, a 290–foot elevation. The entire basin, which touches on fourteen states, supplies the largest volume of water to the Mississippi, even though its sister tributary, the Missouri, claims greater land area. Extending from the Chautauqua Lake region of New York to the prairies of Illinois, it begins in mountains and ends in gentle plains. Comprising only five percent of the land area of the forty-eight contiguous states, in 1965 the Ohio Basin accounted for 20 percent of the gross national product.[2]

The continuing significance of the Ohio River is the product of geography and history. Its strategic location, navigability, and natural resources strongly influenced the economic development of the region through which the river flows. People and commerce moved along it from the populous East Coast to the West, while its tributaries extended the economic influence of the Ohio well beyond its borders. Because of favorable climate, range of geological formations, and rich soils adjoining its banks, the river has proved a major source of agricultural products, forest and mineral resources, and manufactured goods.[3]

Nevertheless, development in the valley has not necessarily proceeded in an orderly or equitable fashion, as evidenced by the contrasts among communities like Pittsburgh, Wheeling, and Cairo. Such varying influences as low water or ice, the absence of bridges, and even the different economic and cultural systems established on its northern and southern shores affect the river's impact on the cities and farms along its banks. The economic development encouraged by the Ohio has in fact contributed, over time, to its relative decline in importance and its pollution by such byproducts of prosperity as sewage or chemicals.[4]

The economic influence of the Ohio is therefore complex and is best understood in five phases: from prehistory to the end of the American Revolution; from the establishment of the national government in the 1780s to the 1850s; from the 1850s to the early 1880s; from the early 1880s to the end of World War I; and from 1920 to the present. Distinctive subdivisions and characteristics mark each era; each contributed in singular ways and at different levels to the growth and development of the region and the nation.

FROM PREHISTORY TO THE 1780S

From the earliest times, the Ohio appealed to those seeking to improve their fortunes. Prehistoric settlements were prevalent along the Ohio and its tributaries, as agriculture and town life emerged where the flood plains offered rich soils, the rivers food and opportunities for trade. These communities were also noted for their distinctive ceremonial and burial mounds. Historic tribes turned as well to the Ohio and its river network for food and trade. One such settlement was the Shawnee town built before the 1740s near the junction of the Scioto and the Ohio (present-day Portsmouth), where the Great Warriors' Path from the Great Lakes to the south crossed the Ohio. The presence of prehistoric mounds there attested to its long-term importance.[5]

Beginning with the French explorer Sieur de la Salle, who "discovered" the Ohio in the late 1660s while seeking a river route to the Pacific, Europeans also realized its significance. Especially interested in New World fur, the French made it part of an extensive trading system protected by a series of posts established between Quebec and Louisiana. A French engineer made a compass survey of the river in 1729, and a second military expedition explored the Ohio ten years later. A post was established at Vincennes on the lower Wabash in 1732.

The intrusion of the British into the Transappalachian West in the 1740s made the Ohio Valley an arena for Anglo-French rivalry. In 1742 four Virginians, led by John Peter Salley, traveled down the Kanawha, Ohio, and Mississippi to New Orleans, seeking to explore the commercial potential of the region. Within two years a delegation of colonists met in Lancaster, Pennsylvania, with representatives of the Iroquois League; the agreement that followed formed the basis for British and later American claims to the furs and land of the upper Ohio valley. In 1749, the crown granted hundreds of thousands of acres to the Ohio Company of Virginia. Such acts precipitated the French to launch a military expedition led by Pierre Joseph Céleron de Bienville, who in 1749 planted lead plates along the banks of the Ohio claiming French ownership. Soon thereafter two Pennsylvania agents, George Croghan and Conrad Weiser, and a Virginian, Christopher Gist, launched an expedition to counter the claims of the French. Fearing British plans, the French began to strengthen their western posts and to build new ones to the east, notably in western Pennsylvania. Undeterred; the Virginians began to build a fort near the forks of the Ohio, and in late 1753 sent Gist and his young aide, George Washington, to strengthen their claim to the region. The French, however, overran that vital but unfinished post in April 1754 and renamed it Fort Duquesne.[6]

The French and Indian War which followed centered on control of the vital Ohio Valley. The struggle altered the economy of the natives, as competition among tribes for furs and booty led to the decline of hunting and gathering as well as to the rise of intertribal warfare, of which the British and the French took advantage. In the long run, the French proved unequal to the task of defending such a large territory with limited resources and trading disadvantages. In the Treaty of Paris (1763), France ceded its North American claims to the British.

During and after this final struggle, the English spoke with increasing enthusiasm of the potential of the Ohio country. In 1750 Lewis Evans, a Philadelphia cartographer commissioned by the governor of Pennsylvania to spy on the land west of the Appalachians, reported that the region provided boundless opportunities, especially because of its navigable Ohio waterway and its tributaries (especially the Monongahela), its forests and meadows, its plentiful wild game, and many mineral resources—salt, iron ore, coal, limestone, sand, and clay. George Washington's topographical and military reconnaissance in the region four years later reinforced the perception.[7]

Interest in these opportunities grew stronger after 1766, when British naval officer Thomas Hutchins prepared the first hydrographic study of the Ohio. Assisting him was an army officer, Harry Gordon, who prepared the first detailed map of the river. Their report "provided reliable information about river navigation, accurate descriptions of transportation routes, and potential sites for camps and fortifications." On their return Hutchins's map was "copied and distributed to the British forces . . . His maps of the Ohio Basin were published in London in 1778 and remained for many years the only reliable source of information about the Ohio Valley frontier." Hutchins, who later joined the Revolutionary cause and became the first "Geographer of the United States," had "a major influence on the opening of the valley to settlement."[8]

Ironically, British efforts to control settlement in the interests of economy and stable relations with the Indians laid part of the foundation for the Revolutionary War and the establishment of the United States. Population pressures, for instance, forced the British government in 1768 to open the region south of the entire Ohio River to white settlement. Settlement of the Ohio Valley below Fort Pitt (earlier Duquesne) followed "through the rather divergent interests of land companies grandly conceived, of frontiersmen in search of hides and pelts and lands to farm, and of Christian missionaries."[9] Ohio Company stockholder George Washington, for example, returned to tour the upper Ohio in 1770, and expressed special interest in the bottomlands of the Great Kanawha. Native Americans invited Moravians to place missions near the Ohio.

While Virginians and Pennsylvanians explored, settled, and laid competing claims to what are now southwestern Pennsylvania and northern West Virginia, an equally dramatic development was occurring in the lower Ohio Valley, as Virginians came down the Ohio or through the Cumberland Gap and established permanent settlements, initially in 1773 at Harrodsburg, on the Kentucky River. Three years later this rapidly growing region became a county of Virginia. Shortly after the Revolutionary War broke out, one of Kentucky's delegates to the Virginia legislature, the youthful George Rogers Clark, obtained permission to drive the British out of the area north of the Ohio, thus to control the river and its tributaries. Clark and his men achieved dramatic results, including the capture of Fort Sackville at Vincennes in February 1779. In the process Clark established several forts in the region, notably Fort Nelson at the Falls of the Ohio (1778), later known as Louisville. The focus of English-American controversy for twenty years, the Ohio Valley fell into American hands as part of the peace settlement. Clark and his men were awarded land grants for their service, and Clarksville, established in 1784 on the north bank of the Ohio, opposite Fort Nelson, was the first American town in the Northwest.[10]

FROM THE 1780S TO THE 1850S

The ending of the Revolutionary War brought even greater American interest in the Ohio River Valley. The "ark of empire"—the sturdy, utilitarian flatboat, which appeared on the river before the war's end—was the principal means of transportation for the thousands who traveled downstream (at about five miles per hour) in search of homesteads. Aided by the national government—via removal of Indian threats, institution of orderly processes for land surveys and sales (1785), creation of a means of forming a republican government (1787), and grants to land companies—pioneers crossed the mountains to the Upper Ohio and its tributaries, where they bought or built flatboats. Construction of these vessels gave rise to some of the earliest crafts and industries in the new river towns, such as Pittsburgh and Wheeling.[11]

The westward pull of the Ohio for settlement and commerce was powerful. In the spring of 1788, for example, 308 flatboats, carrying 6,000 settlers, 3,000 head of livestock, and 150 wagons floated past Fort Harmar (Marietta). By 1790 the valley, sparsely populated in 1775, had 125,000 residents. Because of the difficulty and the cost of reaching eastern markets with agricultural produce, pioneers also began to use the flatboat for trade downriver. A French immigrant, Barthelemi Tardiveau, was probably the first to attempt the downriver trip on the Ohio and Mississippi rivers to New Orleans. Five years later, in 1787, he published an influential tract promoting the establishment of regular trade with New Orleans.[12]

Such development doomed hopes of the British and the Indians that the Ohio would be the barrier to northward and westward white settlement. The importance of the Ohio Valley as an avenue for national expansion was demonstrated by the fact that the first five Indian treaties (1783–1805) and the first grants of land to Revolutionary War veterans were in the valley. The spearhead of this expansion was the town. American settlements began to spring up, joining their older cousins Pittsburgh, Wheeling, Clarksville, and Louisville: Marietta, established at the mouth of the Muskingum in early 1788 by New Englanders of the Ohio Company; Cincinnati, a settlement (1788) in Symmes Purchase; and, in the next two years, Gallipolis, Massie's Station, Columbia, and North Bend. Most of these communities grew quickly: Marietta, for instance, had 2,400 residents by 1790.[13]

Such communities owed their rapid growth to the presence of federal land offices and other agencies of government, the emergence of commercial and financial institutions, the building and outfitting of flatboats, and the development of market-oriented agriculture. Notable products were flour, corn meal, meat, and salt. In general, before 1790 the economy north of the Ohio was less diverse than the settlements to the south and more heavily dependent on furs, the trading of which was seasonal. Still, early manufactures also suffered seasonal fluctuations, as travel was most reliable when the water level rose in the late fall and in late winter to late spring. The New Orleans market thus exerted a substantial and often capricious influence in the region, as water levels and one-directional flatboat travel combined to effect low prices for Ohio Valley commodities.[14]

In the early republic, nevertheless, the Ohio was truly the key to regional development and an essential part of national expansion as well. Between 1792 and 1818, five states in the Ohio River Basin joined the Union—Kentucky, Tennessee, Ohio, Indiana, and Illinois. The population of the Ohio and Mississippi valleys in 1810 was almost seven times its level twenty years earlier. A symptom of that was the growth in receipts at New Orleans from $5,000,000 in 1807 to $22,000,000 in 1830. A shipper of provisions, Cincinnati became the largest city on the Ohio (10,000 in 1818) and one of the leading manufacturing centers in the nation. To take advantage of this rising commerce, entrepreneurs established numerous communities along the river and its tributaries. All of these towns were laid out on the grid plan according to commercial, not aesthetic, considerations. The Ohio was the Main Street in each of these. That was the dream of Hugh McGary, Jr., when he purchased land in March 1812 to establish a town he named Evansville after one of the Indiana Territory's leading politicians. The desire to tap western trade was, moreover, a major factor, if not the most important one, in the nation's economic development before 1850, and was a vital part in the transportation revolution in the building of roads, canals, steamboats, and railroads. Between 1790 and 1850 much of the nation-building occurred in the Ohio River Valley.[15]

The Ohio Valley's growth was, however, uneven. On the one hand, the Treaty of Greenville (1795) opened up most of present-day Ohio to white settlement. By the late 1790s a zone of white settlement paralleling the Ohio, fifty to seventy miles wide, extended from Pittsburgh past Cincinnati. Soon the first new state had been carved out of the Northwest Territory. In addition, the Jay (1794) and Pinckney (1795) treaties removed British troops from the Northwest and opened the Mississippi to American commerce. The purchase of Louisiana in 1803 gave even greater impetus to western commercial development. On the other hand, substantial parts of the western Ohio Valley remained in Indian hands until Governor William Henry Harrison of the Indiana Territory, later commander of American forces in the West in the War of 1812, secured them for white settlement. The long, difficult, and dangerous roads between the valley and economic centers in the East also retarded development.[16]

Despite this, economic development in the Ohio Valley was substantial. Town life, especially on the north bank of the river after 1800, vividly illustrated this. As late as 1797 there were settlements of only thirty or so families every 400 miles, but soon a second generation of settlement emerged: orderly, neat communities contrasting sharply with the rough-hewn, often violent world of the first-generation subsistence farmers only a few miles inland.

Government in such new towns as Shawneetown influenced development in numerous ways: regulating prices of commodities, laying out and maintaining roads, protecting property, and encouraging the growth of financial institutions. Early river towns also boasted newspapers, which, like word of mouth, travel reports, and military campaigns, stimulated westward expansion. Frontier journalists benefited directly from the growth of their communities and unabashedly promoted their towns. Newspapers served also as vital means of communications in the valley, sharing information from boatmen about prices, weather, and river conditions.[17]

By 1815 a distinctive pattern appeared: counterclockwise trade via the Ohio-Mississippi axis. Agricultural goods were sold in New Orleans, finished goods purchased from the East or Europe, and transportation arranged for the shipment of these items to Pittsburgh, whence they were shipped downriver. Intertwined was, for most, a shift from subsistence to commercial agriculture, which in turn gave rise to merchants and commercial brokers. South of the Ohio, agriculture revolved around the cultivation and marketing of staples, especially tobacco and hemp, with the aid of slave labor. To the north there was no dominant commodity or port, and a variety of economic circumstances, conditions, and ventures. Cincinnati did not gain the regional significance of New Orleans until after 1815. Although farming was the prevalent economic activity, substantial trade was developing, as well as some manufacturing, in a number of towns. Waves of newcomers, impelled by determination and faith and characterized by a variety of ethnic, religious, and economic conditions, moved into and through the Ohio Valley.[18]

In the four decades following the ending of the War of 1812 the nation experienced perhaps the greatest period of growth in its history, and the Ohio was central to that drama. A contemporary account claimed that in 1820 approximately 2,400 flatboats passed the Falls of the Ohio carrying 1,804,000 pounds of bacon, 200,000 barrels of flour, 20,000 barrels of pork, 62,000 bushels of oats, 100,000 bushels of corn, 10,000 barrels of cheese, 160,000 pounds of butter, 466,000 pounds of lard, and 11,207,000 fowl. By the late 1820s approximately 4,000 flatboats carrying 160,000 tons annually descended the Ohio. The state of Ohio had a population of over 800,000 by 1830, and Cincinnati, with nearly 25,000 residents, was the dominant city of the West. Other river cities in the Buckeye State, like Steubenville, also thrived. The bulk of the population resided in the Ohio and the Miami, Scioto, and Muskingum valleys. Indiana's population was 343,000, more than twice that of 1820, most of it in the Ohio Valley and in the interior regions north of the river towns of Lawrenceburg, Madison, New Albany, and Evansville. Illinois's population was concentrated in the crescent defined by the Wabash, Ohio, and Mississippi valleys.[19]

The typical settler was caught

> in the restlessness that engulfed the nation in 1815 . . . [He] put his family, livestock, and belongings on a raft or a flatboat and headed down one of the great avenues to the interior of the continent. . . . Once ashore at a likely spot, the emigrant found himself in a new world. On all sides stretched the wilderness, as all-encompassing, frightening, and exhilarating as it had been for the first settlers on the continent. . . . The most important thing about the new world was the land.[20]

Topography made the Ohio "the main thoroughfare between the Atlantic coast and the Mississippi valley. By way of its waters, more than any other route, a whole continent was peopled.[21] It was "the only important navigable river flowing toward the west in eastern North America, serving as a great highway . . . for immigrants . . . [and] for their commerce as well." Henry Clay observed that he had never seen "a section for which God had done so much and man so little."[22] An unobstructed liquid pool from Pittsburgh to Cairo in its seasonal high stages, the river possessed only two major natural obstacles—Letart's Rapids, 234 miles below Pittsburgh, and the Falls of the Ohio, opposite Louisville, both passable during slackwater times. Other obstacles were islands and bars, especially between Pittsburgh and Wheeling, although, by creating slackwater pools, bars could also be a boon to boaters.[23]

The Ohio highway promoted economic development in two other respects: by encouraging boat-building and stimulating a variety of land and water improvements designed to gain better access to the Ohio. The construction of flatboats and their relative, the barge, encouraged the building of sea-going sailing vessels on the Ohio. The river's navigability and proximity to cheap and ample lumber supplies led to the establishment of the first shipyard at Elizabeth, Pennsylvania. Floated downriver, loaded with commodities, these vessels entered foreign trade directly from river ports and thus avoided the payment of duties at New Orleans. This industry continued through the mid–1860s.

To provide a dependable two-way commerce, beginning in the early 1790s merchants and navigators began to use keelboats, which proved profitable, despite their slow upriver speed via arduous labor. One owner in 1817 reported that the cost of operating a thirty-six-ton boat from New Orleans to Louisville was $1,750 and that the profit was $1,490 on each trip. The capital outlay was less than $2,000. Eventually these craft lost passenger and long-distance freighting to steamboats, but continued to be used on short routes, especially near headwaters of tributaries, until railroads and better roads reduced their number.[24]

The steamboat was the most important technological innovation. The first to travel the Ohio, the *New Orleans*, was built at Pittsburgh in 1811 by agents of Robert Fulton, whose efforts to maintain a monopoly were defeated by the U.S. Supreme Court's ruling in 1824 that navigable waters and interstate commerce were under federal jurisdiction. At about the same time, such improvements as broad, shallow hulls, huge wooden superstructures, engines that could run in muddy water, and sternwheel propulsion made the steamboat even more attractive. Also important were business considerations: owners did not have to build or maintain their thoroughfares, capital outlays for boats were relatively modest, and profits were substantial. Before the steamboat, a Pittsburgh to New Orleans passenger paid $60; in 1833 the steamboat rate was $6. Upstream freight from Cincinnati to Pittsburgh dropped from $7 to $10 per 100 pounds to $2 or $3. The steamboat quickened transportation, stimulated other transportation innovations like the canal, gained a virtual monopoly on passenger traffic, and handled most freight, except during low water. As early as 1830, the volume of freight carried on steamboats exceeded that of flatboats and keelboats combined, and in succeeding years gained an even greater share of river-borne freight.[25]

The steamboat contributed to economic development in other ways. In addition to stimulating the development of a variety of new industries and occupations and greatly expanding agriculture and commerce, it provided floating shops and groceries, groggeries, and blacksmith, tinsmith, or cabinet-maker services. It also encouraged towns and cities to provide suitable landing and wharfage facilities, which in turn expanded the impact of this mechanized system. The coming of the steamboat led Congress to appropriate funds in 1824 for channel improvements on the river. This funding not only created many construction jobs, but also produced a 50 percent reduction in steamboat insurance rates between 1827 and 1835. Fires, collisions, and boiler explosions replaced snags as the chief hazards of river travel. The pioneer efforts of the U.S. Army Corps of Engineers laid the basis for countless other river improvement projects, including Charles Ellet's seminal study of river hydrography in 1853.[26]

In addition to innovations in boat-building, the Ohio stimulated economic development through a number of land and water projects intended to secure better access to that great river. Indian trails and military roads were the first—notably Braddock's Trace, Forbes Road, the Genessee Road, and the Cumberland Gap. In the early national period, such enterprises as Zane's Road connected Wheeling with Limestone (Maysville, Kentucky) on the Ohio after 1796; in 1812 an east-west road was developed from Marietta via Chillicothe to Cincinnati. The most significant publicly funded highway was the National Road, which extended from Cumberland, Maryland, following Braddock's Trace to Brownsville, Pennsylvania, on the Monongahela, to Wheeling. Built with revenues from the sale of public lands, it reached the Ohio in 1818 and eventually extended to Vandalia, Illinois. Wheeling thus gained a short-term advantage over Pittsburgh in the 1820s, because the number of islands and bars in the Ohio between those two cities made Wheeling a popular point of embarkation down the river. Such projects attracted not only federal revenues, but even larger amounts from state and local governments and private investors.

They also were the scene of a huge human drama. One traveler on the National Road in Pennsylvania in 1817 observed, "We are seldom out of sight, as we travel on this grand track toward the Ohio, of family groups behind and before us. . . ."[27] More often than not, pioneers rode in a cart pulled by a single horse. The poorer traveled on foot. On reaching the Ohio they encountered a thriving early urban economy: axemen, carpenters, and boatmen capable of supplying a light skiff or a flatboat, and countless others—blacksmiths, glassmakers, saddlers, ropemakers, tanners, chandlers, weavers, and cutlers—to supply their needs for the long journey west.[28]

Canal building also followed westward expansion. The Louisville and Portland Canal, completed in 1830 opposite the Falls of the Ohio with some financial aid from the federal government, was one of the most vital. Canal tolls there were high—up to half of the annual operating cost of a boat—but not nearly as expensive as the cost of transshipment by portage. The canals constructed in the Old Northwest and Pennsylvania in response to New York's Erie Canal (1825), which offered an efficient east-west route to the interior and greatly stimulated the development of the Great Lakes region, had even greater significance. Pennsylvania responded by building a canal from Philadelphia to the Forks of the Ohio. The Chesapeake and Ohio Canal secured access for Baltimore merchants to the beginning of the National Road. Western proponents of state funding for canals argued that they would provide better routes to the Ohio and open up eastern markets, where merchants would obtain higher prices for their goods, have a better selection at lower prices of items they desired to purchase, and be less dependent on the seasonal limitations of Ohio River trade. The state of Ohio built two major canals connecting the Ohio River and Lake Erie and several others from eastern Ohio to the Pittsburgh region. Indiana responded with the Wabash and Erie and the Whitewater, though completed with private funds and much less successful than those of Ohio.[29]

The economic consequences of canals were mixed. In Indiana, canal building helped to bankrupt state government, and the Ohio to Lake Erie route, completed in 1853, was a financial debacle. The Wabash and Erie did, however, open up interior regions in north central Indiana, where the canal continued to operate long after the closing of the southern portion. The prospect of being the terminus of the canal led to the economic takeoff of Evansville, but the city's trading orientation in 1853 remained southward. Ohio canals did shift trading patterns in the central and northern portions of the state, but Ohio River trade continued to be vital in the southern section. On the eve of the railroad era, canals "had not shattered the Ohio Valley trade's dependence upon New Orleans and the

Southern market."[30] Perhaps their positive effects dominated, for canals attracted population, opened multiple market outlets, played a crucial role in the export trade, lowered freight rates, and laid the basis for railroad development.[31]

The railroad was the final ingredient of the transportation revolution. Like the canal, it was originally oriented to the river systems. Not coincidentally, the first operational line was known as the Baltimore and Ohio (1830). Like the steamboat—but to a much more substantial degree—it exerted enormous influence on the economy of the Ohio Valley. Over the next twenty-five years, the construction of a number of north-south lines in the west connected river towns with the interior. In 1852, moreover, two major eastern lines—the Baltimore and Ohio and the Pennsylvania—reached the Ohio at Wheeling and Pittsburgh, respectively.[32]

As a river of opportunity, an avenue for settlers, and the object of many of the internal improvements of the age, the Ohio stimulated expansion of agriculture and commerce, exploitation of natural resources, and development of manufacturing. The valley's topography, fertile soils, temperate climate, abundant forest and mineral resources, and navigable waterways made it an enormous magnet for settlement. By 1825, distinctive agricultural regions were developing in Ohio: a corn, cattle, and hog belt, for instance, in the southwest quadrant, thanks to soil conditions, custom, and market and transportation facilities provided by the river. The Scioto Valley was the state's most productive, due to its rich alluvial soil and its accessibility to southern markets. In addition to corn and hogs, it exported wheat, flour, whiskey, rye, beeswax, beans, hemp, wool, poultry, dairy products, and fruit. The opening of canals in Ohio expanded wheat production in central and northern sections of the state, and by the early 1840s farmers shipped almost all of that grain to the Northeast. Similarly, hemp and wool were produced for the East. By contrast, nearly all of the corn, pork, and whiskey was destined for the South.[33]

Agriculture and commerce grew hand in hand, and each generation built on the gains of its predecessor. The *Evansville Gazette* of January 21, 1824, observed that the principal object of the region was to raise plenty of corn and hogs. Early producers could sell their surplus to new settlers in the region, but now the surplus had to be directed to new markets in the South. Bacon, hams, corn, honey, and other local products were thus shipped downriver, and keelboats returned with sugar, coffee, molasses, and other luxuries. Tributaries of the Ohio became "routes interior for ambitious traders with strong backs, or the means to employ strong backs. . . . "[34] The production of tobacco in Kentucky illustrated another dimension, as it led as early as the 1780s to the establishment of warehouses in Louisville and along the Kentucky River. In these warehouses inspectors graded the crop and gave receipts which circulated as currency. Such patterns helped, in turn, to form a more complex commercial system. As the scale and scope of trade grew, so did the functions of the merchants in the towns and cities of the valley who became the middlemen—shippers, bankers, and the like—in this thriving economy. The growth of Cincinnati most vividly illustrates this process. In 1840, 2,044 of its workers were engaged in commerce, and another 1,756 in transportation and navigation, as compared with 248 and virtually none, respectively, in 1819.[35]

The broadening of transportation networks and markets brought greater wealth and the expansion of commercial capitalism, producing divisions of wealth and power. Order and organization were required to facilitate the smooth flow of commerce and to maximize profit. Cincinnati merchants might have dealings with New York bankers, Pittsburgh merchants, or country storekeepers in the Ohio Valley. Each market was different and fluctuated daily. Newspapers, the mails, and later the telegraph provided vital information. Merchants responded to the increasingly complex economy by forming special interest groups, as in 1823, when they set uniform commission and storage rates, ending rate wars and regularizing relationships. Concern for the quality of goods destined for export led as well to a centralized method of inspection. Control of the local press was also vital, as it was the chief means of securing information about markets and of community promotion. By the early 1830s three distinct groups in the commercial sector existed—wholesale merchants, whose large mercantile firms were competing with eastern wholesalers for control of western trade; commission agents, who were middlemen between local retailers, eastern manufacturers, and regional farmers; and retail shopkeepers. The establishment of a Chamber of Commerce in 1839 underscored the growing divisions in the mercantile community, as it reflected the interests of the larger firms. It also was symptomatic of the city's prosperity. Cincinnati's river trade reached its peak in the early 1850s, when almost 4,000 steamboats arrived annually. Cincinnati was also sixth largest city in the nation.[36]

Numerous other commercial success stories could be told. Because of location, Pittsburgh, the primary origin of western travel and trade, became the object of numerous internal improvements projects, and via the state canal (1834) and subsequent smaller canals became the hub of a three-state region, tripling its population by 1850 and outstripping its Wheeling rival. Downriver, Louisville flourished owing to the firm commercial base established by its canal and by the coming of the steamboat. With access to the interior provided by the Michigan Road and the Madison and Indianapolis Railroad (1847), Madison in southeastern Indiana began to enjoy prosperous times as a trading center. Madison was a point of export for the agricultural goods of its hinterlands, and the lowering of freight rates and the increase in the carrying capacity and the speed of the steamboat made imported goods sold at Madison no more expensive than those sold at Cincinnati or Louisville.[37]

The commercial economy, however, depended on the weather as much as on agriculture. Weather made river transportation seasonal, adversely affected overland transportation and the supply of water for mills, and influenced when agricultural commodities could be processed, since refrigeration was absent. Water levels and ice meant that there were two seasons of trade, and the length of a season depended on the depth and character of a particular channel as well as on the type and size of the boat and the nature of the cargo. Too much water was as much of a problem as too little, because of the debris generated by floods. Crucial coal, lumber, and crude iron—carried in clumsy flat barges—were even more adversely affected by ice and low water. Since most of the initial fuel supply came from the lower Monongahela and the Ohio above Wheeling, serious shortages developed during portions of the year in downriver communities. This was relieved somewhat by the opening of coal mines in the lower valley and the building of coal barges with shallower draught.[38]

Yet Ohio Valley commerce thrived. Combined with the bounties reaped from the agriculture, forests, and minerals of the region, it also contributed to the emergence of a prosperous manufacturing sector. The region was well known as an agricultural cornucopia. Its hardwoods were plentiful. The greatest resource was white oak, used for making agricultural implements, carriages, barrels, and furniture. Much was shipped to

England for shipbuilding. Also important were hickory and black walnut. Cypress, used for shingles, was another unique forest resource in the lower valley. Although the region lacked white pine for construction, that could be obtained from the upper reaches of the Allegheny River and shipped downriver.[39]

In addition the region boasted vast mineral resources, especially in the Upper Ohio, but their full value was not immediately seen. Although "stone coal" and petroleum had little use to early settlers who discovered them while looking for limestone or salt, the earliest stirrings of the Industrial Revolution in the West came from the untapping of these and other bountiful resources—iron ore, lead, sand, and clay.

Salt, which abounded at springs and licks, contributed heavily to early economic development. Saline preserves in nearby southern Illinois, for example, accounted for the settlement of Shawneetown in 1818. Salines on the Muskingum were also essential to the growth of Zanesville. The Scioto Salt Works made seventy to eighty barrels of salt daily and sold it via horseback upwards of 100 miles away. Gallatin County, Illinois, produced 100,000 barrels of salt in 1827 and employed 1,000 persons in making salt from brine. The salt works of the Muskingum country reportedly manufactured 500,000 barrels in 1837. Salines were also abundant in the upper Monongahela country, along the Great Kanawha, and in the Blue Licks region of Kentucky. Hard to handle and store, expensive and risky to ship, salt was nonetheless in great demand. Canals and steamboats, however, introduced cheaper, purer salt from places like Michigan into the valley. That led to a decline in commercial production of Ohio Valley salt, although commercial salt manufacturing in the Kanawha Valley prospered. In 1829 its works manufactured 925,000 barrels of salt, more than twice the amount made in Ohio, the second leading salt producer. Production soared with the expansion of the meat-packing industry in the valley and elsewhere. Kanawha salt was inexpensive and plentiful, and enjoyed the advantages of strong brine (seventy-five gallons made one barrel of salt), improvements in drilling methods, and availability of cheap coal used for heating the brine. Like all salt produced in the valley, however, Kanawha salt contained impurities that rendered it unsuitable for meats destined for distant Southern markets, and its production dropped off by the 1840s as cheaper, purer sources, such as the Saginaw region of Michigan, were found. Salt production survived due to consolidation of factories and improvements in manufacturing techniques. It would also lay the foundation for the chemical industries of later years.[40]

Iron ore was also essential to the valley's development. Here, too, the river played an important part. Small forges using local ore, charcoal, and limestone sprang up throughout western Virginia and southwestern Pennsylvania before 1800. By 1822 the Pittsburgh-Wheeling region was noted for its puddling furnaces and rolling mills. Iron production also thrived from the mid-1820s to the late 1860s in the Hanging Rock region on the north and south sides of the Ohio near Ironton, Ohio, and Ashland, Kentucky. In 1860, Ohio was second only to Pennsylvania in iron production, with a number of furnaces in its southeastern quadrant near the river. These furnaces sent a highly profitable manufacture, pig or bar iron, downstream to blacksmiths and foundries in the West for transformation into such tools as plows and axes or the Kentucky rifle. Iron production stimulated innovations such as crucible steel, which had its roots in Cincinnati in 1832, and the Bessemer process, the brainchild of an Ohio Valley resident. The Pittsburgh-Wheeling region specialized in making heavier iron goods, and Cincinnati in lighter ones. Iron production had other effects—for example, stimulating the wood-cutting and limestone businesses. By the 1840s, anthracite and bituminous coal were being used as a substitute for charcoal because of their low cost and availability. Coke was introduced in western Pennsylvania about 1820. The making of iron goods like plows, boilers, and rails undergirded the agricultural and transportation revolutions of the antebellum era.[41]

Bituminous coal was another important resource, although it remained commercially unimportant as long as wood was plentiful. Not until the 1850s was coal widely used as a fuel for factories, steamboats, and homes in the river valley. Commercial mining of "stone coal"—to distinguish it from charcoal—began in the early nineteenth century in southwestern Pennsylvania, southern Ohio, and southern Illinois, but "Pittsburgh coal" predominated. The depletion of timber resources, the rising iron industry, and the low cost of the fuel made the use of coal more common in the early years in the Upper Valley. In 1827, $1.50 worth of Pittsburgh coal, or 12.5 bushels, produced power equal to a cord of hickory, which cost $2.87. The costs of shipping the bulky commodity by wagon or steamboat, however, were substantial: a ton costing $1.00 in Pittsburgh might cost $10.00 in Cincinnati. Coal barges, moreover, could not be used during large portions of the year because of ice or low water. These factors, combined with the depletion of wood supplies downriver, contributed to the opening of coal mines in the lower Ohio Valley, such as one at Cannelton, Indiana, in the late 1830s. The coming of railroads added still another stimulus. By the 1840s, Ohio produced 3,500,000 bushels annually, Illinois 424,000, and Indiana 242,000. Western Virginia's and Kentucky's coal production remained relatively insignificant.[42]

Other mineral resources contributed to the development of the valley. Limestone abetted not only iron and steel production, but construction as well—as a building material and as an ingredient in mortar and plaster. Also important were the sand and the clay in the Upper Valley, which led by the early 1800s to thriving glass and pottery works in southwestern Pennsylvania, southeastern Ohio, and northwestern Virginia. The later discovery of natural gas in the region aided in the inexpensive production of glass and pottery. Clay, plentiful in the valley, was also used for making brick and tile. Oil and natural gas were additional mineral resources, known to Indians and whites from colonial times onward. Oil was not important until the late 1850s, when the discovery of oil at Titusville on the Allegheny River sparked a commercial revolution. Demand for "coal oil" grew enormously.[43]

Forest and mineral resources were important ingredients in the emergence of manufacturing, the most dramatic aspect of economic development in the valley before the Civil War. Within a generation of the first white settlement at Cincinnati, manufacturing developed to serve distant as well as local markets. The combination of ambitious newcomers, abundant and varied natural resources and agricultural products, local demand, and steam power produced this rapid emergence of manufacturing. Other factors worked against it: the newness of the country, the inexperience of the settlers, the scarcity of labor and of capital, the limited knowledge and skill regarding manufactures, the uneven financial conditions of the region, and the attractiveness of farming and commerce. Yet the cost of importing goods across the mountains from the East made necessary and profitable the production of most of the local wants from local industry, such as pots, kettles, tools, ovens, and furniture. The new manufacturers themselves needed supplies, including machinery, impossible to transport cheaply long distances over land. These circumstances aided related industries, like the foundries which made boilers. The high transportation costs of raw materials to distant markets also encouraged the milling of flour and lumber. "The wide distribution of the grain supply, the simplicity of the manufacture, and the small amount of capital necessary for the erection of a mill, caused the production of flour to become widely distributed. . . . [This also characterized] the preparation of lumber."[44]

By 1830, valley industry had entered the mill era, a period which also witnessed the factory system and the steam engine. The transportation revolution allowed well-established and successful operations serving their immediate locales to penetrate national markets. By the 1850s, Cincinnati, with superior slaughtering and packing facilities, an ample supply of labor, a specialized work force, access to markets, and efficient use of byproducts (for example, lard, soap, candles, and bristles), was known as "Porkopolis." The Ohio Valley led the nation not only in pork products, but also in flour, liquor, lumber, and agricultural machinery.[45]

Manufacturing and commerce also went hand in hand. In the pioneer era, the establishment of western towns, the coming of settlers, the isolation of the region, and the importance of the location for westward migration led Pittsburgh, for example, to develop specialized manufactures—glassware, iron tools, flour, whiskey, and the like. Louisville became a major producer of rope, made from hemp grown in the region, as well as a maker of tobacco goods. In a number of towns, the coming of the keelboat and the steamboat spawned new industries. Because of location, Pittsburgh and Jeffersonville/New Albany, Indiana became major shipbuilding centers. By 1830 Cincinnati and Pittsburgh, the largest cities in the valley, were also the chief manufacturing centers.[46]

The steam engine, closely associated with innovations in river transport, was an essential part of Ohio Valley industrialization, for it reflected the region's weather as well as its receptivity to technological change. Steam dominated the mill period prior to the Civil War, for ice and low water inhibited the growth of water-powered mills. In 1859, for instance, 76 percent of its foundries were steam-powered, as compared with 46 percent nationwide. Climate also dictated seasonal meat-packing and the making of lager beer—from late fall to late winter, when temperatures were lower; before the advent of artificial refrigeration these industries required thick walls, deep cellars, and river and lake ice. In 1871–1872, for instance, 88 percent of Cincinnati's pork was packed between November 1 and March 1.[47]

The mill period was distinguished by the importance of manufacture of grain and timber products; the dispersion of factories (for example, the manufacture of liquor, beer, wagons, carriages, leather goods, flour and meal, agricultural implements, and lumber) throughout the region; the growing likelihood of corporate ownership of mills; the attraction of newcomers from Western Europe as well as rural regions to urban areas; and the quickening of commerce, as city leaders sought to extend their influence into even larger portions of the interior. By 1860 flour, meal, and lumber accounted for 51 percent of the value of manufactured products in Indiana and 42 percent in Illinois. The relatively low level—28 percent—in Ohio reflected the industrial diversity of the Upper Ohio Valley, an attribute which came later to the more western regions. Valley manufacturing nevertheless reflected the primacy of agriculture.[48]

The economic takeoff of the Ohio Valley after 1815 was also demonstrated in its urbanization. Towns both spearheaded economic development and reflected the vast changes that were occurring. In the boom years of 1815–1850, the rate of urbanization in the valley was the highest in the nation. Thereafter the rate of growth was uneven. In 1790, the combined populations of Cincinnati, Louisville, and Pittsburgh totaled less than 600; by 1830, they reached 51,000, about 5 percent of the total urban population of the nation. Immigration helped to fuel that growth. In much of the Ohio Valley the dominant group of immigrants, particularly after 1848, was German. Victor Hugo captured that drama in his observation of the thousands of ordinary people leaving the Rhineland. "They were not flying to the sound of the trumpet," he said, but "were hurrying from misery and starvation. They could not obtain a living in their native land, but had been promised one in Ohio."[49]

The first frontier of the Ohio Valley had been the town—whether offering markets or government for the hinterlands. Most did not turn out as their founders planned, however, and those that prospered did so for a number of reasons. Location was essential: Louisville was located on a natural break in transportation; Pittsburgh lay at the Forks of the Ohio, Cincinnati at the mouth of the Little Miami and across the river from the mouth of the Licking River, and Paducah near the mouths of the Cumberland and the Tennessee. Wheeling benefited from its being on the National Road and the Baltimore and Ohio Railroad.[50]

The success of towns depended, however, on more than location. Other factors included federal Indian policy and land development, political organization of their territories, access to and development and control of hinterlands, local investment in rivercraft and other means of tapping the interior, the development of commercial agriculture, the quality of boosterism via editors or intellectuals, commercial and industrial expansion, and the abundance of regional resources.

Luck also counted. The towns of the Ohio Valley offer countless examples of varying degrees of success and all-too-frequent failure. Despite optimistic names—Aurora and Rising Sun, Indiana, or Metropolis, Illinois, for example—most never developed as their founders had planned they would.[51] An early star, Lexington faded somewhat by 1840, in part due to the Panic of 1837 and the rising success of Louisville. Marietta, despite its favorable location at the mouth of the Muskingum, its salt springs, stone, and coal, grew less rapidly than Zanesville, an interior town on the Muskingum that benefited from canal building, access to the National Road, and the natural resources of its region. Wheeling grew unevenly, despite the advantages of location. Although Pittsburgh sought unsuccessfully to block the construction of a river bridge there, Wheeling nonetheless saw only a brief period of glory in the 1820s, for Pittsburgh possessed superior transportation connections. The building of a railroad bridge across the Allegheny in the late 1850s offered Pittsburgh uninterrupted rail access into northern Ohio and Indiana. Location, transportation improvements, and resources, especially coal and iron ore, combined to make it the dominant city in the three-state region and a rising national star.[52]

The fate of four southern Indiana towns—Newburgh, New Albany, Madison, and Evansville—is instructive. Though settled last, by the late 1850s Evansville's star was clearly rising, while those of Madison and New Albany were falling. Newburgh's star never really rose. The second largest city in Indiana in 1850, Madison suffered from a paucity of public and private capital, as demonstrated by the low level of its industrial development. That meant that much of the region's resources had to pass through for processing elsewhere. Railroad construction across Madison's hinterlands, especially by Cincinnati investors, also had a devastating effect. New Albany, located below the Falls of the Ohio, took advantage of its location to become an important shipbuilding center, and rail and road transportation into its interior encouraged the development of manufacturing. Yet New Albany's growth rate dropped by the 1850s because of limited availability of capital, strong competition from the mills and meat processing facilities across the river in Louisville, and sparsely populated and undeveloped hinterlands. Newburgh remained a sleepy river town, its opportunity for greatness removed by the railroad's bypassing it. By contrast, Evansville grew rapidly after 1840, becoming a chartered city in 1847 and tripling its population in the 1850s. The prospect that the Wabash and Erie Canal would be completed there helped boost its growth, as did its ability to develop strong commercial ties to its hinterlands, which included southwestern Indiana, southeastern Illinois, and western Kentucky. Local leaders established an aggressive Board of Trade in 1857, a year after Evansville was made a federal port of entry. Coal mining and industry—especially foundries and flour and lumber mills—flourished, but the chief reason for Evansville's success was commerce, notably wholesale dry goods and groceries.

The southern Illinois towns of Shawneetown and Cairo also illustrate this pattern. The Shawneetown land office opened in 1812 with great initial promise, as it offered wealth in furs and salines. The community suffered, however, from flooding, the absence of water and other easy access to the interior, the Panic of 1837, and the competition from northern towns. Cairo, which possessed an advantage in location, suffered from flooding and disease, and despite two speculative efforts in 1818 and 1837 did not take hold until the construction of levees and the completion of the Illinois Central Railroad to the community in 1857. Even then, Cairo remained small.[53]

The Ohio also exerted a force in state-building. The lure of Western trade, for example, powerfully influenced public and private investment patterns in Pennsylvania, contributing to the completion of the state canal and the Pennsylvania Railroad. In Ohio, the river served as a means of exploration, migration, and commerce, and in the 1850s virtually every hamlet and town boasted a steamboat landing. To the west, Indiana was also heavily indebted to the river, to which it owed most early road, canal, and railroad projects. The Ohio contributed, as in Pennsylvania, to major public investment schemes, whether the massive Internal Improvements Act of 1836 or the many riverfront improvement projects undertaken by its river towns. Perhaps least influenced by the Ohio was the last state formed in the Ohio Valley—Illinois—which was more indebted for its development to the Erie Canal, the opening of the Great Lakes trade, and the railroad age.[54]

Like towns and states, the steamboat and the railroad were important economic consequences of the Ohio River, which in turn exerted profound effects upon the economic development of the Ohio Valley. Each illustrated the close interrelation of the navigability and location of the river and its tributaries, the development of natural resources, and the technological changes of the era. The fifty years following the introduction of the steamboat on the Ohio represented a period of extraordinary regional growth. By 1860, half of the pork and other meat packed in the nation came from Ohio and Indiana, and 40 percent of its pig iron was made in the upper reaches of the valley. Without the steamboat, declared Louis Hunter, the advance of the frontier, the rise of river cities, the growth of manufacturing, and the decline of subsistence agriculture would have been infinitely slower. The rise of the steamboat also contributed greatly to population growth and dispersal west of the Appalachians and accelerated the demand by civic and business leaders in the valley for river improvements and the establishment of a slackwater system via locks and dams.[55]

The steamboat was an attractive addition to Ohio River transportation for several reasons. Relatively inexpensive to purchase, between 1830 and 1860 more than half of these craft on the Ohio were owned by a single person or two to four partners. They also operated on a publicly maintained right-of-way. As population and traffic increased, moreover, individualistic and haphazard business practices like carrying small cargoes and using capricious schedules and rates grew unprofitable and disappeared.

The effects of steamboat technology on speed, direction of trade, and freight and passenger costs were gigantic. One particularly dramatic effect, the replacement of counterclockwise trading patterns with up- and downriver trade, encouraged Ohio Valley interdependence and greatly increased trade eastward. Hence farmers and merchants in the Ohio Valley gained advantage as the prices of Southern commodities and finished goods from the East or Europe declined, while the gap between the prices for Western export staples sold in the Ohio

Valley and those sold at New Orleans significantly narrowed. In 1816–1820, a farmer's barrel of flour purchased twenty-seven pounds of sugar, as compared with thirty-nine in 1826–1830. In the same period, the amount of sugar a barrel of pork could purchase rose from thirty to fifty-two pounds. As the volume of trade on the Ohio soared between 1820 and 1860, the number of steamboats rose with it.[56]

Early Ohio Valley railroads also owed their growth to the river, designing lines such as the Evansville and Crawfordsville and Madison and Indianapolis to extend the trading regions of river cities. Like the steamboat, they increased the speed of travel, lowered freight costs, and helped to alter the direction of Ohio Valley trade. Railroads, however, offered the advantage of speedier, year-round travel. This freed merchants from the need to build up stocks for the one or two times a year that navigation was possible and freight rates low. The railroad boosted the fortunes of river towns that secured rail connections, as the case of Pittsburgh so dramatically illustrated. Smaller communities like Parkersburg, Virginia (now West Virginia), and Henderson, Kentucky, also benefited from rail connections. Although railroads in the 1850s produced a decline in downriver trade by steamboat, they encouraged upriver trade to the early railheads at Pittsburgh and Wheeling and contributed to the rise in riverborne coal traffic, as the demand for that fuel for locomotives increased. As the river's economic importance grew, the demand for river improvements also increased. Railroads offered definite threats to river transport—for example, by opening up interior markets, cutting off river towns from their trading hinterlands, encouraging bridge-building across the Ohio, or carrying passengers and many kinds of freight rapidly, cheaply, and year-round. Such challenges were, however, not apparent to most immediately before the Civil War.[57]

FROM THE 1850S TO THE 1880S

In the 1850s, the Ohio reached its peak as a force in regional and national economic development. As the demand for the building of bridges indicated, however, it could also function as a barrier. Nature had created a formidable waterway to cross or to navigate, especially in the winter and summer. Yet human beings also exploited the Ohio as a barrier, whether by using it to separate Native Americans from early settlers or to delineate state lines or spheres of economic activity. Most strikingly, the Ohio defined two cultures—one shaped by the plantation and human slavery, the other by a more diversified economy and free labor. Many contemporary observers, such as Alexis de Tocqueville, contrasted the types of settlements and economic endeavors on the north and south banks of the Ohio and noted that the river of opportunity seemed to favor the former more than the latter. One Michigan soldier wrote during the Civil War, as he traveled between Ohio and Kentucky, of the differences in appearance between the two states. Ohio's shore, he reported, seemed "a continual garden," its lands dotted by home and vineyards, while Kentucky appeared to be "in a state of nature with now and then a cabin and truck patch to mar the scenery."[58]

As John Barnhart observed, this reflected a more fundamental matter: the struggle between planter and yeoman, extending west of the Appalachians after the 1790s.

> [O]nly north of the Ohio were the forces working for democracy strong enough to check the advance of the planter. . . . Not slavery alone, not lack of the franchise, not property qualifications, unequal representation, and unjust taxation, but something larger than these were at stake. The basic issue was the right of the people to establish a democratic society.[59]

The river—the River Jordan to African Americans, a line delineating slavery and freedom—would become a road to new opportunities for runaways and, after Emancipation, freed slaves. Not coincidentally, Evansville's first black Baptist church, formed in the spring of 1865, was named Liberty. Nor was it accident that the African American population in river communities on the north bank grew significantly thereafter—for example, from about 100 in Evansville in 1860 to 1,400 in 1870 and 7,500 in 1900, or 13 percent of the city.[60]

The Civil War era proved, in a larger economic sense, a transitional time for the Ohio Valley. Into the 1880s, "river intelligence" sections in the newspapers of river towns remained a vital source of information for local merchants. Yet change was occurring, although perhaps not perceptible at the time: the critical decade was the 1850s. This has to be seen in the larger context of regional specialization and of the westward movement of population and settlement. The railroad came after this process was well underway, and did not cause the shift of river valley trade to the east, but merely accelerated that process. Rail traffic was revolutionary, however, as the large scale of railroad operations allowed and practically required frequent, regular service. That meant corporations dominated the rail system, which held virtual monopolies in the territories they served, unlike the highly competitive steamboat lines which were generally owned by a few persons. Railroads offered through service over long distances, sometimes via connecting lines or even steam packets. The steamboat, in capacity and cost of service, retained an advantage over railroads, but railroads were at the beginning of technological development and steamboats at maturity. One Cincinnati commercial reviewer spoke of that in 1858 when he observed that "[e]xcept those engaged in the New Orleans and lower Mississippi trade, the business on the Ohio, owing to Railway competition, has become generally unprofitable and exceedingly precarious, so that few are disposed to build new boats, or to enter the business. . . . "[61] This pattern also appeared in the steady decline in tonnage carried by Ohio Valley steamboats after 1856. The number of steamboats arriving from all points at Cincinnati averaged 3,633 annually between 1851 and 1855, but dropped to between 2,800 and 2,950 annually from 1856 to 1870, and declined thereafter.[62]

In some respects the Civil War contributed to economic difficulties, as Confederate control over some Ohio River tributaries as well as the lower Mississippi and New Orleans disrupted river trade until mid-1863. The war also slowed the work on such transportation projects as the Roebling suspension bridge connecting Covington and Cincinnati, completed in 1866.

In other respects the war was a boon. River trade at Cincinnati, for example, increased with the use of river transports for moving Union troops. Cities like Louisville, Pittsburgh, Evansville, and Cincinnati, even small towns like Cannelton, Indiana, thrived as suppliers of food, boots, clothing, and the tools of war. Other important products were gunboats and rams, notably those made by James B. Eads and Charles Ellet. James Hollenshade of Cincinnati manufactured not only army weapons, but also pontoon bridges and wagons. Cairo prospered when the Union Army used it as a major point of departure for western campaigns. The coal trade, perhaps the most directly benefited, flourished as the demand for the fuel in factories and river craft increased significantly. The war also aided Northern railroads, given the disruption of Southern trade and the needs of the war effort in the North. The Indianapolis and Terre Haute Railroad profited so much that in April 1864 it paid a 25 percent stock dividend, a regular cash dividend of 5 percent, and an extra cash dividend of 5 percent. Interior cities like Indianapolis and Chicago rivaled Cincinnati as meat-packing centers.[63]

Through the 1880s, the river remained a vital part of the valley economy. It was, as Charles Ambler pointed out, a "poor man's highway" even after railroads crossed it at right angles and usurped much of the river's role in regional development. Rich bottomlands and hinterlands not served by rail remained open to steamboat traffic. Riverboats, moreover, continued to receive government mail contracts through the turn of the century. After the war, as shown by the experiences of Evansville and Cincinnati, tobacco and cotton trade with the South grew. Evansville merchants, for example, established packet service to the upper Tennessee River, where wholesalers and foundry proprietors found new markets; in turn, the city became a thriving tobacco market as well as a manufacturer of cotton textiles. The river was also an important artery for iron ore: before the opening of the Mesabi Range, Cumberland Valley and Missouri Valley sources met the raw material needs of the Upper Ohio Valley as its local supplies dwindled. Shipbuilding, especially the building of barges, remained important to the valley's economy, as the successes of the Dravo Company at Pittsburgh and the Howard Brothers at Jeffersonville demonstrated. Cincinnati, Paducah, and other smaller towns also ran important shipbuilding and repair yards.[64]

The Ohio may, in fact, have enjoyed a second "golden age" prior to the 1880s. Barge traffic supplied an important ingredient, hauling coal, iron ore, iron, petroleum, even new commodities like bauxite from Georgia and Alabama for the new aluminum mills in Pittsburgh. Coal, by far the most important commodity in postwar river freight, met the increased demands of industrialization and electrification. Pittsburgh was initially the major shipper. Low water and ice continued to pose a problem, however, and due to that, the price of Pittsburgh coal, and the increasing demand for coal in the Upper Valley, downriver fields greatly expanded. In Indiana, coal production in its southwest counties increased from 1.45 million short tons in 1880 to 29.35 in 1920. Petroleum was also an important item of freight, since independent producers sought to compete with Standard Oil, which controlled the rails. Where rails did not parallel the river, moreover, farmers depended on packet and barge traffic. Immigrants also used packets, for they offered good service at low cost.[65]

FROM THE 1880S TO THE FIRST WORLD WAR

The river was becoming a less important part of the economy of the region, as shown by the decline in packet service due to the failure of the "Big Seven" lines, rate wars, new railroad service connecting river towns (such as the Louisville, Henderson, and St. Louis, 1886–1891), the building of railroad bridges, and the continuing challenge of floods and ice. The number of packets operating out of Cincinnati dropped to ninety in 1879–1880, with arrivals and departures only a third of what their numbers had been in the early 1850s. Packets continued to function through the turn of the century because they carried small lots of freight cheaply and offered excursion services. "Floating palaces" remained a part of the Cincinnati riverfront into the 1890s, and the Louisville and Evansville Packet Line operated until 1909—one of the last to survive. By 1886, steamboats accounted for less than 5 percent of most commodities, such as cotton, corn, and hams and bacon, shipped to and from Cincinnati and Louisville. Steamboat tonnage in the Ohio Valley declined 75 percent between 1870 and 1910, with the sharpest drop occurring between 1900 and 1910 (49 percent).[66]

The usual explanation offered is the inherent superiority of railway transportation. This view possesses some substance, although the answer is infinitely more complex. To be sure, rail freight and passenger service was faster, more reliable, and in most matters less costly, and it was year-round. One must also consider the fact that the river valley was becoming economically fragmented; the hinterlands, once its tributaries, were now formidable competitors in their own right. The Upper Valley had become more self-contained: much of the Monongahela and the Ohio from Pittsburgh to Wheeling emerged as the nation's workshop, their banks lined with iron and steel mills and coal mines. South of Wheeling, the region remained heavily agricultural, with pockets of industry and coal mining.

Ironically, the population dispersed throughout the inland

west with the aid of river transport, to such places as Columbus, Indianapolis, or Chicago, were now more easily reached by rail. Hence the earlier dependence of railroads on the river to reach markets was reversed. Pittsburgh—a city of bridges—symbolized that shift. Eventually this meant that the river towns lost their economic supremacy. Superior access to livestock and grain by extensive rail connections, coupled with such innovations as the refrigerated rail car, enabled Chicago to eclipse Cincinnati as the nation's leading meat producer. Even Indianapolis posed a great threat: Kingan and Company, shortly after the end of the Civil War, was the first meat packer to operate year-round, an innovation which offered farmers a more reliable market and producers a more stable source of revenue.[67]

The decline of the steamboat stemmed from other sources. To suggest that rail lines singled out riverboats for rate wars, for instance, ignores the bloody rate wars that railroad companies waged against each other. The railroad, inherently more reliable because it operated year-round, also required a more sophisticated economic system in which to operate, thus threatening the small-scale, unorganized steamboat operators. Railroads also could carry specialized cargoes in separate cars and offer local and express service. Steamboats required large crews to fuel and maintain the engine, a distinct disadvantage. Perhaps most important, steamboats remained vital only so long as people were concentrated along the trunk lines of the river system.[68]

The packet's demise may in fact have resulted from factors other than the railroad. Charles Ambler pointed to the shortsightedness of Ohio Valley communities and states in seeking local "pork-barrel" aid and not improvements in the waterway as a whole. Moreover, large corporations such as U.S. Steel, although using their own barges for shipping, relied on rail systems they controlled or favored. In addition, as industry marched westward, suppliers did not need to transport raw materials over such long distances to reach the factories of the late nineteenth century. Steamboat packets were also hurt by the introduction of the diesel engine and the screw propeller on river towboats in the 1920s, as well as by gasoline-powered motorboats and trucks, which provided speedier deliveries. Ambler added that low wages paid to rivermen made for a lower caliber of worker as time passed and that "way charges" collected by wharves and levees grew increasingly costly.

Weather counted too, as the river offered uncertain deliveries three to five months a year.[69]

While the steamboat faded from the scene, and with it a number of Ohio River communities, a number of river cities prospered. With its many bridges and rail connections, its vast natural resources, its application of the new processes of making steel, and its protected location west of the Appalachians, Pittsburgh became by the turn of the century not only the center of America's iron and steel industry, but also a major manufacturer of glass, machine and foundry products, electrical equipment, and aluminum. In 1903, the city shipped 48 million bushels of coal downriver—almost twenty times the level of 1844. A major shipper and refiner of petroleum, Pittsburgh benefited from the major oil fields in the Allegheny Valley and northwestern Ohio. The heart of the giant U.S. Steel Corporation, it included a new industrial satellite community, Ambridge, incorporated in 1905 on the site of the former Indian community of Logstown, later the location of the Harmonist community of Economy. Named after the American Bridge Company, this industrial city made steel for bridges and buildings and such other producer durables as pipes and barges. At the completion of the pioneering 1907 Pittsburgh survey, whether seen "as a city, a district, or a region," Pittsburgh—by far the largest city on the Ohio—"was an economic rather than a civic entity." Pittsburgh's region was a scattering of desolate villages—grimy mill and mining towns dominated by their factories—set in a scarred landscape, its peoples fragmented by ethnicity as well as governmental disorganization. "A relentless economic discipline" shaped everything.[70]

Downriver, a new city in the new state of West Virginia also attested to the importance of the railroad and the far-flung urban market it was helping to create. Named after Collis P. Huntington, who acquired control of the Chesapeake and Ohio in 1869, the community was chartered two years later, and in 1873 became a major railhead on the Ohio. The city's growth was largely due to the C&O, as it was also the site of a major yard and shops. Rail lines along the river subsequently gave Huntington connections to the north as well as the south. By 1941 it was West Virginia's largest city.[71]

The railroad also contributed significantly to Cincinnati's development. As river trade declined in the 1870s, in part because railroad lines now paralleled the river, the city's hub shifted from the riverfront to the rail terminals to the north. The city secured a direct southern connection in the early 1880s, underscoring its dependence on railways. No longer the industrial leader in the Northwest, Cincinnati nonetheless prospered with its new connections to a national urban market. The success of its Procter and Gamble Company in marketing a pioneer "brand name" product, Ivory Soap, attested to that.[72]

Louisville as well traced its growth in this era to railroads, not to the river. Greatly aided by L&N connections southward, the city's industrialists benefited too from new postwar rail ties to other parts of the South and, with the completion of a bridge in 1870, to the North as well. Louisville's manufactures, like those of Cincinnati, reflected the resources of the region: tobacco and meat products, whiskey, flour, farm implements, and the like. With the enlargement of the Portland Canal, the city's importance as a river transshipment center grew. But a Factory Fund drive on the eve of World War I reflected the gap created by the loss of river trade. Leaders of the drive secured Reynolds Metals and Ford Motor Company factories in the city that helped to fill that void.[73]

Evansville too demonstrated that the railroad, with the subsequent access it provided to a national urban market, was the key to its continued development. With rail connections to Chicago, St. Louis, Nashville, and Louisville, Evansville had become Indiana's second largest city by the early 1890s. The completion of the L&N railroad bridge and the building of the Howell yard and shops for that line in the mid–1880s gave the city an important economic boost and allowed its newly formed Business Men's Association (1886) to boast of Evansville as "Gateway to the South." Newer industries in the city of nearly 90,000 included the Hercules Buggy Works, Bucyrus-Erie, and Mead Johnson. Evansville's economy, like Louisville's, still largely reflected the resources of its region. In value, the leading manufactures in 1919 were flour, furniture, and tobacco. Like Cincinnati, the development of brand name products such as Swan's Down Cake Flour demonstrated Evansville's entry into the national urban market.

Because of rail connections, access to resources and the national market, and availability of capital, these five cities enjoyed a scale of economic development which was not shared by many river towns or interior communities near the river. Evansville was the only river city in Indiana to prosper in the age of industry. New Albany, with only tenuous ties to its hinterlands and a fragile factory base, lost its boatyards after the

Civil War. A brief period of prosperity as a major producer of plate glass ended when the firm moved to the natural gas belt near Muncie which opened up in the 1880s. Thereafter the town stagnated, as Madison had a few decades earlier. In the forty years between 1880 and 1920, New Albany gained only 6,000 in population; it reached 23,000, 66,000 less than Evansville. Despite its having the Howard Boatyards and a railroad repair facility, Jeffersonville achieved a population of only slightly over 10,000–less than 1,000 more than in 1880. Paducah, although its boatyard survived the packet era, benefited even more from being a rail center, aided by the railroad bridge across the Ohio and the Illinois Central shops in the city.[74]

More often than not, however, river towns like Smithland, Kentucky, languished because they failed to obtain railroads. Similarly, a number of Ohio and West Virginia river valley communities experienced little substantial growth. In the Buckeye State, most of the economic expansion occurred in the north, where rail and lake connections, oil and natural gas, and iron, steel, and rubber combined to produce an industrial explosion.

Along the river, noteworthy exceptions to the rule of economic stagnation were places like Steubenville and East Liverpool (part of the coal, iron and steel, and ceramics and glass manufacturing network centered in Pittsburgh), and the Ironton region, noted for coal, iron, and steel. In West Virginia, a substantial proportion of economic activity after the 1870s was allocated to coal mining. Railroad building focused on opening of coal-producing areas to the river and rail network and to timber regions which could provide construction material for the mines. Wheeling, dominant in the early 1800s, managed modest growth after the B&O reached it in 1852, perhaps in part because the railroad did not make Wheeling its only railhead on the Ohio or build a yard and shops there. Certainly Pittsburgh's economic power, however, provided the chief reason.[75]

Despite the effects of the railroad and later the automobile and truck—symbolized by the building of Ohio River bridges, twenty-four of them between 1922 and 1933 alone—the river remained an important part of the economic life of the region, if not necessarily the nation. For example, the towboat and barge helped to maintain the Ohio as a major transportation artery. In 1908, in fact, the Inland Waterways Commission identified Pittsburgh, not New Orleans, as the leading river port of the nation. In 1910, 236 towboats worked the river, with annual tonnage of 26,077–as compared with 171 and 23,619, respectively, in 1870. Barge tonnage exceeded that of steamboat packets by over 8,000 tons. The continued importance of the river also explained the demand for canalization. The Corps of Engineers completed the first dam of the "slackwater" system on the Ohio slightly south of Pittsburgh in 1885. Ten years later the Ohio Valley improvement Association was formed by a group of Cincinnati business leaders, many of them suffering from the declining fortunes of the packet lines. The proposal to establish a minimum year-round depth of water by locks and dams all the way to Cairo had widespread appeal. When the third annual convention of the Ohio Valley Improvement Association (OVIA) met in Evansville in October 1897, delegates from Wheeling to Cairo attended what the editor of the *Evansville Daily Journal* called one of the most important meetings in the city's history. On several occasions, Evansville leaders boarded the steamer *Hopkins* to visit other river cities to lobby for cooperation in the securing of river improvements.[76]

Between initial Corps of Engineers river improvements in 1827 and 1903, Congress appropriated 6.6 million dollars. Animated especially by the commercial and military activity on the river during the Civil War, the Corps not only increased dredging and snag removal, but also installed beacons and buoys. Initially proposed in the 1870s, its plan for a six-foot slackwater system achieved by locks and dams was implemented very slowly. The OVIA was organized to reverse this dilatory situation. One of its goals was to give Congressmen a first-hand look at the condition of the river. Barge traffic in bulky goods, argued the OVIA, had enormous economic impact. The valley could become, as Andrew Carnegie declared, "the workshop of the world." Congressman Augustus Stanley of Kentucky insisted at an early OVIA meeting that "your hills along this valley [contain] wealth unknown to any citizen of the plain. . . ."[77]

With the support of key congressional leaders, President William Howard Taft, and the newly formed (1907) Inland Waterways Commission, Congress in 1910 approved the building of fifty-four locks and dams providing for a nine-foot channel, to be completed in 1922. Congress appropriated little money initially, however, and coal traffic on the Ohio concurrently declined, reaching an all-time low of 4.6 million tons in 1917. This decline was attributable to the abrupt halt of coal shipments from Pittsburgh to New Orleans because of demand for coal by Upper Valley steel makers, damage to barges on the unimproved Ohio, and competition from Alabama coal and Oklahoma oil in the New Orleans market. This reduced waterborne commerce on the Ohio by 50 percent and raised questions about the economic justification for canalization.[78]

FROM THE FIRST WORLD WAR TO THE PRESENT

During World War I, shipping demands overburdened the rail system and led the federal government not only to assume control of the railroads but also to rediscover the benefits of river transport. In the process, the Federal Barge Line was created, subsequently becoming part of the Inland Waterways Corporation (1924) when the river was opened to private carriers. Inland in turn (1928) became the American Barge Company of Louisville. Simultaneously, congressional appropriations for canalization increased substantially. The final dam, Number 53, opened on August 27, 1929, and the OVIA staged a dedication cruise from Pittsburgh to Cairo to celebrate the opening of a new age of river commerce: tonnage in the 1920s had already doubled, much of that in steel and petroleum products. A closely related reason for this growth was the replacement of the less efficient steam-powered sternwheelers by more powerful, diesel-powered towboats equipped with screw propellers. These modern craft, pushing modern steel barges, were as important as canalization in river revitalization.[79]

Several related developments of long-term import also occurred. First, wartime shortages of chemicals had encouraged development of new sources, aiding the rebirth of the Kanawha Valley, with its access not only to water but also to vital ingredients—coal, brine, chlorine, and carbon. (The region went on to become a major producer of synthetic fabrics, especially nylon, by the eve of World War II.)

Second, the Ohio, a river of opportunity, could also be a river of danger, as evidenced in its winter and spring floods. The flood of 1913 in particular caused an estimated $180 million in damage, a vivid revelation of its awesome power. In response, Congress authorized several flood control surveys and projects; after the even more deadly flood of 1937, which left 500,000 homeless and paralyzed business, additional legislation was passed.[80] Also important was the work of local and state governments, most notably the Miami Watershed Conservancy District. Completed in 1922 at a cost of 40 million dollars, the Ohio-funded project, directed by Arthur E. Morgan, was the first major river basin flood control program in the nation, a forerunner of conservancy programs in the Muskingum Conservancy District, the Tennessee Valley Authority, and the Southwest. Through dams, levees, and reservoirs, such subsequent projects provided not only flood control but improved river access for commerce, recreational opportunities, and soil conservation. Thus responses to flooding—a negative effect of the river—produced economic benefits.[81]

Such developments—especially canalization, accompanied by technological improvements in river transportation—produced a renaissance after 1930. Although initially inhibited by the Great Depression, the positive economic impact of these changes soon made itself felt. The 22.5 million tons shipped in 1930 dropped somewhat until 1933, when the level increased every year, reaching 36.5 million in 1941. In the same period, the average distance of river tows nearly tripled, to 142 miles. River carriers chiefly shipped coal, but petroleum, iron, and steel provided business as well. Canalization also led to the construction, mostly by private funds, of a series of terminals capable of handling the new barges. Whether distributing waterborne commerce inland or collecting inland commodities for river transport, these terminals attested to the complex transportation network's creation by barge, rail, and truck. Evansville's 90,000–square-foot Mead Johnson Terminal, opened in January 1931, epitomized the dawning of this new era. Such facilities allowed standardization of transportation schedules and cooperation among rail, truck, and water lines.[82]

Other effects of canalization included the revival of boatbuilding and new forms of river economic activity. The Dravo Contracting Company near Pittsburgh, one of a number of yards in the valley to benefit from these changes, was producing ten to twelve barges a month by 1925, in addition to doing general contracting and building locks, dams, bridges, and houses. Other notable manufacturers were located at Charleston, Point Pleasant, Jeffersonville, and Paducah. Technological innovation combined with wartime congestion, moreover, to produce greater water transport of basic, heavy, and bulky commodities such as iron and steel, petroleum, and agricultural and forest products—items of low value per unit which need not necessarily reach their destinations speedily. Owing to the limitations imposed by rail transport during the war and the paucity of barges, a number of corporations, such as Wheeling Steel and Jones and Laughlin Company, marketed their products in their own tows and barges with fuel supplied by their own companies after the early 1920s. New barge lines were also formed. Improvements on the tributaries of the Ohio—most of which offered access to vast coal resources—expanded greatly after the 1920s. The most dramatic was the Tennessee Valley Authority during the New Deal.[83]

Transportation improvements also figured heavily during the Second World War. Defense contracts were awarded to heavy industries in the Upper Valley, and to various other industries, including boatyards such as the one in Jeffersonville. Slightly over 4,000 small vessels and landing craft were built on inland rivers and floated to the Gulf of Mexico, approximately 1,000 of them constructed in the Ohio Valley. Location and navigability figured heavily, for instance, in the awarding of an LST contract to the Missouri Bridge and Iron Company, which built a shipyard in Evansville and launched its first LST in October 1942. The most prolific boatyard in the Ohio Valley, the Evansville shipyard had produced its hundredth ship by June 1944. At its peak it employed 19,500 and had subcontracts with twenty-seven Evansville firms. It brought over 300 million dollars in defense contracts to the city.[84]

From 1946 to 1953, "approximately 2,500 new industries located in the valley, and 5.5 billion dollars was spent to create or expand industries set on or near the navigable streams of the Ohio River system." This expansion depended largely on the growing national demand for electricity and such consumer durables as electrical appliances, which the Ohio Valley could meet because of its cheap water transport and abundant coal. Steam electric plants grew up rapidly along the river, and by the mid-fifties "30 million tons of the fuel were helping to produce some 12 million kilowatts of electric power annually." In addition, "dependable water supplies and savings derived from transporting petroleum, coal, sulfur, and crude ores . . . caused an expansion of the chemical industry." By the early 1950s, river traffic was increasingly being handled by river-truck-rail terminals, such as large new ones at Louisville and Pittsburgh, which permitted transshipment of coal and coke, oil and gasoline, iron and steel, and gravel, chemicals, and automobiles. Private interests built most, but local and state governments learned quickly of the economic benefits derived from such terminals, the newer ones of which were "highly mechanized operations that permit fast unloading and reduce turnaround time."[85] Most ports on the Ohio also added specialized grain- and coal-loading facilities.

In addition to the spawning of coal-fired generators, chemical plants, and freight facilities, the modernized river also created some new industries. A striking example was offered in Louisville, where cheap water transport and location gave rise to General Electric's huge Appliance Park, announced in 1951. Accessible by water year-round, Louisville could obtain Pittsburgh steel by water, while trucks and trains shipped the appliances to market. Water transport rates and cheap electricity led Alcoa six years later to locate a major smelting facility slightly upriver from Evansville, where ore could be easily shipped and whence the finished product could be transferred by land.[86]

By the late 1950s the Ohio had reassumed an important role in the life of the region and the nation, though not in its pre-1880s form. Employment directly related to river transportation, for example, remained a minute part of the work force in river communities, but employment indirectly supported by the river, such as coal mining and aluminum work, existed in impressive numbers. The volume of river traffic continued to grow significantly. Tonnage carried on the river increased from about 34 million in 1940 to nearly 80 million in 1960. The number of ton-miles trebled, to 18 million. Coal and coke accounted for most of the tonnage, but the river carried such other items as (in order) petroleum products, aggregates, iron and steel, and chemicals.[87]

The composition of river traffic changed as well: in relative terms, in the ability of the waterway to hold its own against expanded truck, pipeline, and air traffic, and in the expanded use of barges to carry bulky, heavy commodities. The Ohio was the chief mover of the nation's energy supplies by 1957, whether by tonnage or ton-miles (75 and 67 percent, respectively).[88]

The revival of the river was the product of the diesel tow, larger steel barges, and canalization. Barge-carried freight, though slower, profited through its inherent advantage of lower costs than that of rail. It also benefited from the expenditure of public funds on the right-of-way, and paid no user fees for the river. It depended heavily on coal production, an industry booming in the Ohio Valley in part because of low freight costs and because of expanding generation of electric power along the river, carried inland by long distance transmission lines—12 percent of the nation's power in 1957, as compared with 6 percent in 1939. The Port of Huntington, which shipped coal, grew impressively as a result. Cheap electricity and freight also stimulated the development of a host of new satellite industries, such as aluminum smelters, as well as older ones, and were responsible for the burgeoning chemical and petroleum facilities in the valley. In short, a new industrial boom began, although the region was relatively less prosperous than it had been in the days of the steamboat. Ample water, cheap barge transportation, and plentiful coal helped return the Ohio River "to a position of major significance as part of the nation's transportation system."[89]

The Corps of Engineers in the early 1950s began planning modernization of the slackwater system in response to deterioration of locks and dams; increased volume of freight, especially upriver; traffic jams at locks; larger number of barges used in each tow; and demand by riverside industries, terminals, and pleasure boat operators for uniform water supplies and stable pools.[90] This modernizing meant that riverborne commerce and river valley economic activity continued to develop hand in hand. Longer tows of coal and other primary materials could move more efficiently and safely, in greater volume, in both directions on the river, contributing substantially to the industry and commerce of the Ohio River Valley. Access to raw materials was improved, costs of those materials were kept relatively low, contact between internal and external markets was improved, and expenses for fuel and energy remained low. The valley gained dependable year-round transportation and opportunity for economic development near the river. Agriculture and industry gained strength from better access to markets with low cost transportation. River modernization also encouraged technological change in towboats and barges. Towboats with ratings of 7,000 horsepower were increasingly common, and "jumbo" and "superjumbo" barges, some 52 feet wide and 290 feet long and carrying 3,000 tons, three times the load of those in the 1920s, appeared. In 1986, a typical 1,500–ton-barge, carrying 52,500 bushels of grain or 453,600 gallons, equaled the loads of fifteen large railroad hopper cars or fifty-eight trucks. A typical tow, consisting of fifteen barges and extending 1,500 feet, required for land travel 870 trucks and two and one-fourth unit-trains.[91]

Not surprisingly, the amount of tonnage carried on the river grew steadily: in 1965, total tonnage swelled to 103 million, while ton-miles rose to 23 billion. By 1977 these amounts were, in order, 151 million and 37 billion. Coal accounted for about 82 million tons, followed by petroleum products, aggregates, chemicals, and iron and steel. All of the commodities except coal expanded somewhat unevenly since the early 1950s. Especially striking in the recent period was the increased shipping of grain due in part to agreements after 1972 with the Soviet Union. Aluminum traffic also expanded notably: buildings, automobiles, and other consumer durables. A capital intensive industry, aluminum had few mills on the Ohio—chiefly Huntington, Evansville, and Pittsburgh—and shipped its products by truck or rail rather than the river because users were widely scattered and time important, given the costs of investment and the high value of the products manufactured at facilities like Alcoa's near Evansville.[92]

Similar trends continued through the 1980s. Freight traffic continued to grow, with the notable exception of recession years of the early 1980s. Thereafter tonnage climbed, reaching 197.1 million in 1987. The Port of Pittsburgh, with 28.6 million tons in 1985, remained the largest inland port in the nation. The other leading Ohio ports were, in order, Huntington (19.6), Cincinnati (16.2), Louisville (8.0), and Mt. Vernon, Indiana (5.8)—the latter the result of the opening of the state subsidized Southwind Maritime Centre in 1979. Bulk commodities—especially coal and coke, which annually accounted for about 60 percent of the total—constituted most of this traffic. Reflecting changes in American heavy industry, iron and steel products, both in tonnage and ton-miles, accounted for a smaller portion of the total (in 1986, in order, 5.7 million tons, or 3 percent of the total, and 3.4 billion ton-miles, or 7 percent). By contrast, aggregates had climbed to second in total tonnage, followed by petroleum products, chemicals, and grain. In billions of ton-miles, coal and coke, with 28.3, led other commodities by far, followed by chemicals, petroleum, iron and steel, aggregates, and grain. Ton-miles increased for all commodities except ores and minerals, and petroleum fuels. The average haul distance remained about 250 miles. Such growth encouraged continued improvements, including development of the Tennessee-Tombigbee waterway, completed in the 1980s.[93]

The internal dynamics and the varying types of economic impact of river traffic are worth noting. Through the mid-1980s, several of the major river ports (Pittsburgh and Louisville) received far more than they shipped, while Huntington and Mt. Vernon shipped substantially more than they received (coal in the former case and grain, coal, and oil in the latter). Cincinnati received approximately the same amount as it shipped. In 1986, moreover, the greatest share of Ohio River freight (56.9 million tons) was shipped from its docks to other inland waterways, while 44.6 million tons came from other inland waterways to Ohio docks. Another 30 million tons were dispatched upstream between Ohio River ports, and 26 million more were sent downstream to other Ohio ports. In short, 56 million tons, or about 29 percent of total river tonnage, were shipped between Ohio River ports. Much of the coal and coke of the Pittsburgh region, for instance, continued to be consumed in the Upper Ohio Valley. One-quarter of West Virginia's coal in 1985 was transported from ports in the Kanawha Valley and at Huntington, and most of that coal was used for coke producers and electric generators in the Ohio, West Virginia, and Pennsylvania.[94]

The Ohio continued to exert an enormous effect on the region. Sometimes, as in the case of Jeffboat, the heir of Jeffersonville's Howard Boatyards, that consequence resembled nineteenth-century patterns. Aided by its two state-funded ports, southern Indiana river commerce regained its supremacy over that of the state's Lake Michigan region. Much continuity also existed in the economies of such cities as Lawrenceburg, Owensboro, Steubenville, and Ashland. In other cases, the impact appeared in a somewhat different fashion. By the mid-1980s, West Virginia had two Quaker State refineries, and Kentucky had fifty-eight coal-loading facilities. Cargill Corporation had become the largest supplier of grain in the valley. The Dravo Corporation was a major supplier of aggregates as well as other river-related products and marine equipment.[95]

As the transformation of post–World War II Pittsburgh from "Smoky City" to "Golden Triangle" so dramatically illustrated, economic development of the Ohio Valley had to be seen as a multifaceted issue. Pittsburgh's flood control, water quality, and sanitation programs, combined with the renaissance of its parks and other recreational projects along its three rivers, demonstrated a recognition of the importance of public health and the quality of life. Commercial and industrial use of riverside space, for example, prevented recreational use, and was unsightly. Industrial and mine waste and residential sewage created severe water pollution problems exacerbated by canalization, which impeded the free flow of the Ohio, a dirtied and dammed river. Such matters awakened concern in Ohio as early as 1913 and prompted the Surgeon General to call for an interstate conference on public health in 1924. Sparked by Cincinnati business and civic leaders after 1935 and supported by congressional legislation in 1948, the governors of the eight states in the Ohio watershed signed an interstate compact in June 1948 creating the Ohio River Valley Sanitation Commission (ORSANCO). At the time, only a few communities had any sort of sewage control projects. By 1968 substantial progress had been made. Much work, however, remained.[96]

Concerns about the negative economic implications of valley development could also be seen in the establishment of a research laboratory for the infant Environmental Protection Agency in Cincinnati in 1970 and the formation of numerous citizens' committees on health and quality of life issues in the 1970s. A pioneering interagency investigation, the Ohio River Basin Energy Study or ORBES (1981), underscored the tensions: concerns about the consequences of development for the environment and society as well as the economy versus the economic advantages to be gained from the bountiful coal and water in the region. ORBES concluded that the development of the chief commodity of the valley had enormous implications—for example, the effects of sulfur dioxide on crops—and that numerous private and public agencies with decision-making powers were creating Balkanization in the valley. ORBES insisted that the diversity of the region and its main street, the Ohio, must be understood before progress could be made. This diversity could lead to apparently conflicting needs. Thus, residents in Madison, Indiana, had formed a "Save the Valley" organization to block the building of power plants, while others in eastern Ohio had organized "Save Our Valley" to prevent the loss of industrial jobs and to attract new industry. ORBES concluded that growth and clean air and water were not irreconcilable, and that the first step needed to be the uniting of the disparate factions served by the Ohio River.[97]

All of this indeed posed a challenge, as shifting consumer

demands and foreign competition in the 1970s and 1980s brought economic devastation to the coal mines and the iron and steel industries of the Upper Valley. In April 1990, for instance, the number of jobs in the mines and mills south of Wheeling was less than half of the 60,000 available in 1975. Despite dramatic increases in river traffic, the economy of the Ohio Valley was, according to the ORBES study, generally only stable, and in some places like West Virginia and Kentucky, actually depressed, whether measured by gross regional product or per capita income. That suggested that the impact of canalization on job creation and income may have been greater outside the Ohio Valley than in it and helped to explain why many valley residents were reluctant to endorse clean air legislation in 1990.[98]

However much the manner of its influence had changed, in numerous ways the Ohio River remained vital to the well-being of the people of the region and created, however tenuous, a bond from Pittsburgh to Cairo. The spilling of diesel oil or gasoline into the waters near Pittsburgh in 1989 and 1990 had dire implications for jobs as well as public health for hundreds of miles downriver, as did the discharge of raw sewage from Louisville. Nature, too, provided a linkage, whether because of flooding, drought, or ice. In the summer of 1988, for instance, the Ohio and Mississippi valleys suffered a severe regional drought. The Corps of Engineers estimated costs to the Ohio Valley, in delays, light loadings, and diversions, at 60.6 million dollars. Much of this was due to the poor condition of the uncanalized Mississippi, not the Ohio, where only a few miles near Cairo were closed. The cold weather of December 1989 created similar problems. In both cases, shippers turned to port facilities on the Ohio because the Mississippi was inaccessible, and also loaded their cargoes from barges in ports like Mt. Vernon onto trucks and railcars.[99]

As the premier highway to the West in the early days of the nation, the Ohio provided an avenue for settlement and development. Location, agriculture, natural resources, and technology joined to that to make for an extraordinary era in American history. Distinctive commercial and industrial responses emerged. Although relatively dispossessed by the advent of the railroad and the very national population dispersal it figured heavily in producing, the Ohio Valley experienced a renaissance after World War I. The nature of economic activity after canalization appeared heavily oriented to traffic in bulky commodities, especially coal, but that belied the diversity and the vitality of the life of the valley, as new industries grew up and many discovered the recreational and aesthetic value of the river. Admittedly the results of the renaissance have not been uniform, and some of the products of the valley, especially electricity, may have benefited residents to the north more than those of the valley. There is no doubt, however, that the Ohio River has been, and will continue to be, a powerful force in the economy of the region and the nation.

NOTES

1. Fernand Braudel, *The Identity of France*, Volume I, *History and Environment* (New York: Harper and Row, 1988), 264.

2. Ohio River Basin Survey Coordinating Committee, *2020 A.D.: A Survey of the Ohio River Basin* (Cincinnati: Ohio River Division, U.S. Army Corps of Engineers, 1969), 2, 7–9, 14.

3. Ibid., 10–11; Ohio River Basin Survey Coordinating Committee, *Ohio River Basin Comprehensive Survey*, Volume I: *Main Report* (Cincinnati: Ohio River Division, U.S. Army Corps of Engineers, 1969), 1–11; Isaac Lippincott, *A History of Manufactures in the Ohio Valley to the Year 1860* (reprint of 1914 publication, New York: Arno Press, 1973), 1–19.

4. Edward J. Cleary, *The ORSANCO Story: Water Quality Management in the Ohio Valley under the Interstate Compact* (Baltimore: Johns Hopkins University Press, 1967), 10–12. The population growth rate in the valley since 1900 was, to the mid-1960s, about half to two-thirds of the national rate.

5. Writers Program, Works Progress Administration, *The Ohio Guide* (New York: Oxford University Press, 1940), 9–14; Writers Program, Works Progress Administration, *West Virginia: A Guide to the Mountain State* (New York: Oxford University Press, 1941), 30; John D. Barnhart and Dorothy L. Riker, *Indiana to 1816: the Colonial Period* (Indianapolis: Indiana Historical Society, 1971), 49–50; R. E. Banta, *The Ohio* (New York: Rinehart and Company, 1949), 25–43, 61; James H. Madison, *The Indiana Way: A State History* (Indianapolis: Indiana Historical Society, 1986), 3–35.

6. Michael C. Robinson, *History of Navigation in the Ohio River Basin* (Fort Belvoir, Va.: U.S. Army Corps of Engineers, 1983), 53; Barnhart and Riker, *Indiana to 1816*, 54–79; Frank E. Ross, "The Fur Trade of the Ohio Valley," *Indiana Magazine of History*, XXXIV (December 1938), 417–43; George A. Rawlyk, "The 'Rising French Empire' in the Ohio Valley and the Old Northwest: The 'Dreaded Juncture of the French Settlements in Canada with Those of Louisiana,' " *Contest for Empire 1500–1775: Proceedings of an Indiana American Revolution Bicentennial Symposium*, John B. Elliott, ed. (Indianapolis: Indiana Histori-

cal Society, 1975), 45; James A. Brown, "The Impact of the European Presence on Indian Culture," *Contest for Empire*, 10–12, 24; Banta, *The Ohio*, 44–49; Leland D. Baldwin, *Pittsburgh: The Story of a City* (Pittsburgh: University of Pittsburgh Press, 1937), 1–12; Philip S. Klein and Ari Hoogenboom, *History of Pennsylvania* (New York: McGraw-Hill, 1973), 56, 59.

7. Brown, "The European Presence," 10–12, 19; Klein and Hoogenboom, *History of Pennsylvania*, 69; Baldwin, *Pittsburgh*, 1–12; Banta, *The Ohio*, 110.

8. Robinson, *History of Navigation*, 2–3.

9. Banta, *The Ohio*, 118.

10. Ibid., 117–69; Robinson, *History of Navigation*, 3; John Alexander Williams, *West Virginia: a Bicentennial History* (New York: W. W. Norton, 1976), 5–6; George H. Yater, *Two Hundred Years at the Falls of the Ohio: A History of Louisville and Jefferson County* (Louisville: Heritage Publishing Co., 1979), 1–10; Barnhart and Riker, *Indiana to 1816*, 192–236.

11. Robinson, *History of Navigation*, 3–5; Charles H. Ambler, *A History of Transportation in the Ohio Valley* (Glendale, Calif.: Arthur H. Clark Co., 1932), 31–80.

12. Robinson, *History of Navigation*, 3–5; Barnhart and Riker, *Indiana to 1816*, 34–44.

13. Walter Havighurst, *River to the West: Three Centuries of the Ohio* (New York: G. P. Putnam, 1970), 32–104; Malcolm J. Rohrbough, *The Land Office Business: The Settlement and Administration of American Public Lands, 1789–1837* (New York: Oxford University Press, 1969), 3, 4, 14–16; Barnhart and Riker, *Indiana to 1816*, 246; *Ohio Guide*, 432–46; Reginald Horsman, "The Collapse of the Ohio River Barrier: Conflict and Negotiation in the Old Northwest, 1763–1787," *Pathways to the Old Northwest: An Observance of the Bicentennial of the Northwest Ordinance* (Indianapolis: Indiana Historical Society, 1988), 42; Walter Havighurst, *Ohio: a Bicentennial History* (New York: W. W. Norton, 1976), 10–11; Robinson, *History of Navigation*, 3; Madison, *Indiana Way*, 39.

14. Lippincott, *History of Manufactures*, 20–48.

15. Richard B. Morris, ed., *Encyclopedia of American History* (Bicentennial edition, New York: Harper and Row, 1976), 715; Francis P. Weisenburger, "The Urbanization of the Middle West: Town and Village in the Pioneer Period," *Indiana Magazine of History*, XLI (March, 1945), 19–30; Richard C. Wade, *The Urban Frontier: The Rise of Western Cities, 1790–1830* (Cambridge, Mass.: Harvard University Press, 1959), 1–35; Darrel E. Bigham, *An Evansville Album: Perspectives on a River City, 1812–1988* (Bloomington: Indiana University Press, 1988), 1.

16. Barnhart and Riker, *Indiana to 1816*, 370–404; R. C. Buley, *The Old Northwest: Pioneer Period, 1815–1840*, Volume I (Bloomington: Indiana University Press, 1950), 1–93, passim; John D. Barnhart, *Valley of Democracy: The Frontier versus the Plantation in the Ohio Valley, 1775–1818* (Bloomington: Indiana University Press, 1953), 49.

17. Malcolm J. Rohrbough, *The Transappalachian Frontier: People, Societies, and Institutions* (New York: Oxford University Press, 1978), 53, 132, 138, 145, and 400; Rohrbough, *Land Office Business*, 28; Buley, *Old Northwest*, I:11–14, 17–20, 103, and 124–25. See, for instance, the *Evansville Weekly Journal*, August 10, 1848–a vivid illustration of newspaper boosterism.

18. Rohrbough, *Transappalachian Frontier*, 93–114.

19. Buley, *Old Northwest*, I:530–32 and II:46–55; Rohrbough, *Land Office Business*, 136; Donald T. Zimmer, "The Ohio River: Pathway to Settlement," *Transportation and the Early Nation: Papers Presented at an American Revolution Bicentennial Symposium* (Indianapolis: Indiana Historical Society, 1982), 61–88; Barnhart, *Valley of Democracy*, 27–33.

20. Rohrbough, *Land Office Business*, 89.

21. Zimmer, "The Ohio River," 62.

22. Buley, *Old Northwest*, I:410.

23. Zimmer, "The Ohio River," 62–63; Buley, *Old Northwest*, I:1–6.

24. Robinson, *History of Navigation*, 5–6; Buley, *Old Northwest*, I:444–49.

25. Robinson, *History of Navigation*, 7–11; George Rogers Taylor, *The Transportation Revolution, 1815–1860* (New York: Harper and Row, 1951), 64–73; Buley, *Old Northwest*, I:444; Louis C. Hunter, *Steamboats on the Western Waters: An Economic and Technological History* (Cambridge, Mass.: Harvard University Press, 1949), 29–32.

26. Robinson, *History of Navigation*, 12–15; Banta, *The Ohio*, 282–307.

27. Frederick Jackson Turner, *Rise of the New West, 1819–1829* (reprint of 1906 edition, Gloucester, Mass.: Peter Smith, 1961), 78. Also note Buley, *Old Northwest*, I:444–49.

28. Buley, *Old Northwest*, I:1–6; Taylor, *Transportation Revolution*, 15–31; Turner, *Rise of the New West*, 78–83.

29. Buley, *Old Northwest*, I:435–36, 490–508; Paul Fatout, *Indiana Canals* (West Lafayette, Ind.: Purdue University Press, 1972), 1–21; Taylor, *Transportation Revolution*, 46–55; Donald F. Carmony, "The Mammoth Internal Improvement Fiasco," *The Hoosier State: Readings in Indiana History*, Ralph Gray, ed., Volume I (Grand Rapids, Mich.: W. B. Eerdmans, 1980), 236–37; Harry N. Scheiber, *Ohio Canal Era: A Case Study of Government and the Economy, 1820–1861* (Athens: Ohio University Press, 1969), 9–17, 134–35, 185–86, and 206; Ronald E. Shaw, "The Canal Era in the Old Northwest," *Transportation and the Early Nation*, 89–107; Benjamin F. Klein, ed., *The Ohio River: Handbook and Picture Album* (Cincinnati: Young and Klein, 1969), 297, 303.

30. Scheiber, *Ohio Canal Era*, 237. See also Ralph Gray, "The Canal Era in Indiana," *Transportation and the Early Nation*, 128–29.

31. Scheiber, *Ohio Canal Era*, 206, 212, 237.

32. John F. Stover, *American Railroads* (Chicago: University of Chicago Press, 1961), 13–14, 41–42; Havighurst, *Ohio: Bicentennial History*, 88; Bigham, *Evansville Album*, 2–4.

33. Lippincott, *History of Manufactures*, 6–13, 56–66; Buley, *Old Northwest*, I:527–36; Steven J. Ross, *Workers on the Edge: Work, Leisure, and Politics in Industrializing Cincinnati, 1788–1890* (New York: Columbia University Press, 1985), 1–30.

34. Rohrbough, *Transappalachian Frontier*, 176.

35. Ibid., 42–44.

36. Ross, *Workers on the Edge*, 30–32; Rohrbough, *Transappalachian Frontier*, 171, 176; Taylor, *Transportation Revolution*, 8–9, 10–11; Charles N. Glaab and A. Theodore Brown, *A History of Urban America* (Third ed., New York: Macmillan, 1983), 124–27; Federal Writers Project, *Cincinnati: A Guide to the Queen City and Its Neighbors* (Cincinnati: Wiesen-Hart, 1943), xxi, 54, 59, and 60–61.

37. Thomas C. Cochran, *Pennsylvania: A Bicentennial History* (New York: W. W. Norton, 1978), 59–60, 116–17; Baldwin, *Pittsburgh*, 192–99; (no author) *History of the Ohio Falls Cities and Their Counties*, Volume I (Cleveland: L. A. Williams and Co., 1882), 53; Yater, *Two*

Hundred Years, 34–45; John T. Windle and Robert M. Taylor, Jr., *The Early Architecture of Madison, Indiana* (Madison and Indianapolis: Historic Madison and the Indiana Historical Society, 1986), 3, 8, and 9; Zimmer, "The Ohio River," 65–70.

38. Louis C. Hunter, *Studies in the Economic History of the Ohio Valley: Seasonal Aspects of Industry and Commerce before the Age of Big Business and the Beginnings of Industrial Combination* (Northampton, Mass.: Smith College, 1934), 5–49.

39. Lippincott, *History of Manufactures*, 11–13.

40. Ibid., 13–19; Banta, *The Ohio*, 485–507; Buley, *Old Northwest*, I:543–46.

41. Banta, *The Ohio*, 490–97; Lippincott, *History of Manufactures*, 14–15; Buley, *Old Northwest*, I:547–49.

42. Buley, *Old Northwest*, I:546–47; Banta, *The Ohio*, 497–500; Lippincott, *History of Manufactures*, 13–14.

43. Banta, *The Ohio*, 500–04; Buley, *Old Northwest*, I:549–50; Lippincott, *History of Manufactures*, 17–19.

44. Lippincott, *History of Manufactures*, 195 (see also 63–65, 193–95); Ambler, *History of Transportation*, 81–106.

45. Lippincott, *History of Manufactures*, 182–84, 195–97; Taylor, *Transportation Revolution*, 246.

46. Lippincott, *History of Manufactures*, 49–126; Rohrbough, *Transappalachian Frontier*, 38.

47. Hunter, *Studies in Economic History of the Ohio Valley*, 32–49.

48. Ibid., 50–126; Lippincott, *History of Manufactures*, 129–92; Taylor, *Transportation Revolution*, 207–208.

49. Victor Hugo, quoted in Havighurst, *Ohio: Bicentennial History*, 50. Also note Blake McKelvey, *American Urbanization: A Comparative History* (Glenview, Ill.: Scott, Foresman and Company, 1973), 14, 24, 37.

50. Rohrbough, *Transappalachian Frontier*, 348–49; Wade, *Urban Frontier*, 39–71, 161–202, 304–42; Glaab and Brown, *History of Urban America*, 29–31.

51. McKelvey, *American Urbanization*, 14, 17, 44; Taylor, *Transportation Revolution*, 10–11, 67–68; Glaab and Brown, *History of Urban America*, 30–31, 33; Buley, *Old Northwest*, I:20–50; Rohrbough, *Transappalachian Frontier*, 360–64.

52. Glaab and Brown, *History of Urban America*, 29–33; Banta, *The Ohio*, 13–14; Rohrbough, *Transappalachian Frontier*, 134, 157, 171, 176, 214; Buley, *Old Northwest*, I:20–50; McKelvey, *American Urbanization*, 46, 47, 50, 60; Williams, *West Virginia*, 50–51; *West Virginia Guide*, 254; Baldwin, *Pittsburgh*, 140–49, 190–99; Roy Lubove, ed., *Pittsburgh* (New York: Franklin Watts, 1976), 112–20, 177–80; Ambler, *History of Transportation*, 295–318; Archer B. Hulbert, *Waterways of Western Expansion: The Ohio River and the Tributaries* (Cleveland: A. H. Clark, 1903), 209–11.

53. Bigham, *Evansville Album*, 2–3; Victor M. Bogle, "New Albany: Mid-Nineteenth Century Economic Expansion," *Indiana Magazine of History*, LIII (June 1957), 127–46; Windle and Taylor, *Early Architecture of Madison*, 3, 8, 9, 11, 13; Zimmer, "The Ohio River," 65–84; Federal Writers Project, *Kentucky: A Guide to the Bluegrass State* (New York: Harcourt, Brace and Co., 1939), 56–57, 139–43, 147–58, 221–25, 408–09, 413–16; *West Virginia Guide*, 8, 14, 32, 97–98, 102, 260–64; Richard J. Jensen, *Illinois: A Bicentennial History* (New York: W. W. Norton, 1978), 3–31; Robert P. Howard, *Illinois: A History of the Prairie State*

(Grand Rapids, Mich.: William B. Eerdmans, 1972), 122–23; Federal Writers Project, *Illinois: A Descriptive an Historical Guide* (revised edition, Chicago: A. C. McClure, 1947), 54, 56, 58; John M. Lansden, *A History of the City of Cairo, Illinois* (Reprint of the 1910 edition, Carbondale: Southern Illinois University Press, 1976), 32–33, 76, 85; Rohrbough, *Transappalachian Frontier*, 357–59.

54. *Ohio Guide*, 319–21; Cochran, *Pennsylvania*, 59–60; Havighurst, *Ohio: Bicentennial History*, 35–43, 437–38; Madison, *Indiana Way*, 75–93; Lee Burns, "The Ohio River, Its Influence on the Development of Indiana," *Indiana Magazine of History*, XIX (June, 1923), 169–81; Jensen, *Illinois*, 3–31.

55. Hunter, *Steamboats on the Western Waters*, 29–32, 37–40; Zimmer, "The Ohio River," 84; Buley, *Old Northwest*, I:431; Taylor, *Transportation Revolution*, 64–69. According to Hunter (654), in 1860 Pittsburgh, Cincinnati, and Louisville had twenty-eight shipyards employing about 1,400 workers, and the three cities had another thirty-eight machine shops and seventy-one foundries related to steamboats which employed about 3,400 and 4,400, respectively. The largest number, by far, were in Pittsburgh.

56. Hunter, *Steamboats on the Western Waters*, 644, 657, 658–59, 660, 662; Taylor, *Transportation Revolution*, 69–73, 135–36, 143, 159–160, 443; Ambler, *History of Transportation*, 295–318.

57. Taylor, *Transportation Revolution*, 74–103; Havighurst, *Ohio: Bicentennial History*, 88; *Kentucky Guide*, 62; Baldwin, *Pittsburgh*, 97–99; Stover, *American Railroads*, 139, 150–51; Scheiber, *Ohio Canal Era*, 320; Ambler, *History of Transportation*, 197; Lippincott, *History of Manufactures*, 129–44; Emma Lou Thornbrough, *Indiana in the Civil War Era, 1850–1880* (Indianapolis: Indiana Historical Society, 1965), 332–37.

58. Quoted in Reid Mitchell, *Civil War Soldiers: Their Expectations and Their Experiences* (New York: Viking Press, 1988), 103–04. A similar perspective is found in Alexis de Tocqueville, *Democracy in America*, I (New York: 1945), 361–62. See also Rohrbough, *Transappalachian Frontier*, 5–6, 64–85, 114, 345, 353; Barnhart, *Valley of Democracy*, 4, 8, 19, 105, 218, 234; Banta, *The Ohio*, 459–84; and Havighurst, *River to the West*, 236–49.

59. Barnhart, *Valley of Democracy*, 4, 19.

60. Darrel E. Bigham, *We Ask Only a Fair Trial: A History of the Black Community of Evansville, Indiana* (Bloomington: Indiana University Press, 1987), 21–23.

61. Hunter, *Steamboats on the Western Waters*, 500, 503.

62. Ibid., 660.

63. *Ohio Guide*, 200; Yater, *Two Hundred Years*, 82–94; *Kentucky Guide*, 147–50; Banta, *The Ohio*, 497–500; *Cincinnati Guide*, 66–67; Ambler, *History of Transportation*, 239–63; Klein, *Ohio River*, 271; Lippincott, *History of Manufactures*, 258–60; Thornbrough, *Indiana in the Civil War Era*, 337, 412–13; Allan Nevins, *The Ordeal of the Union*, Volume VII; *The War for the Union: The Organized War, 1863–1864* (New York: Charles Scribner's Sons, 1971), 212–70.

64. *Evansville Daily Journal*, July 17, 1868. See also *Kentucky Guide*, 139–43, 221–25; *Illinois Guide*, 169–76; Burns, "The Ohio River," 180; Ambler, *History of Transportation*, 266–70, 272–73, 278, 285–91, 318–45; Havighurst, *Ohio: Bicentennial History*, 45–50.

65. Hulbert, *Waterways*, 209–11; Roy Lubove, *Twentieth Century Pittsburgh: Government, Business, and Environmental Change* (New York: John Wiley, 1969), 24–25; Clifton J. Phillips, *Indiana in Transition: The*

Emergence of an Industrial Commonwealth, 1880–1920 (Indianapolis: Indiana Historical Society, 1968), 186.

66. Havighurst, *Ohio: Bicentennial History*, 45–50; Daniel Lynn Bolin, *Ohio Valley History: West Point to Lewisport, A Bibliography* (New Orleans: Polyanthos, 1976), 7–8; Ambler, *History of Transportation*, 245–91; Bigham, *Evansville Album*, 51; Hunter, *Steamboats on the Western Waters*, 332, 639; Phillips, *Indiana in Transition*, 225.

67. Thornbrough, *Indiana in the Civil War Era*, 418–19; Bogle, "New Albany," 127–46; Taylor, *Transportation Revolution*, 165, 443; Rohrbough, *Transappalachian Frontier*, 310–14; Klein and Hoogenboom, *Pennsylvania*, 265; *Ohio Guide*, 349–51.

68. Hunter, *Steamboats on the Western Waters*, 418–519.

69. Ambler, *History of Transportation*, 347–63.

70. Lubove, *Twentieth Century Pittsburgh*, 2. See also ibid., 4–7, 8, 17–18, 24–25, 27; Baldwin, *Pittsburgh*, 221–22, 358–66; Cochran, *Pennsylvania*, 122, 130, 137, 160; Bayard Still, *Urban America: A History with Documents* (Boston: Little, Brown and Co., 1974), 210; Klein and Hoogenboom, *Pennsylvania*, 24; Havighurst, *River to the West*, 21–31; Edward K. Muller, "Metropolis and Region: A Framework for Enquiry into Western Pennsylvania," *City at the Point: Essays on the Social History of Pittsburgh*, Samuel P. Hays, ed. (Pittsburgh: University of Pittsburgh Press, 1989), 181–212.

71. *West Virginia Guide*, 235, 238–39, 240–42.

72. *Ohio Guide*, 201; *Cincinnati Guide*, 60–61, 245; Ross, *Workers on the Edge*, 133–34, 194–96.

73. *Kentucky Guide*, 176–85; Yater, *Two Hundred Years*, 95, 141, 145, 162, 164; *History of Ohio Falls Cities*, 53–56.

74. Bigham, *Evansville Album*, 15–21; *Evansville Daily Journal*, June 13, 1888; Vanderburgh County Recorder, Articles of Association, Book 1, 291–94; Madison, *Indiana Way*, 156; Phillips, *Indiana in Transition*, 274–75.

75. Thornbrough, *Indiana in the Civil War Era*, 404–60; Phillips, *Indiana in Transition*, 274–75, 367; *Illinois Guide*, 169–76, 435–37; Donald F. Tingley, *The Structuring of a State: The History of Illinois, 1899 to 1928* (Urbana: University of Illinois Press, 1980), 56–57, 291–92; *Kentucky Guide*, 139–43, 221–25, 406–07, 412; *Ohio Guide*, 266–72, 319–21; Havighurst, *Ohio: Bicentennial History*, 111–13, 115, 150–51; Williams, *West Virginia*, 52, 79, 114; *West Virginia Guide*, 61, 83, 85.

76. Klein, *Ohio River*, 235–39; Hunter, *Steamboats on the Western Waters*, 639; Robinson, *History of Navigation*, 53–58; *Evansville Daily Journal*, October 12, 1897; *Evansville Journal-News*, October 24, 1929; Hulbert, *Waterways*, 216–19; Charles K. Palmer, "Ohio Valley Commerce, 1787–1936," *Indiana Magazine of History*, XXXVII (June 1937), 157.

77. Archer B. Hulbert, *The Ohio River: A Course of Empire* (New York: G. P. Putnam, 1986), 359.

78. Robinson, *History of Navigation*, 25–29; Ambler, *History of Transportation*, 393–422; Havighurst, *Ohio: Bicentennial History*, 45–50, and *River to the West*, 204–07; Palmer, "Ohio Valley Commerce," 157; Klein, *Ohio River*, 371–72.

79. Robinson, *History of Navigation*, 29–30; Havighurst, *River to the West*, 257–60; Ambler, *History of Transportation*, 414–17, 423–25; Joseph R. Hartley, *Economic Effects of Ohio River Transportation* (Bloomington, Ind.: no pub., 1957), 37.

80. *West Virginia Guide*, 83, 85; Amber, *History of Transportation*;

Ohio River Basin Coordinating Committee, *2020* A.D., 31–37; Bigham, *Evansville Album*, 71, 76.

81. Klein, *Ohio River*, 337–57; Havighurst, *Ohio: Bicentennial History*, 188–92.

82. Robinson, *History of Navigation*, 35; Palmer, "Ohio Valley Commerce," 163–68; *Cincinnati Guide*, 203; *Evansville Press*, November 23, 1930 and February 27, 1931.

83. Ambler, *History of Transportation*, 425–28, 430–37; Palmer, "Ohio Valley Commerce," 158–70; Hartley, *Economic Effects*, 20, 32a, 76, 97, 100, 103.

84. Robinson, *History of Navigation*, 35; James H. Madison, *Indiana through Tradition and Change: A History of the Hoosier State and Its People, 1920–1945* (Indianapolis: Indiana Historical Society, 1982), 373–77; Missouri Valley Bridge and Iron Company, *Pictorial History of the Evansville Shipyard, January 1942–December 1944* (Evansville: Missouri Bridge and Iron Co., 1944), 1; Bigham, *Evansville Album*, 99.

85. Robinson, *History of Navigation*, 35–36.

86. Yater, *Two Hundred Years*, 221; Bolin, *Ohio Valley History*, 7–8; Bigham, *Evansville Album*, 145.

87. Clarence W. Newman, *Ohio River Navigation: Past-Present-Future* (Cincinnati: U.S. Army Corps of Engineers, Ohio River Division, 1979), 22; Ohio Valley Improvement Association, Annual Report, 1972, passim. Information about river-related employment in one city, Evansville, may be found in Bureau of the Census, U.S. Department of Commerce, *Census of the Population: 1950*, Volume II: *Characteristics of the Population*, Part 14; *Indiana* (Washington, D.C.: Government Printing Office, 1952), 265; *Census of the Population: 1960*, Volume II: *Social and Economic Characteristics of the Population*, Part 16; *Indiana* (Washington, D.C.: Government Printing Office, 1962), 235; and *Census of the Population: 1970*, Volume I: *Characteristics of the Population*, Part 16: *Indiana* (Washington, D.C.: Government Printing Office, 1972), 362.

88. Hartley, *Economic Effects*, 3, 5, 76, 97, 103, 110, 111–16.

89. Ibid., 123. See also ibid., 117–23, and Robinson, *History of Navigation*, 39–40.

90. Robinson, *History of Navigation*, 39–40, 51; Klein, *Ohio River*, 57.

91. Newman, *Ohio River Navigation*, 22; Robinson, *History of Navigation*, 40; *1986 Report on the Ohio River Navigation System* (Cincinnati: U.S. Army Corps of Engineers, Ohio River Division, 1986), 7, 39. The author wishes to thank Augustine J. Fredrich, professor of engineering technology at the University of Southern Indiana, and Arlene Dietz, staff member of the Navigation Data Center, Army Corps of Engineers, Fort Belvoir, Virginia, for their assistance in securing recent statistical data on the Ohio River system.

92. Ohio River Basin Coordinating Committee, *2020* A.D., 27–32.

93. Ibid., 14; Madison, *Indiana Way*, 272–73; Corps of Engineers, *1986 Report*, 13, 16; *Waterborne Commerce of the United States, Calendar Year 1987*, Part 2: *Waterways and Harbors, Gulf Coast, Mississippi River System, and Antilles* (New Orleans: U.S. Army Corps of Engineers, 1987), 35–38; *Ohio River Basin Navigation System, 1987 Statistical Supplement* (Cincinnati: U.S. Army Corps of Engineers, 1987), 16, 17, 20; *The Ohio River Basin Navigation System, 1988 Report* (Cincinnati: U.S. Army Corps of Engineers, 1988), 16–17, 40; Institute for Water Resources, Report 88–R–7: *The 1988 Inland Waterway Review* (Fort Belvoir, Va.: U.S. Army Corps of Engineers, 1988), 35–38.

94. Corps of Engineers, *Ohio River Basin Navigation System, 1987*

Statistical Supplement, 6, 17; Corps of Engineers, *Ohio River Basin Navigation System 1988 Report*, 46, 58.

95. Corps of Engineers, *Ohio River Basin Navigation System, 1987 Statistical Supplement* 6–13. Klein, *Ohio River*, 19–160, provides a useful if sketchy profile of each community along the Ohio ca. 1960.

96. Lubove, *Pittsburgh*, 181–97, 212–18, and *Twentieth Century Pittsburgh*, especially chapters 6–7; Madison, *Indiana through Tradition and Change*, 311; Cleary, *The ORSANCO Story*, 3, 6, 10, 12–19, and 20–82, passim; Sherman L. Frost and William J. Mitsch, "Resource Development and Conservation History along the Ohio River," *Ohio Journal of Science*, 36 (Dec. 1988), 66–67.

97. Environmental Protection Agency, *Ohio River Basin Energy Study (ORBES): Main Report* (Washington, D.C.: 1981), 1–81, 295–96.

98. *New York Times*, Apr. 1, 1990; *ORBES Main Report*, 67–69.

99. Klein and Hoogenboom, *Pennsylvania*, 477–78; Corps of Engineers, *Ohio River Basin Navigation System, 1988 Report*, 41–42; *Evansville Press*, Dec. 27, 1989.

Leland R. Johnson ENGINEERING THE OHIO

Draining an area the size of France and serving a population larger than Canada's, the Ohio River has been altered, or engineered, for human use since prehistoric times. Indians canoed its currents, drank its water, and ate its fish and shellfish. They apparently dammed it with large rocks placed in a V configuration to trap fish. Broad scale alterations of the Ohio and its tributaries began, however, after the arrival of Euro-American pioneers, who cleared the streams of snags—fallen trees—and boulders for safe passage of their boats and who dammed streams to produce power for grinding grain, sawing lumber, spinning fabrics, and other early industrial manufacturing. Our focus, however, is not these early and relatively minor adaptations of the Ohio's water resources for human purposes; rather, it is the long-term and immense engineering of the Ohio River system for public service by the U.S. Army Corps of Engineers.

As a result of engineering, the Ohio today does not much resemble the turbulent, free-flowing, and obstructed stream it was when French and British army engineers seeking control of the strategic river first mapped it. Then, it resembled its larger free-flowing tributaries of today. Its channel was littered with snags and strewn with boulders, its flow broken by sand bars, rock ripples, and falls, especially the Falls of the Ohio where it dropped twenty-five feet over a two-mile stretch of limestone. In 1990, twenty dams impounded most of its 981–mile course, submerging its natural obstructions; and boats had to leave its marked channel to encounter snags, bars, or falls. The natural river fluctuated wildly from a series of shallow pools during puny drought flows to a raging torrent rising eighty to a hundred feet in flood season. In 1990, its flow was managed through timed releases from its dams to increase flow during droughts and decrease the crests of floods.

Except on the Tennessee River, where the Tennessee Valley Authority has built dams since 1933, federal engineering of the Ohio River Basin's water resources has been managed by the U.S. Army Corps of Engineers, specifically by its Ohio River Division headquartered at Cincinnati with subordinate Districts at Pittsburgh, Huntington, Nashville, and Louisville. Districts are the Corps' engineering, construction, and operations field offices, while the Division is its management review agency. District and Division Engineers are Corps officers commanding forces of civilian engineers, technicians, and scientists. Although the Ohio River Division in 1990 commanded about 4,000 personnel, during the Second World War its command surpassed 11,000 because it is responsible for mobilizing the Ohio Valley for national defense as well as engineering of its water resources. This dual mission capability brought the Corps its engineering assignment for the Ohio in 1824 and has sustained it since.

Located on the top floors of a nondescript building in downtown Cincinnati, with little external evidence of its existence other than a satellite downlink scanning the sky, is the Ohio River's engineering control center. Responsible for defense and water resource development in America's heartland, when established in 1901 it was first named the Central Division, and it became the modern Ohio River Division in 1933. Even its own personnel admit the Division is a "grey eminence," largely unknown to the people it serves. Herein, the Division's plans and work in the twentieth century, and those of Army Engineers who preceded it in the nineteenth century, are revealed and their engineering of the Ohio's riverine environment examined.

Among their profession, it is a truism that engineers should "plan their work and work their plan." This is precisely what

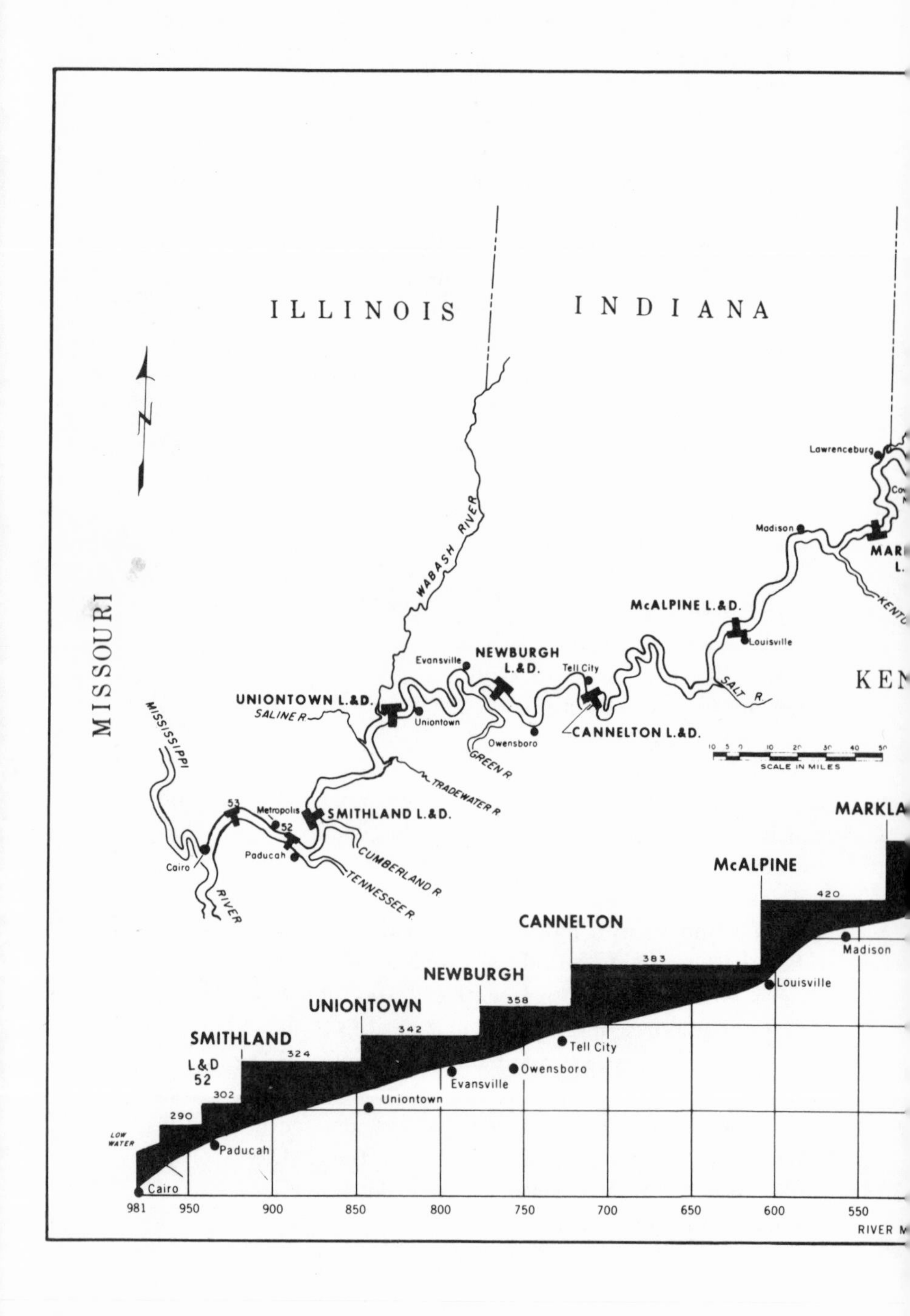

ILLINOIS
INDIANA
MISSOURI
KEN
N
WABASH RIVER
MISSISSIPPI
RIVER
Lawrenceburg
Madison
McALPINE L.&D.
Louisville
NEWBURGH
L.&D.
Evansville
Tell City
UNIONTOWN L.&D.
SALINE R.
Uniontown
Owensboro
GREEN R
SALT R.
CANNELTON L.&D.
SCALE IN MILES
TRADEWATER R
SMITHLAND L.&D.
Metropolis
53
52
Paducah
Cairo
CUMBERLAND R
TENNESSEE R.
MARKLA
McALPINE
420
CANNELTON
383
NEWBURGH
358
UNIONTOWN
342
SMITHLAND
324
L&D
52
302
290
LOW WATER
Madison
Louisville
Tell City
Owensboro
Evansville
Uniontown
Paducah
Cairo
981
950
900
850
800
750
700
650
600
550
RIVER M

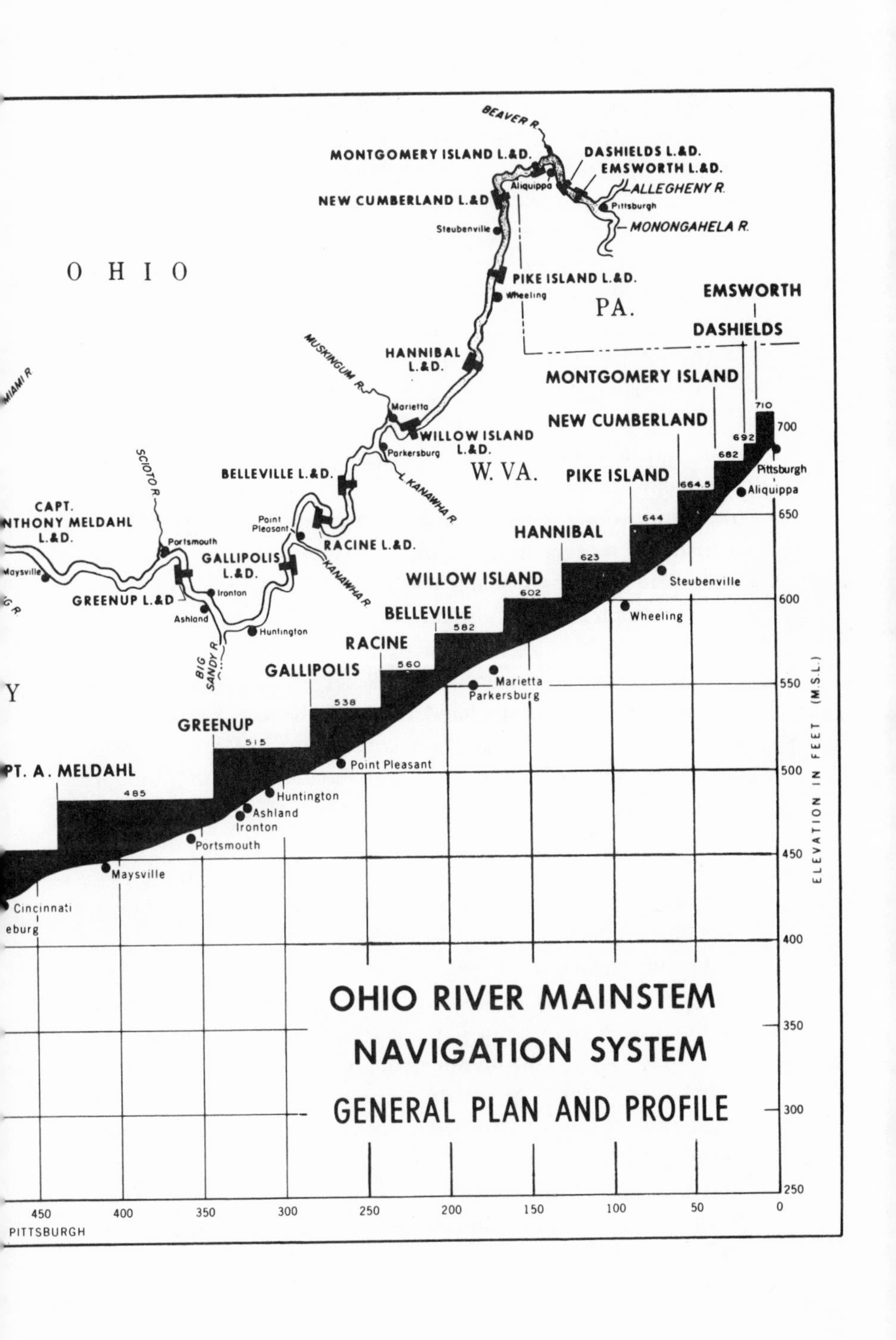

BEAVER R.
MONTGOMERY ISLAND L.&D.
DASHIELDS L.&D.
EMSWORTH L.&D.
ALLEGHENY R.
Aliquippa
Pittsburgh
NEW CUMBERLAND L.&D
MONONGAHELA R.
Steubenville
OHIO
PIKE ISLAND L.&D.
Wheeling
PA.
EMSWORTH
DASHIELDS
MUSKINGUM R.
HANNIBAL L.&D.
MONTGOMERY ISLAND
MIAMI R.
Marietta
WILLOW ISLAND L.&D.
NEW CUMBERLAND
Parkersburg
SCIOTO R.
BELLEVILLE L.&D.
L. KANAWHA R.
W. VA.
PIKE ISLAND
CAPT.
NTHONY MELDAHL
L.&D.
Point Pleasant
Portsmouth
RACINE L.&D.
HANNIBAL
GALLIPOLIS L.&D.
KANAWHA R.
Maysville
Ironton
WILLOW ISLAND
GREENUP L.&D
Ashland
Huntington
BELLEVILLE
BIG SANDY R.
RACINE
GALLIPOLIS
Y
GREENUP
PT. A. MELDAHL
710
692
682
664.5
644
623
602
582
560
538
515
485
Pittsburgh
Aliquippa
Steubenville
Wheeling
Marietta
Parkersburg
Point Pleasant
Huntington
Ashland
Ironton
Portsmouth
Maysville
Cincinnati
eburg
ELEVATION IN FEET (M.S.L.)
700
650
600
550
500
450
400
350
300
250
OHIO RIVER MAINSTEM
NAVIGATION SYSTEM
GENERAL PLAN AND PROFILE
450
400
350
300
250
200
150
100
50
0
PITTSBURGH

the Corps and its Divisions have done since 1824. When planning locks and dams, the Corps has used fifty years as the anticipated economic life. Like Oliver Wendell Holmes's wonderful one-horse shay, the Corps' perfectly engineered lock should serve its purpose at least fifty years without major repairs and be entirely replaced at the end. Such design precision rarely occurs, although once an Ohio lockgate at Pittsburgh collapsed near the end of its design life as it was being replaced. It surely is more than coincidence, however, that the Corps and its Division have adopted four central plans for Ohio River engineering, each being worked during a fifty-year span.

The Corps' four central plans for Ohio River engineering have been implemented in fifty-year phases. The first phase began in 1824, aiming to clear the Ohio's channel of obstructions and to achieve a low-water depth of at least thirty inches for shallow-draft steamboat commerce. Although interrupted by political disagreements and civil war, and hampered by irregular and meager funding, the Corps used channel clearance as its principal engineering method on the Ohio until 1874, when it adopted a second plan.

Authorized in 1875, construction of the second plan began in 1879 and continued until 1929. Referred to as the canalization project because it aimed to make the Ohio resemble a slackwater canal, it began with construction of Davis Island Lock and Dam (Lock and Dam 1) at Pittsburgh in 1879 under Colonel William E. Merrill's management. Merrill, at Cincinnati, managed the project until his death, and in 1901 the Central Division opened at Merrill's office to direct its completion. This was achieved in 1929 when Lock and Dam 53 opened near the Ohio's mouth.

The third plan, the flood control program, began in 1938 when the Ohio River Division completed a comprehensive plan for building seventy-eight dams and reservoirs on the Ohio's tributaries. Devised during the droughts and devastating floods of the 1930s, this plan sought to reduce flooding below the dams, and, through coordinated operation of the dam system, to control the Ohio's water, reducing flow during floods and increasing it during droughts. Its Districts operated the dams on the tributaries, and the Division managed the system as a whole for flood control and accessory purposes on the mainstem. Many modifications of the 1938 plan occurred during its fifty years of implementation, but by 1988 the Division had its seventy-eighth flood control dam under construction.

The Division's fourth central plan was named the Ohio River modernization project because it proposed to modernize the river, converting it from a local into an interstate highway for commerce. By 1955, traffic using the Ohio had grown to the extent that the wicket dams completed in 1929 had become obsolete. The Division therefore planned to replace the old dams with nineteen higher and larger locks and dams of modern design. By 1990, eighteen of the modern locks and dams had replaced all wicket dams except Dams 52 and 53 near the Ohio's mouth and design of the nineteenth to replace them had begun. The Division expected to complete the Ohio's modernization by 2005, concluding another fifty-year cycle.

As a rule, the Corps and the Division did not anticipate that implementing the four engineering plans for the Ohio would require fifty years each; they hoped to do the work in half the time. Why implementation took longer than expected is traced in the following discussion of the plans and how they worked. In aggregate, they have engineered massive changes in the Ohio River.

CHANNEL CLEARANCE, 1824–1874

Origins of Corps engineering on the Ohio may be traced to intercity rivalry between Pittsburgh and Wheeling and the droughts of 1818–1819. Long the head of Ohio River navigation, Pittsburgh faced a challenge in 1818 when the National Road bypassed it to strike the Ohio at Wheeling. To westward-bound pioneers, Wheeling advertised that most boats sunk on the Ohio wrecked above Wheeling and that the river was six inches deeper below Wheeling than above. Wheeling declared that it headed the Ohio's low-water navigation.

The opening of the National Road eroded Pittsburgh's economic status as "Emporium of the West," and the extended droughts of 1818–1819 multiplied its loss. "Our rivers are so low as to render navigation very difficult, and at this moment there is probably near a million worth of merchandize laying along our shores," lamented a Pittsburgh editor in 1818. Before rains ended the 1818 low water, more than $3 million worth of commodities waiting delivery rotted on Pittsburgh's wharf. When the drought resumed in April 1819, the captain of a boat drawing only fourteen inches reported it took him thirty-five days to navigate from Pittsburgh to Cincinnati because he grounded fifty times on shoals where the river was ten inches deep and "worked as hard as ever I did in my life" prying his boat over the shoals. This extended drought and a resulting economic recession shook Pittsburgh and the Ohio ports below.

Deciding during the drought that hazardous rocks obstructing the Ohio should be removed, Pittsburgh's civic leaders collected donations for the purpose and called for volunteers. "If a party of fifty or sixty would assemble on any given day, and go down," wrote an editor, "the removal of these rocks would only afford a pleasant picnic. Fellow citizens, what say you?" The picnic began in October, as civic-spirited Pittsburghers waded down the Ohio, dragging rocks from the channel and blasting them to bits.[1]

As they worked, a joint state commission appointed to survey and plan improvement of the Ohio navigation passed on its way to Louisville. Ohio's governor in 1817 had invited states bordering the river to appoint representatives to this joint commission, and the 1818–19 droughts had encouraged their participation. The commissioners started their survey at Pittsburgh, and as they descended the Ohio they saw more than thirty boats "worse than dead, ruinously expensive to their owners, lying in all directions, chiefly high and dry, some half in and half out of water, all sustaining incalculable injury from an exposure of six or eight months, waiting the returning flood." Delivering their reports and maps to the state governments, they recommended that each state appropriate $10,000 to remove the boulders, snags, rock ledges, and gravel bars obstructing the Ohio's navigation.[2]

The only state responding was Pennsylvania, which appropriated $15,000 in 1821 to clear the channel. Paying laborers fifty cents a day, plus all the food and whiskey they could consume, the Pennsylvania commissioners cleared snags and boulders from the Ohio, blasted obstructive rocks, and, with teams of oxen pulling plows and scrapers, dredged channels through gravel bars. This continued each low water season until the state appropriation was exhausted in 1824, and it opened a low-water channel deep enough for small boats to Wheeling.[3]

Congressmen from states bordering the Ohio and Mississippi rivers in 1820 secured a federal appropriation to continue the survey begun by the states. Responsibility for the survey went to Secretary of War John C. Calhoun, who then supported federal transportation improvements to bolster national defense and economic prosperity. "It is in a state of war," Calhoun declared, "when a nation is compelled to put all of its resources in men, money, skill, and devotion to country into requisition, that its Government realizes in its security the beneficial effects from a people made prosperous and happy by a wise direction of its resources in peace."[4]

Troubled by difficulties the Army had experienced when striving to reinforce New Orleans, Washington, and other points against British attack during the War of 1812, Calhoun had his Engineer officers planning transportation improvements useful during military mobilization. These included Colonel Joseph Totten, Chief Engineer of the Army, and General Simon Bernard, formerly one of Napoleon's engineers. Calhoun ordered these officers to repair to Louisville and resume the survey where the state commission had stopped, extending it to the Ohio's mouth and on to New Orleans. When the officers completed their survey in 1822 and submitted their maps to Congress, they reported the rivers so obstructed that boats dared not run at night; even in day, wrecks caused significant economic losses. To reduce risks to navigation, they recommended that the federal government sponsor research into methods of removing snags from channels and fund hydraulic experiments with wing dams as a means of deepening channels at shoals.[5]

With this report at hand, Congress in 1824 took up the question of improving navigation on the Ohio and Mississippi. Henry Clay of Kentucky contended that because these rivers bordered several states and were the "common commercial highway of all," their improvement clearly lay within federal powers. Clay and his friends reminded Congress that people in the Ohio valley before 1803 had contemplated separation from the Union to secure free river navigation and warned that navigation improvements might be undertaken by a state confederacy, if not by Congress. Interdepartment conflict reared its head when a Virginia congressman suggested sidestepping Constitutional issues by assigning the work to the U.S. Navy instead of Army Engineers. The Navy could build its gunboats at Pittsburgh and direct gunboat crews to clear river obstructions as they sailed to New Orleans to enter foreign service.[6]

As enacted in May 1824, the first inland river navigation bill appropriated $75,000 for improving the Ohio River and the Mississippi below St. Louis, generally in accordance with the

Totten-Bernard plan, and Congress delegated the experimental research and engineering to the U.S. Army Corps of Engineers. Henry Clay jubilantly pronounced the law a precedent for treating the inland rivers "as our SEAS—as our Atlantic ocean and Mexican gulf, and as such are considered as entitled to special care and attention."[7]

To direct hydraulic research with wing dams, the Army's Chief Engineer sent Major Stephen H. Long to the Ohio, and Long in 1824–25 built the Corps' first dam on the river near Henderson, Kentucky. He drove parallel rows of wooden pilings in the riverbed, filled the space between with stone, and experimented with differing lengths, widths, and heights until he identified a design answering the purpose. Unlike slackwater dams that cross a river, the wing dam extended from one bank toward the channel at a forty-five-degree angle downstream to confine river flow at low-water stages, thereby increasing current velocity to erode an obstructive gravel bar and deepen the channel. Though renamed "spur dikes" to prevent confusion with slackwater dams, wing dams to deepen river channels were still used by the Corps for open-channel regulation, notably on the Missouri River, in the twentieth century.[8]

To secure a machine capable of removing snags, the Chief Engineer offered engineers and scientists a $1,000 prize for the best design, and during the summer of 1824 an avalanche of entries arrived. "The Amazing Quantity of Goods, of all Descriptions, and Lives lost on these Rivers, is Frightful in the Extreme to the Human Heart," asserted one engineer when submitting his design: "Could I cast in a Mite to Prevent this Wonderful Devastation, it would be a lasting Source of Consolation, and to the People of the United States an Unknown Saving."

Most designs found inspiration in twin-hull ferryboats propelled by horses walking the deck in circles and turning capstans geared to paddlewheels. Captain John W. Bruce of Vanceburg, Kentucky, submitted the winning design for a twin-hulled boat with a windlass between the two hulls that he called a "machine boat." Attaching a cable from the windlass to a snag, workers turned the windlass to raise the snag from the river for disposal. This may not have been the most effective design submitted, however, because the Chief Engineer selected it after awarding a contract for clearing the Ohio and Mississippi rivers to Bruce, who made his bid contingent on the use of his own "machine boat."[9]

Directed by law to "promptly" remove all snags from the Ohio and Mississippi, the Chief Engineer accepted an astonishingly low bid of $60,000 from Captain Bruce, a member of Kentucky's legislature and campaigner for Henry Clay. Although the Chief thought Bruce's bid too low, Clay and other congressmen assured him that Bruce would remove the snags as specified. To inspect the snagging, the Chief selected Major Samuel Babcock, an officer who had distinguished himself during the War of 1812 but who was unfamiliar with the Ohio. This proved a mistake.

Bruce started work at Pittsburgh in late 1824 and continued downriver in 1825, with Major Babcock following on inspection. Bruce removed snags only from the low-water channel, however, not from the entire riverbed, and Senator William H. Harrison and the Ohio delegation soon protested this neglect. After investigation, the Chief suspended Bruce's contract and arrested Major Babcock. Babcock was court-martialled for neglect of duty and sentenced to dismissal from the Army, but President John Quincy Adams, after reviewing the case, remitted the sentence.[10]

Heeding this debacle's lessons, Congress in its Rivers and Harbors Act of 1827 mandated the removal of obstructions of every description endangering navigation at any river stage, and it ordered that a "practical agent" with long experience with river navigation be placed in charge of the project. This "practical agent" proved to be Henry M. Shreve, the famous steamboat builder and river captain. Establishing his office at Louisville, Shreve designed and built steam-powered, double-hulled snagboats that were to roam the rivers during the following half century seeking snags to devour. Supervision of Shreve's work went to Major Stephen H. Long, who was to manage the channel clearance project until the Civil War.[11]

Shreve's snagboats proved too large to ascend through the small canal and locks completed around the Falls of the Ohio in 1830. Built by the independent Louisville and Portland Canal Company with federal funding assistance, this canal passed down the Kentucky side of the Falls and ended in a set of three locks capable of raising small steamboats about thirty feet from below to above the Falls. During the following forty years, the company collected enough tolls from boats using the canal to reimburse its investors and buy out stockholders, delivering the stock to the U.S. Treasury. By 1855, the federal government owned 9,995 shares of canal stock, leaving only 5 shares in the

hands of the company's directors. It appears, in fact, that the federal government collected more tolls from the Louisville canal than it expended on improving the entire Ohio before the Civil War. Congress did not accept control of the canal from the company, however, until 1874.[12]

Because Shreve's snagboats could not work upstream of the Falls, Congress in 1835 removed the Upper Ohio from Shreve's management, and the Chief Engineer appointed Captain John Sanders to direct work on the upper river from an office at Pittsburgh. Sanders built smaller snagboats to clear the Upper Ohio, along with dredges to cut through gravel bars, and constructed wing dams and dams closing secondary channels behind islands to concentrate the river's low flow.[13]

Shreve worked to achieve a minimum channel depth on the Lower Ohio of thirty-six inches, while Sanders aimed to open a channel at least thirty inches deep at low water on the Upper Ohio. During the economic depression of 1838, however, Congress and President Martin Van Buren suspended work on the Ohio and other rivers. Shreve mothballed his snagboats at St. Louis, Sanders stored his at Steubenville, and from 1839 to 1842 no snag removal or channel clearance was accomplished. During these years, 136 steamboats went to the river bottom, causing losses estimated at a million dollars annually. "We are not aware of the causes which have induced the discontinuance of this valuable service," complained boatmen, "but we know that the consequences have been disastrous."[14]

When President John Tyler signed the River and Harbor Act of 1842, funding resumption of the Ohio River project, Captain Sanders collected his equipment at Steubenville and resumed work. The Tyler administration, however, replaced Shreve with Captain John "Roaring Jack" Russell, a giant river captain of Frankfort, Kentucky, capable of "knocking down six of the best men in his employment at any time." Working under the supervision of Colonel Stephen H. Long, Russell put Shreve's snagboats back at work and built more to clear the Ohio and inland rivers. These renewed efforts to open a three-foot channel continued only three years until President James K. Polk took office and vetoed project appropriations on Constitutional grounds. Long and Sanders again mothballed their snagboats and mobilized during the following years for the Mexican War.[15]

Clearance of the Ohio's channel began a third time in 1852 when President Millard Fillmore approved the first River and Harbor Act since 1844. Colonel Long and "Roaring Jack" Russell built new snagboats and a dredge, again desnagged the rivers, and repaired the wing dams built earlier. Although reporting 124 lives lost in 85 steamboat wrecks in 1854, Long's request for $600,000 to finish channel clearance projects was ignored by the Franklin Pierce and James Buchanan administrations. The work did not resume until 1866, much to the regret of Union Army commanders who needed steamboat service for logistical support. During the Civil War, 144 steamboats transporting army supplies went to the bottom, some under Confederate shelling but most from collisions with snags and obstructions.[16]

At war's end, Congress funded renewed improvement of Ohio River navigation, and the Chief of Engineers sent William Milnor Roberts, U.S. Civil Engineer, to Pittsburgh and General Godfrey Weitzel to Louisville to resume the work. Roberts secured workboats, cleared snags, and rebuilt wing dams. From 1867 to 1872, Weitzel completed larger locks and enlarged the Louisville and Portland Canal around the Falls of the Ohio, and in 1874 Congress acquired the last five shares of company stock and assigned canal operations to the Corps of Engineers.[17]

The Corps' fifty-year effort to establish a safer and somewhat deeper channel on the Ohio approached its end in 1874 when

Congress approved new plans. Sporadic, meager funding for the channel clearance from 1824 to 1874 had hampered efforts aimed at providing an open channel with wing dams concentrating the river's low flow. Even had a thirty-inch channel depth been achieved, by 1874 it would have become obsolete as waterborne commerce began its transition from shallow-draft steamboat packets to a towboat-barge system for transporting bulk commodities. The Corps continued channel clearance engineering where necessary while implementing its canalization plans, and in the late twentieth century it still undertook dredging and clearing work where conditions required.

CANALIZATION, 1879–1929

When sending William Milnor Roberts to Pittsburgh in 1866 to resume channel clearance, the Chief of Engineers also directed him to survey the Ohio, identify its commercial trends, and plan its future. Roberts soon recognized that towboats pushing barges would in time supplant steamboat packets, and heavily laden barges would need more than thirty inches of water to navigate. In 1870, he proposed canalizing the Ohio with locks and dams to a six-foot depth. Having earlier designed locks and dams to canalize the Monongahela River, he proposed similar structures on the Ohio, estimating that sixty-six locks could raise boats from Cairo about 450 feet up to Pittsburgh's elevation.[18]

After Roberts had submitted his recommendation, Colonel William E. Merrill took charge of the Ohio, reviewing Roberts's and other plans for increasing its depth. One engineer proposed building a canal alongside the river; another suggested pumping enough water from Lake Erie to maintain a constant six-foot depth on the Ohio; and a third recommended dams on its tributaries to release water during dry seasons, thereby maintaining a boating stage. Merrill selected Roberts's plan as the best because his low dams would inundate little bottomland; the engineering they involved was well understood; and the dams could establish harbors for riverside cities.[19]

Public support for canalization arose in 1871 when the Ohio fell below boating stage in May, not to rise again before the following winter. By October, barges laden with coal waited above dams on the Monongahela for an Ohio rise to permit descent to Cincinnati, Louisville, and other ports, where fuel shortages occurred. Because coal barges could not leave the Monongahela and circle up the Allegheny to Pittsburgh's industrial north side, wagons hauled coal across downtown Pittsburgh, causing traffic jams and destroying city streets. Calling this intolerable, Pittsburghers demanded a dam on the Ohio to get coal wagons off the streets. "Let us no longer depend upon the rain from Heaven for conducting our chief employment," a newspaper editor implored.[20]

Pittsburgh's ironmasters, marine insurance agents, and businessmen in October 1871 petitioned Colonel Merrill and Congress to start building the Ohio's first lock and dam to form Pittsburgh's harbor. Towboat owners, on the other hand, objected that their barge fleets were too large to pass locks without breaking the tows apart above the locks and reassembling them below. They demonstrated on Pittsburgh's streets against locks and dams on the Ohio, protesting that its canalization would "annihilate" their coal towing business and, moreover, increase flooding heights and at low flows form stagnant pools that might be sources of disease.[21]

Merrill dismissed their environmental concerns by pointing out that navigation dams had functioned on the Monongahela since 1841 without the deleterious effects boatmen feared. Recognizing, however, that small locks and fixed dams could disrupt profitable coal-towing to Cincinnati and New Orleans, he initiated engineering investigations of locks and dams throughout the world, seeking a design suitable for Ohio River conditions. To meet the towing industry's needs, he wanted locks large enough to pass small coal tows; and to provide an open channel for the passage of large tows he wanted a movable dam—one holding a deep pool for boats during droughts and collapsing to the riverbed at high water, thereby passing boats over the dam without lockage.[22]

Merrill personally designed the largest locks in the world for the Ohio. Then, the Louisville and Portland Canal locks, at 78 feet wide, were the largest, but he designed a lock that was 110 feet wide and 600 feet long, spacious enough for a ten-barge tow in a single lockage. His principal engineering challenge involved designing wooden lockgates capable of closing a 110-foot lock, and he resolved it with his "rolling lockgate," which was a wooden truss lockgate on wheels rolling on rails across a lock chamber to close it.[23]

After testing many movable dam designs, Merrill found a suitable design on the Seine River near Paris, where French

engineers had built wicket dams. Large wooden panels called wickets were placed side by side atop a dam foundation. When the Seine was high, the panels lay flat on the foundation, allowing boat passage over the dam; at low water, raising the panels and propping them upright could hold the required pool depth for navigation.[24]

In 1874, Merrill recommended that locks and wicket dams be built on the Ohio. In the face of the towing industry's continued opposition, however, he suggested the lock and dam at Davis Island nearest Pittsburgh be built first as an experiment to prove its value. Congress approved this in 1875, appropriating funds to start work in accordance with Merrill's plan. After a delay while the lock site was purchased, Merrill began clearing the site and opening quarries to obtain the stone needed for construction. When construction was fully underway in 1879, he noted that opposition from the towing industry had diminished and declared it his opinion that "the chief benefits to be derived from the construction of the Davis Island dam will be reaped by the shippers of coal."[25]

Davis Island Lock and Dam, which became Ohio River Lock and Dam 1, opened to navigation in 1885 and served its purpose well. In addition to a year-round depth for navigation, it provided more reliable water supply for industry and it submerged noxious effluents threatening public health. Coal shippers in 1888 attributed the saving of their barges from flood and ice to the dam's operations, and lent their support to constructing similar locks and dams farther down the river. By 1900, however, coal barge tows had increased in number and draft, often drawing nine feet of water, and Merrill's successor in charge of the Ohio's canalization urged that the minimum depth be increased to nine feet. He said that depth stood "a fairly good chance of giving all the draft that can go through the Mississippi River during the life of the present generation and perhaps during the present century."[26]

In 1901 the Chief of Engineers established a Central Division at Cincinnati to manage the Ohio canalization project and ordered a restudy of the project's future. After extensive review, the Corps recommended and in 1910 Congress approved canalizing the river with up to fifty-four locks and dams similar to Merrill's Davis Island design and providing a nine-foot channel throughout the Ohio's 981-mile course. Under this plan, the Central Division first constructed dams providing harbors for the Ohio's largest port cities, then built the dams needed between them.[27]

Although the plan initially included fifty-four locks and dams from Dam 1 near Pittsburgh to Dam 54 near Cairo, the Division modified this plan to save funding as work progressed. It retained the original numbering system for the dams, but reduced the total number of wicket dams built to fifty-one by rearranging dam locations and increasing the height of some. Raising Dam 41 at Louisville eliminated the need to build Dam 40, and rearranging the dam sites between Dams 41 and 48 eliminated Dam 42. Nearest Cairo, the Division decided to rely on dredging to maintain a nine-foot depth instead of building a Dam 54. Lock and Dam 53 therefore became the last dam, and its completion in 1929 signaled the opening of nine feet of slackwater from Pittsburgh to Cairo.[28]

As an aid to navigation, the project proved successful when traffic using the locks and dams multiplied with resulting savings in transportation costs. The pools created by the dams also proved beneficial for industrial and municipal water supply. Averaging about ten feet deep, the pools inundated little bottomland along the river when the wickets were up; and at high water, when the wickets were dropped to the riverbed, the Ohio resumed its natural free-flowing character. In 1990, Dams 52 and 53 remained in operation as the only two extant from the original canalization project.[29]

FLOOD CONTROL, 1938–1988

In the early twentieth century, independent engineers and conservationists criticized the Corps for opposing flood control. Actually, it disapproved, not of flood control, but of using navigation improvement as the justification for federal funding of flood control. For example, when an Ohio River flood in 1884 overtopped city-built levees at Lawrenceburg, Jeffersonville, and Shawneetown, Congress ordered Colonel Merrill to investigate, and he reported that, although the towns needed flood protection, higher levees would not benefit navigation. Congress nevertheless funded restoring and raising these levees to help keep boats and water in the channel during floods, and there the Corps built its first levees in the Ohio valley.[30]

In another case, the Corps, after an 1898 Muskingum flood inundated Zanesville, reluctantly built its first concrete floodwall. Ohio's Senator Marcus Hanna had inserted funds for building Zanesville's floodwall in a navigation appropriation for Cleveland's harbor, and the Corps officer sent to Zanesville protested that the floodwall had nothing to do with navigation, was not even in the same watershed as Cleveland's harbor, and building it would be a "decided impropriety." The Chief of Engineers responded that Congress obviously intended to build the floodwall and it would be done as directed. When Senator Theodore Burton of Ohio, known nationally for opposing "porkbarrel" projects, shepherded another appropriation through Congress for raising Zanesville's floodwall as a benefit to navigation, a Corps officer commented that "the wisdom of Congress surpasses all understanding."[31]

The Corps took a similar position regarding flood control dams and reservoirs. After suffering severe flooding in 1907, Pittsburgh advocated flood control dams in the valley. The city funded pioneering studies by a Flood Commission, which in 1912 recommended building flood control dams in the Allegheny and Monongahela valleys above Pittsburgh. Reviewing this multipurpose plan, the Corps found it meritorious, but with so few benefits to navigation that Corps participation was unwarranted. This remained Corps policy until 1930: flood control dams contributed little to navigation improvement and would not merit federal funding until Congress accepted flood control as a purpose for water projects.[32]

Initiative was taken at the state level in Ohio after disastrous flooding in 1913. The Miami Conservancy District to protect Dayton became the first major watershed district in the United States. Under the leadership of Arthur E. Morgan, it constructed five detention dams and related local protection works for flood control in the Miami River basin. After completing this pioneering work, Morgan became a director of the Tennessee Valley Authority, a New Deal initiative for flood control and other purposes.

The first crack in federal policy came after a 1930 drought parched the Ohio River basin and the Monongahela River's flow nearly ceased, threatening to suspend navigation on that busy river. To maintain a boating stage, the Corps had to request a private company to release water stored by a hydroelectric power dam on a tributary, and this clarified the navigation benefits that a high, storage dam might provide. The Corps began studies of building its own high dam for navigation and flood control on the Tygart River, a Monongahela tributary in West Virginia.[33]

An opportunity to build Tygart Dam arose when President Franklin D. Roosevelt established New Deal agencies in 1933 to relieve unemployment and economic distress. Pittsburgh's civic leaders and the Corps in 1933 persuaded the Public Works Administration to fund Tygart Dam's construction for unemployment relief, flood control, and navigation. It was the first Corps dam for flood control in the Ohio River Basin and at its completion was the highest concrete dam east of the Mississippi. Completed in 1938, it stored flood flows to help protect the industrial Monongahela Valley from damage, and released water during droughts to support river navigation.[34]

As Tygart's construction proceeded, flood control and water project development also began on the Tennessee and Muskingum rivers, two Ohio River tributaries, as components of the New Deal program for economic recovery. The Tennessee Valley Authority, established in 1933, initiated comprehensive flood control and multipurpose dams on the Tennessee and its tributaries. In Ohio's Muskingum River Basin, multipurpose water resource development began under a cooperative arrangement between local, state, and federal agencies.

Built as a system under the Muskingum Watershed Conservancy District's aegis and also as a Public Works Administration project to relieve unemployment, fourteen dams were completed from 1934 to 1938. This was a fully cooperative project, with the Conservancy District purchasing the land, the State of Ohio relocating the roads, and the Public Works Administration funding construction under supervision of the Corps, which established a Zanesville Engineer District for the work. Completed in 1938, initial plans called for the Conservancy District to operate the dams, but Congress in 1939 assigned this to the Corps.[35]

As Tygart and the Muskingum dams rose from the valleys, they became components of a comprehensive plan for flood control under preparation at the Ohio River Division. Formed in 1933, the Division succeeded the old Central Division at Cincinnati in charge of Ohio valley water resources; and it drew up the Ohio River's "308 Report," a comprehensive planning study authorized by House Document No. 308 of 1927. In its "308 Report" of 1934, the Division recommended thirty-nine dams and reservoirs for flood control on the Ohio's tributaries, together with floodwalls and levees to protect urban areas along the mainstem. It expected these eventually to be constructed under cooperative arrangements similar to those in the Muskingum Valley. The Public Works Administration funded only Bluestone Dam in the Kanawha Valley, however, before widespread flooding in 1936 encouraged congressional approval of a national flood control policy.[36]

The flood of March 1936 set new records in the Upper Ohio Valley, inundating and severely damaging Johnstown, Pittsburgh, Steubenville, Wheeling, and communities upstream of Cincinnati. Two months later, Congress recognized floods as a menace to national welfare and directed the Corps to cooperate with state and local governments in the construction of flood control dams and local protection projects, provided that the projects were justified by estimated economic benefits in excess of costs. In its 1936 Flood Control Act, Congress approved fourteen flood control dams that the Ohio River Division had planned. Nine were upstream of Pittsburgh, three were in the Kanawha Valley above Charleston, and two on Licking River where they could reduce flooding at Cincinnati. Added to Tygart and the fourteen Muskingum dams, these brought the number of authorized dams to twenty-nine, but all were in the Upper Ohio basin where the 1936 flood had set records.[37]

Ironically, within months of the passage of the 1936 Flood

Control Act, the Ohio River went on a rampage, setting new crest records from Huntington to Cairo. Notable for its damage and disruption to human life and property, the 1937 flood also was of unprecedented duration. At Evansville, for example, the river passed flood stage on January 10 and did not recede below this level until February 19, some forty days later.

The 1937 flood revealed weakness in the Corps' original plans by proving the need for flood control on the Lower as well as the Upper Ohio. Even as the flood passed, the Ohio River Division reassessed its flood control plans for the basin, and in 1938 presented the revised plan to Congress. It proposed forty-nine more flood control dams on the Ohio's tributaries, including the Wabash, Green, and Cumberland rivers in the lower basin, plus many floodwalls and levees for the protection of urban areas. Congress approved this plan in its 1938 Flood Control Act, and together with the twenty-nine dams previously approved, it increased the number of flood control dams authorized for the Ohio River basin to seventy-eight. It also gave the Corps discretionary power to establish construction priorities and to modify the comprehensive plans as need arose.[38]

In 1938, therefore, the Ohio River Division had an approved plan for achieving basin flood control that was to guide its work during the following half century. The majority of the seventy-eight dams in time were built. As dictated by detailed studies, however, the Division modified its plan, relocating the sites of specific dams, eliminating some for engineering, economic, or environmental reasons, and adding others as substitutes. After fifty years of work, the Division was building its seventy-eighth flood control dam in 1988 and had finished it by 1990.

After 1938 Congress approved more dams on the Ohio's tributaries, increasing the number authorized to more than a hundred. From 1974 through 1988, however, it added no new flood control dams to the authorized plan and it deauthorized many. Varying degrees of public interest have been expressed in a few dams remaining on the books and some may be completed in the twenty-first century, but the Division's flood control dams of the twentieth century were in place by 1990.[39]

None of the Division's seventy-eight flood control dams are on the Ohio's mainstem, but their control of river flow has substantial effects on the Ohio. The river's floods are not so high, nor its low flows so puny. Coordinated operation of tributary dams commonly clips as much as ten feet off the top of mainstem floods, and during droughts more than half the Ohio's flow may be provided by releases from the dams on the tributaries.

Although its Districts operate the dams, guidance to coordinate the system as a whole emanates from the Division's Reservoir Control Center in Cincinnati. With an aggregate of thirty million acre-feet of storage, the seventy-eight dams control 39 percent of the drainage area above Pittsburgh, 31 percent above Cincinnati, and, together with TVA's dams on the Tennessee River, 32.5 percent of the area above Paducah. Built in a half century at a cost of $2.9 billion, the dams, by Corps estimate, have prevented $9 billion in flood damages, or about a three to one return on the investment.[40]

Although floods and droughts can occur at any season, the Division's scientists through long experience have identified the hydrologic pattern. Because the average pattern varies from high flows in March to low flows in September of each year, the Division normally manages its dams to store floods in March and release water in September. Because flows may require thirty days to travel from headwaters to the Ohio's mouth, the Division anticipates hydrologic sequences at least a month in advance. This is not so difficult because the Division's command center has computers, automatic surveillance, satellite data, and related electronic equipment. It can detect whether the hydrologic pattern for a year varies from the average cycle and can alter dam operations guidance accordingly.[41]

The Ohio River's flow thus has been engineered by the Division though the construction and management of seventy-eight flood control dams on the tributaries. This management aims to serve the basin's twenty-six million people by reducing flood damages and providing improved flow during droughts. Most of the dams also impound lakes for recreation and a few produce hydroelectric power. The resulting flow changes on the Ohio inevitably affect its riverine environment, over time establishing an ecology differing from that existing before the flood control program began. Analysis of these effects continually occupies the Division's hydrologists and scientists.

NAVIGATION MODERNIZATION, 1955–2005

None of the dams on the Ohio's mainstem serve flood control purposes, nor can they. Their principal function is to provide deep pools for commercial navigation, and when floods approach, the dams' gates are raised high to give them unimpeded passage. Except Locks and Dams 52 and 53 near the mouth, all locks and dams on the river in 1990 were part of the Ohio River Navigation Modernization project, begun by the Division in 1955 after years of study. Dams 52 and 53 are the last wicket dams built as part of the canalization project from 1879 to 1929.

Some "modern" locks and dams on the river, however, were built long before the Division began its modernization program in 1955. Even before canalization with wicket dams had been completed in 1929, replacement of the oldest wicket dams had become necessary. Emsworth Locks and Dam, the structure nearest Pittsburgh, replaced old Dams 1 and 2 in 1922; and Dashields Locks and Dam, next below Emsworth, replaced Dams 3 and 4 in 1929. During the 1930s, Montgomery Dam replaced Dams 5 and 6, and Gallipolis Dam replaced Dams 24, 25, and 26. Rather than movable wickets collapsing to open passage over the dam at high water, these replacement dams were fixed, built of concrete and steel to provide stable pools for navigation. Each new dam had two locks, allowing boats to use one when the other was repaired. The largest lock at these early replacement dams, however, was only 110 by 600 feet, the same as the single locks at the old wicket dams.[42]

After a setback during the Depression, commercial traffic on the Ohio spiraled upward for a half century. New chemical, steel, aluminum, and coal-fired electric plants were built along the Ohio to take advantage of economical transport and abundant water supply, and their location in the valley had a "ripple" effect, attracting industry that used the primary products and power manufactured along the river. By the 1950s, moreover, upbound traffic on the Ohio had nearly equalled downbound traffic, and the heaviest traffic density had shifted downriver from Pittsburgh. Barge tows moving the river's length in 1955, however, still suffered delays at forty-six locks, and by then the standard tow configuration had surpassed 600 feet, meaning that tows had to be broken apart to pass each lock in two sections and be reassembled after exit.[43]

Like Holmes's one-horse shay, the capacity of the old 600-foot locks had become inadequate, the system design had become obsolescent, and the structures had neared the end of their economic life simultaneously. According to the Division's planners, this congruence indicated that Colonel Merrill and the Central Division staff "were either very good engineers or remarkably lucky."[44]

To convert this obsolete system from a highway for local delivery into an interstate, the Division planned to reduce the number of lockages needed to transit the river from 46 to 19. Fourteen locks and dams of a new design would in time replace the remaining wicket dams, and five existing structures would continue in service: Emsworth, Dashields, and Montgomery dams would be renovated to extend their useful life, and new 1,200-foot locks would be added at Gallipolis Dam and at Louisville's Dam 41. Although these five dams retained their existing pool levels, the fourteen new dams would increase pool elevations because each replaced two or more low wicket dams.[45]

Division studies indicated lock dimensions of 110 by 1,200 feet, double the old locks' length, could handle the largest barge tows operating efficiently on the Ohio, and the Division adopted these dimensions for the main lock at each new dam. An auxiliary lock, 110 by 600 feet, would provide additional capacity and serve traffic when the larger lock needed repairs. Where locks at the old wicket dams lifted boats an average of 7 to 8 feet, the new locks would have lifts ranging from 12 to 37 feet. An improved valve and culvert system, moreover, would permit filling the new locks in 8 minutes, compared to 18 minutes at the old locks.[46]

The Division adopted tainter gates as the standard crest gates atop the concrete sills of the new dams. Steel tainter gates up to 110 feet long and more than 40 feet high surmounted the concrete sills between piers. Anchored into the piers on both sides, tainter gates could be pivoted up or down to control the pool, holding it at a stable level. When floods approached, however, the gates moved out of the way, and the dams had little effect on flood flows. Other significant features of dam design included pedestals to support bridges and weirs where hydroelectric plants might be installed. In time, many of the dams also served as highway crossings and as sources of electric power.[47]

With these plans completed, the Division started construction of the Ohio's modernization project in 1955 at New Cumberland Locks and Dam, followed in 1956 by Greenup and Markland dams. These extended and improved the harbors of Pittsburgh, Huntington, and Cincinnati. Work followed at Louisville's Dam 41 and the old Louisville and Portland Canal around the Falls. There, a concrete dam with tainter gate control replaced old Dam 41 with no change in pool elevation. With a wider canal and a new 1,200-foot-long lock, this structure was renamed McAlpine Locks and Dam after William H. McAlpine, a senior engineer who had participated in planning both the canalization project of 1929 and the modernization project of 1955.[48]

After New Cumberland, Greenup, Markland, and McAlpine Locks and Dams had begun, the Division next built locks and dams located between these, working its way downstream toward Cairo. The Division first hoped to start one new structure each year, thereby finishing the Ohio's modernization in a quarter century. Budgetary constraints prevented meeting this schedule, and increasingly complex planning and legal requirements further extended the time. Thirteen of the planned fourteen modern structures were in service by the end of the 1970s, however, and during the 1980s the Division rehabilitated the old Emsworth, Dashields, and Montgomery Locks and Dams and began installation of a new 1,200-foot lock in a canal past Gallipolis Dam. Foundation and design difficulties delayed starting the structure nearest the Ohio's mouth to eliminate Locks and Dams 52 and 53, but in 1988 Congress approved a replacement. The Division expected the Lower Ohio Replacement Structure to be completed about 2005, when Dams 52 and 53 would be removed.[49]

Engineering of the nineteen modernization structures effected major changes in the Ohio's regimen. The five rehabilitated and modernized structures kept their old pool levels, but the fourteen new dams created deeper, wider pools than the wicket dams they replaced, converting the river into a staircase of nineteen "lakes" up to a hundred miles in length. While advantageous for commercial tows and recreation craft, these lakes inundated floodplain farmlands and caused other riverine alterations. Although unjustly faulted for environmental problems of various kinds, the modern dams have produced such challenges as embayment siltation and oxygen depletion that require the Corps' closest attention. On the other hand, the large lakes also resulted in some environmental improvements; the Corps performs far less dredging in the new lakes than it did above the wicket dams, and the islands and adjacent lands of the lakes have become wildlife refuges.[50]

CONCLUSION

Although American Indians and pioneers altered the Ohio and its tributaries for human use, the resulting changes in the riverine environment were transitory. States bordering the Ohio during the early nineteenth century undertook to improve the Ohio's navigation, and when their resources had been exhausted they requested federal assistance for their "common commercial highway." Then, the U.S. Army took interest in improving the Ohio as a logistical artery, and its Engineers before 1824 were practically the only professional engineers in federal service. Congress therefore, in 1824, assigned navigation improvement of the Ohio and other inland rivers to the Corps of Engineers.

In performing its missions on the Ohio, the Corps has adopted four grand plans, each requiring about fifty years for implementation. The first plan from 1824 to 1874 sought to make the river safer and slightly deeper to support steamboat commerce. Irregular and inadequate funding prevented full development of this clearance project, although it did reduce navigation hazards. A channel only thirty inches deep, however, could not have served deep-draft towboat and barge commerce.

Initiated during the 1870s, the Ohio River canalization project involved constructing fifty-one locks and dams to provide a minimum channel depth of nine feet. Completed in 1929 after fifty years of construction, these structures had 600-foot-long locks and movable wicket dams that collapsed to the riverbed during high flows. These served commercial navigation perhaps better than their planners, Colonel William E. Merrill and the Central Division of the Corps, had expected. Tonnages traveling the Ohio multiplied many fold as industry moved to riverside to use the water and economical transportation supplied by the project. A catalyst for regional industrial development, the project also changed the river's environment, containing its low flow in pools at least nine feet deep. At high river stages when the dams collapsed, however, the river regained its natural flow characteristics.

Since 1933 the Ohio River Division at Cincinnati has directed the comprehensive engineering of the river, devising two central plans for the purpose. One called for constructing dams for flood control and related purposes on tributary streams and the other for modernizing the Ohio's navigation project to increase its capacity to match developing commercial navigation.

The flood control program began during the 1930s, in part as an effort to provide work during the Depression. From this foundation, the Division developed a grand plan to control the Ohio River's flow through construction of storage dams on tributaries. As formulated in 1938, the plan had seventy-eight authorized dams for flood control, and by 1988, when the Division was building its seventy-eighth dam, considerable control over the Ohio's flow had been achieved. By storing flood water, the dams reduced the Ohio's flood flows, and by subsequently releasing water they increased the river's drought flows by half or more. Because these dams control only about a third of the Ohio's drainage area, however, they cannot entirely eliminate flooding or water shortages in the basin.

The Ohio's navigation modernization project, begun during the 1950s, has substantially reduced the number of locks and dams operating on the river and also the amount of dredging required to maintain a nine-foot depth. From fifty-one navigation pools, the Ohio by 2005 will be converted into nineteen lakes each up to a hundred miles in length. Although maintaining a nine-foot depth on the river during even the most severe drought, these dams have insignificant effects on flood flows. They vastly improve conditions for commercial navigation and recreation, support bridges, and generate hydroelectric power. They alter the river's natural regimen, sometimes with negative and sometimes with beneficial environmental effects.

No river in America has been altered by engineering more than the Ohio. In 1990, with 91 locks in use at 60 dams on the Ohio and its tributaries, the Ohio River Division operates more locks than any Corps Division in America. With 78 high dams on the Ohio's tributaries, the Division manages more flood control dams than any Division in the Corps. The Ohio surely is the most comprehensively engineered river in the nation, and the resulting alterations of its environment have been pervasive.

Plans for engineering the Ohio have been prepared and implemented with remarkable persistence by the Corps and its Ohio River Division. No matter what the national administration changes, policy shifts, or political controversies, once adopted, the Corps' four grand plans have been inexorably worked by two to three generations of engineers during fifty-year cycles. The key to understanding the Ohio's engineering therefore is found on the top floors of the Cincinnati Federal Building where the Ohio River Division has its headquarters.

The historic pattern indicates a new engineering plan will be required for the Ohio as its existing structures deteriorate, probably within fifty years. Although 1990 was too early to perceive a definitive outline of future engineering on the Ohio, doubtless any plan will strive to meet the needs of the basin's ever increasing human population.

NOTES

1. *Pittsburgh Gazette*, 1818–19 files, Carnegie Library, Pittsburgh, Pa.; Louis C. Hunter, *Studies in the Economic History of the Ohio Valley*, Vol. 9, *Smith College Studies in History* (Northampton, Mass.: Smith College History Department, 1933–34), 5–23; James M. Callahan, "The Pittsburgh-Wheeling Rivalry for Commercial Headship on the Ohio," *Ohio Archaeological and Historical Publications* 22 (1913):40–54.

2. "Reconnaissance of the Ohio River above the Falls Made in 1819 by Commissioners Appointed by the States of Virginia, Kentucky, Pennsylvania, and Ohio," 2 Nov. 1819, Cartographic Records, National Archives, Washington, D.C.

3. *Pittsburgh Gazette*, 1821–24 files, Carnegie Library, Pittsburgh, Pa.; Ohio River Improvement Papers, Record Group 26, Pennsylvania State Archives, Harrisburg, Pa.

4. Secretary of War John C. Calhoun, "Roads and Canals," 14 Jan. 1819, *American State Papers*, Class X: *Miscellaneous*, II, 533–37.

5. U.S., Congress, House, *Message from the President transmitting a Report of the Board of Engineers*, H. Exec. Doc. No. 35, 17th Cong., 2d Sess., 1823.

6. Curtis Nettels, "The Mississippi Valley and the Constitution, 1815–1829," *Mississippi Valley Historical Review* 21 (Dec. 1924):332–38; *Annals of Congress*, 18th Cong., 1st Sess., 1824, 1021, 2578–83; Henry Clay, "Speech on Internal Improvements," 14 Jan. 1824, in James F. Hopkins and Mary W. M. Hargreaves, eds., *The Papers of Henry Clay*, Vol. III: *Presidential Candidate, 1821–1824* (Lexington: University of Kentucky Press, 1963), 572–93.

7. Washington *Daily National Intelligencer*, 31 July 1824.

8. U.S., Congress, Senate, *A Report of the Chief Engineer Relative to the Application of the Appropriation for Removing Obstructions to the Navigation of the Ohio and Mississippi Rivers*, S. Doc. No. 14, 19th Cong., 1st Sess., 1826, 28–31; Louisville *Public Advertiser*, 6 Nov. 1824, 23 Nov. 1825, 25 Feb. 1826.

9. "Plans for Removal of Obstructions in the Mississippi and Ohio Rivers, 1824–25," Records of the Office of the Chief of Engineers, Record Group 77, National Archives, Washington, D.C. (cited hereafter as NARG77). The quotation is from the entry of Henry Vose.

10. Henry Clay to John C. Calhoun, 15 Aug. 1824, in Hopkins and

Hargreaves, eds., *The Papers of Henry Clay*, III, 810; U.S., Congress, Senate, *A Report of the Chief Engineer Relative to the Application of the Appropriation for Removing Obstructions*, S. Doc. No. 14, 19th Cong., 1st Sess., 1826, 9–12; Samuel Babcock, "Journal of a Tour of Duty" 30 June 1825–15 Apr. 1826, Court Martial Case Files, 1809–1894, Records of the Judge Advocate General of the Army, Record Group 153, National Archives, Washington, D.C.

11. U.S., Congress, House, *Sand Bars of the Ohio River*, H. Exec. Doc. No. 145, 19th Cong., 1st Sess., 1826, 1–5; U.S., Congress, House, *Obstructions in the River Ohio*, H. Doc. No. 213, 20th Cong., 1st Sess., 1828, 1–3; U.S., Congress, House, *Navigation Ohio and Mississippi Rivers*, H. Rept. No. 379, 21st Cong., 1st Sess., 1830, 3.

12. Paul B. Trescott, "The Louisville and Portland Canal Company, 1825–1874," *Mississippi Valley Historical Review* 44 (Mar. 1958):686–708; Heber P. Walker, "Louisville and Portland Canal," *Indiana Magazine of History* 27 (Mar. 1932):21–30.

13. James St. Clair Morton, *Memoir of the Life and Services of Capt. and Brevet Major John Sanders* (Pittsburgh, Pa.: W. S. Haven, 1861), 43–60.

14. Joseph H. Harrison, "Martin Van Buren and His Southern Supporters," *Journal of Southern History* 22 (Nov. 1956):438–58.

15. U.S., Congress, House, *Henry M. Shreve—Snag Boat*, H. Rept. No. 272, 27th Cong., 2nd Sess., 1843, 1–5; Ella H. Ellwanger, "One of Kentucky's Gallant Old-Time River Captains," *Ohio River and Inland Waterways Magazine* 2 (July 1920):20–24.

16. Victor L. Albjerg, "Internal Improvements without a Policy," *Indiana Magazine of History* 28 (June 1932):176; Richard G. Wood, *Stephen Harriman Long, 1784–1864: Army Engineer, Explorer, Inventor* (Glendale, Calif.: Arthur Clarke Co., 1966), 209–10; U.S., Congress, House, *Vessels Bought, Sold, and Chartered by the United States*, H. Exec. Doc. No. 337, 40th Cong., 2d Sess., 1868, lists boats sunk in war.

17. Brig. Gen. Richard M. Delafield to Edwin M. Stanton, 2 Aug. 1866, "Letters Sent, 1866," NARG77; U.S., Congress, House, *River and Harbor Improvements*, H. Exec. Doc. No. 56, 39th Cong., 2d Sess., 1867, 1–10; U.S., Congress, House, *Ship Canal around the Falls of the Ohio River*, H. Exec. Doc. No. 181, 40th Cong., 2d Sess., 1868, 1–8.

18. U.S., Congress, House, *Survey of the Ohio River*, H. Exec. Doc. No. 72, 41st Cong., 3rd Sess., 1871, 3–25.

19. U.S., Congress, House, *Plans for the Improvement of the Ohio River*, H. Misc. Doc. No. 33, 46th Cong., 2d Sess., 1880, 4–23; Felix R. Brunot, "Improvement of the Ohio River," *Journal of the Franklin Institute* 97 (May 1874):315–17, 327.

20. *Pittsburgh Daily Gazette*, 23 Oct. and 9 Nov. 1871.

21. Jones and Laughlin, Oliver and Phillips, Moorhead Adams & Co., et al., to Maj. William E. Merrill, 17 Oct. 1871, File 202, Letters Received, 1871–1886, NARG77; Maj. William E. Merrill to Brig. Gen. A. A. Humphreys, 30 Jan. 1872, ibid.; James Henderson, "Reminiscences of the Rivers," *Western Pennsylvania Historical Magazine* 12 (Oct. 1929):235–36.

22. William E. Merrill, "Movable Dams," *Engineering News* 5 (28 Mar. 1878):100–01; Willam E. Merrill, *Improvement of Non-Tidal Rivers* (Washington, D.C.: Government Printing Office, 1881), 3.

23. Maj. William E. Merrill to Maj. Gen. A. A. Humphreys, 2 Apr. 1877, File 532, Letters Received, 1871–1886, NARG77; William L. Sibert, "The Improvement of the Ohio River," *Transactions of the American Society of Civil Engineers* 63 (1909):405–10.

24. Jacques Henri Maurice Chanoine, *Memoire sur les barrages a hausses mobiles* (Paris: Dunod, 1862), 1–179.

25. Maj. William E. Merrill to Maj. Gen. Horatio G. Wright, 28 Nov. 1879, File 5121, Letters Received, 1871–1886, NARG77; Leland R. Johnson, *The Davis Island Lock and Dam, 1870–1922* (Pittsburgh, Pa.: U.S. Army Engineer District, 1985), 63.

26. William E. Merrill, "Historical Sketch of the Work of the United States in the Improvement of the Ohio River," *Proceedings of the Engineers' Club of Philadelphia* 4 (Feb. 1885):331–38; Maj. William H. Bixby to Brig. Gen. John Wilson, 30 Jan. 1900, File 33792, General Correspondence, 1894–1923, NARG77.

27. John L. Vance, "Sketch of Ohio River Improvements," *Ohio Archaeological and Historical Publications* 18 (1909):418; William M. Hall, "Some Notes on the Location and Construction of Locks and Movable Dams on the Ohio River," *Transactions of the American Society of Civil Engineeers* 86 (1923):107–108, 162–64.

28. Edmund L. Daley, "Mastery of the Ohio River," *Military Engineer* 19 (May 1927):188–93; C. W. Kutz, "Ohio River Canalization," *Engineering News-Record* 104 (13 Mar. 1930):436–37.

29. C. W. Kutz, "Ohio River—An Economic Epic," *Military Engineer* 21 (Nov. 1929):509–10; C. L. Hall, "Economics of the Ohio River Improvement," *Transactions of the American Society of Civil Engineers* 103 (1938):1527–78.

30. "Regulation of Western Rivers," *Engineering News* 11 (23 Feb. 1884):92; U.S. Army, Chief of Engineers, *Annual Report of the Chief of Engineers for 1885* (Washington, D.C.: Government Printing Office, 1886), 1796–98; William E. Merrill, "The Ohio River Floods," *Engineering News* 11 (22 Mar. 1884):137.

31. Zanesville Chamber of Commerce, *Levee at Zanesville, Ohio* (Zanesville: Chamber of Commerce, 1910), 1–9; Maj. William H. Bixby to Brig. Gen. John Wilson, General Correspondence, 1894–1923, NARG77.

32. F. W. Altstaetter, "The Ohio River," *Professional Memoirs, Corps of Engineers* 2 (Jan. 1910):35–44; U.S., Congress, House, *Reservoirs at the Headwaters*, H. Doc. No. 1289, 62d Cong., 3rd Sess., 1912; U.S., Congress, House, *Flood Protection and Prevention*, H. Doc. No. 1792, 64th Cong., 2d Sess., 1916.

33. "When Power Aids Navigation," *National Waterways* 9 (Oct. 1930):38–40.

34. W. D. Styer, "Pittsburgh Area Inaugurates Its Flood-Control Program," *Engineering News-Record* 113 (12 July 1934):48–50; W. D. Styer, "The Tygart River Reservoir Project," *Civil Engineering* 5 (June 1935):342.

35. Hal Jenkins, *A Valley Renewed: The History of the Muskingum Watershed Conservancy District* (Kent, Ohio: Kent State University, 1976), 1–24; U.S. Army Engineer District, Zanesville, *History and Development of the Muskingum Watershed Conservancy District Project, Ohio* (Zanesville, Ohio: U.S. Army Engineer District, 1938), 6.

36. U.S., Congress, House, *Ohio River*, H. Doc. No. 306, 74th Cong., 1st Sess., 1934, 1–9.

37. E. K. Morse and Harold Thomas, "Floods in the Upper Ohio River and Tributaries," *Transactions of the American Society of Civil Engineers* 103 (1938):624–30; Joseph L. Arnold, "The Flood Control Act of 1936: A Study in Politics, Planning, and Ideology," in Howard Rosen and Martin Reuss, eds., *The Flood Control Challenge, Past, Present, and Future: Proceedings of a National Symposium, New Orleans, Louisiana,*

September 26, 1986 (Chicago: Public Works Historical Society, 1988), 13–25.

38. W. G. Hoyt, "Unusual Events and Their Relation to Federal Water Policies," *Transactions of the American Society of Civil Engineers* 108 (1943):290–316; "$800,000,000 Flood Control Plan," *Engineering News-Record* 118 (10 June 1937):852; U.S., Congress, House, Committee on Flood Control, *Comprehensive Flood-Control Plan for Ohio and Lower Mississippi Rivers*, Comm. Doc. No. 1, 75th Cong., 1st Sess., 1937; U.S., Congress, House, Committee on Flood Control, *Comprehensive Flood Control Plans, Hearings on Report of Chief of Engineers*, H. Rept. No. 2353, 75th Cong., 3rd Sess., 1938, 9–10, 125–27.

39. Douglas L. Weart and James W. Bruce, "Ohio River Basin Flood Control Plan," *Military Engineer* 40 (Aug. 1948):345–49. Interest continued in 1990 in the proposed Rowlesburg, Haysi, Station Camp, and Celina dams, but none were near construction.

40. U.S. Army Corps of Engineers, Ohio River Division, *Ohio River Basin Flood Control and Multipurpose Reservoir Data* (Cincinnati: U.S. Army Engineer Division, 1984), passim.

41. Ronald Yates, "Water Control Management in the Ohio River Basin," Paper presented at Central State University Water Management Seminar, 21 Feb. 1989, Reservoir Control Center Files, U.S. Army Engineer Division, Cincinnati, Ohio.

42. Charles M. Wellons, "Construction and Operations of a Modern River Lock," *National Waterways* 5 (Jan. 1929):57–58; Wilfred Bauknight, "New Crest Gate for Dams," *Engineering News-Record* 118 (6 May 1937):665–66; Roger G. Powell, *Lock and Dam Replacement* (Cincinnati: U.S. Army Engineer Division, 1939), 1–24.

43. P. W. Loveland and T. P. Bailey, "Navigation on the Ohio River," *Military Engineer* 41 (May 1949):174; John Lane, "Lifeline to Mid-America," *Water Spectrum* 1 (Summer 1969):15–18.

44. Charles F. Michiels, William F. Lail, and Robert E. Mytinger, "Current Trends in Ohio River Traffic," *Journal of the Waterways and Hydraulics Division, American Society of Civil Engineers* 87 (Dec. 1956):paper 1123.

45. James W. Bruce, Dwight W. Keller, and James A. Neill, "Modern Facilities for Ohio River Navigation," *Journal of the Waterways and Hydraulics Division, American Society of Civil Engineers* 88 (May 1957):paper 1239; James Wolfe, "The Damming of Pittsburgh," *Greater Pittsburgh* 50 (Oct. 1968):36–40.

46. Edwin E. Abbott, "Design for a New Ohio River," *Civil Engineering* 32 (Oct. 1962):46–49.

47. Ibid.

48. Modernization project details and bibliographic citations provided in Leland R. Johnson, *The Falls City Engineers: A History of the Louisville District, Corps of Engineers, United States Army, 1970–1983* (Louisville: U.S. Army Engineeer District, 1985), 28–47, 134–59.

49. Ibid. The author's forthcoming history of the Ohio River Division will provide project details and bibliographic citations.

50. Robert W. Schmitt, "Some Environmental Concerns Associated with Modern Navigation Projects," in U.S. Army Corps of Engineers, Navigation Workshop, 18–21 May 1987 (San Francisco: U. S. Army Engineer District, 1987), 342–45; U.S. Army Corps of Engineers, Ohio River Division, Ohio River Bank Erosion Study (Cincinnati: U.S. Army Engineer Division, 1977), II–1 to II–19; *Louisville Courier-Journal*, 15 Oct. 1989.

Boyd Keenan

AN ECOPOLITICAL SYSTEM OF GLOBAL SIGNIFICANCE

"The Valley of the Ohio, without doubt, comprehends a larger quantity of fertile land, a more extensive and diffused interior navigation, together with a more salubrious climate, than any other portion of the temperate zones of the globe. . . . The resources of the finest iron and lead, of coal and salt, are spread over this section of the United States in a profusion unequalled in the world" (Mann Butler, *Valley of the Ohio*, 1853). Butler's flattering characterization of the Ohio Valley contrasts starkly with its current image as a pariah or outcast—the source of water, land, and air pollution that threatens the ecological health of great portions of our nation as well as Canada. At the time Butler penned his tribute, the Ohio River and its valley were central to many of the great political issues of that era. But concerns about the environment were not among them.

Today the broader Ohio Basin is increasingly embroiled in political battles at every level of government that involve ecological questions. This final chapter encourages the use of an enlarged concept—that of an "ecopolitical system"—to examine these conflicts. Viewed as such a system, the Ohio Basin has significance for other sections of the country and the world. Improved understanding of the ecological challenges it faces may not only help to remove the stigma from the valley but also contribute to the quality of life around the planet.

The notion of an ecopolitical system may need elaboration. Occasionally used by writers, public officials, and scientists seeking to describe new kinds of problems, the term has become more familiar in the aftermath of recent ecological disasters in the Soviet Union and Eastern Europe. Political commentator Georgia Anne Geyer has quoted Sovietologists and European specialists who warn that "the ecological has become the metaphor for national protest." Geyer continues:

> The words "ecological" and "environmental" are far too weak for the life-and-death fight that is already developing. . . . How rapidly will the ecological fears and protests be translated into political forms? My suspicion is, very quickly. At the same time, the Soviet Union, as well as other countries, is facing a whole new genre of political issues that I can at the moment only call part of "ecological politics." These issues cross borders and pose bedeviling new threats. . . . Once the problems behind these complaints become life-threatening, they also become basically non-negotiable, posing frightening political questions.[1]

These issues that "cross borders" and pose "frightening political questions" are almost always confronted in the context of river basins. Many rivers in Eastern Europe, including the Danube, the Elbe, and the Volga, form basins which sprawl across several countries or, in the case of the Soviet Union, republics. Others, such as the Amazon in South America, contain vast rain forests whose ability to regenerate is very limited and whose gradual disappearance may threaten the entire globe. Thus, river basins are becoming the sites of new kinds of ecological battles for which, as Geyer implies, we have neither adequate vocabularies nor conceptual frameworks. Politics and policymaking are now embedded in ecosystem science as phenomena to be studied along with the biology, geology, and history of a region. The term ecopolitical system reflects a growing societal conviction that ecological and political systems are now inextricably linked.

Before proceeding, we must ask whether ecosystem scientists would accept the term "ecopolitical system" as helpful. Would they approve its use as the conceptual foundation for this chapter? Two prominent American ecologists who have argued, if not for the term itself, at least for such an approach are Barbara L. Bedford and Simon A. Levin, both of Cornell University. Noting that the new ecosystem science should be aimed ultimately at policymakers, Bedford and Levin describe it as "the only discipline that deals explicitly with integration of physical, chemical, and biological systems at the scales of concern to *policymakers* . . . it is particularly important, therefore, that the link between ecosystem science and environmental agencies be a strong one." The two ecologists emphasize that ecosystem scientists can provide "the understanding of environmental systems operating across jurisdictional boundaries." While acknowledging that these kinds of scientists "are not likely to become involved in solving the problem," they imply that political scientists and the general public should blend ecosystem concepts with those of policymakers. Keeping in mind Bedford and Levin's warning that "ecosystems are not well-defined and homogeneous units in space and time," most ecologists would surely agree that the unique physical and political aspects of the Ohio River Basin, together with decades of study by practitioners and scholars, have positioned the river's broad basin as an ecosystem of global significance.[2]

The Ohio River is understood to be that body of water that flows from Pittsburgh to Cairo, Illinois, before joining the Mississippi River. River specialists disagree about the meaning of hydrological terms such as river "reaches," valleys, basins, and watersheds. Most difficult, perhaps, is the notion of a "valley." Some argue the valley is simply that portion of land on either side of a river. But how much land? A few hundred yards? A mile? Two miles? One county? Two counties? There seems to be no simple answer. Many hydrologists and related specialists prefer to dispose of the concept of "valleys" altogether, favoring instead either "drainage basin" or "watershed." These two terms are indeed based on exact hydrological phenomena. But because we are considering politics and government—both inexact fields—we shall not become preoccupied with rigid definitions.

To distinguish a large river like the Ohio from the system formed by its various tributaries and the broader drainage basin, the main river is usually called the "mainstem" or "main channel." The Ohio River Basin refers to the drainage basin or watershed area of the Ohio and its tributaries, encompassing portions of fourteen states. These usages will generally be followed here. An infinite number of ecosystem regions are found within the Ohio River Basin. Each of these regions, ranging from small areas within tributary subbasins to the Ohio Basin's total watershed, has its own ecopolitical system. This conclusion is in keeping with Bedford and Levin's precept that ecosystems are defined by the researcher and may "range from small ponds to the entire globe."[3]

This final chapter presents an ecopolitical perspective on the Ohio River and its environs. The issues dealt with here will help us better understand the growing importance of ecopolitical systems as we seek to learn from past attempts by public and private sector leaders to manage the natural resources of a great American river and its basin.

Coal has long been "king" in the Ohio River Valley. The presence of massive coal reserves, most of them with high sulfur content, necessarily dominates any discussion of environmental and/or ecological issues in the valley and the broader basin. From the early years of the Republic until the past few decades, this presence was viewed as an unmitigated blessing, a source of heat to protect humankind against the cold. In the nineteenth century, coal replaced wood and water power as the key energy source essential to the development of products which all civilized societies now take for granted. Throughout the twentieth century, steel factories and other industries powered by coal from the Ohio Basin have contributed mightily to U.S. strength as a world power.

But over the past two decades, American attitudes have changed dramatically about the utilization of coal, and high sulfur coal in particular. Any claim today that coal is an "unmitigated blessing" faces serious challenge. Indeed, no contemporary issue so forcefully undergirds this chapter as the reality that a great many Americans and Canadians fear the widespread burning of coal in the Ohio Valley. (A map of air dispersion from the Ohio Valley is shown in Figure 1.)

Political leaders and environmental groups have argued that coal-powered Ohio Valley electric power plants are the main culprits in the formation of acid rain which falls in the Northeast and Canada. While the debate continues, most scientists agree that some abuses to lakes, forests, and other natural resources can be traced to coal use in the Ohio Valley area. Beneath the acid rain controversy is the uncertainty surrounding the comparative merits of coal, other fossil fuels, nuclear power, and alternative sources of energy. Understanding the

Figure 1

Ohio Valley Air Mass Trajectories

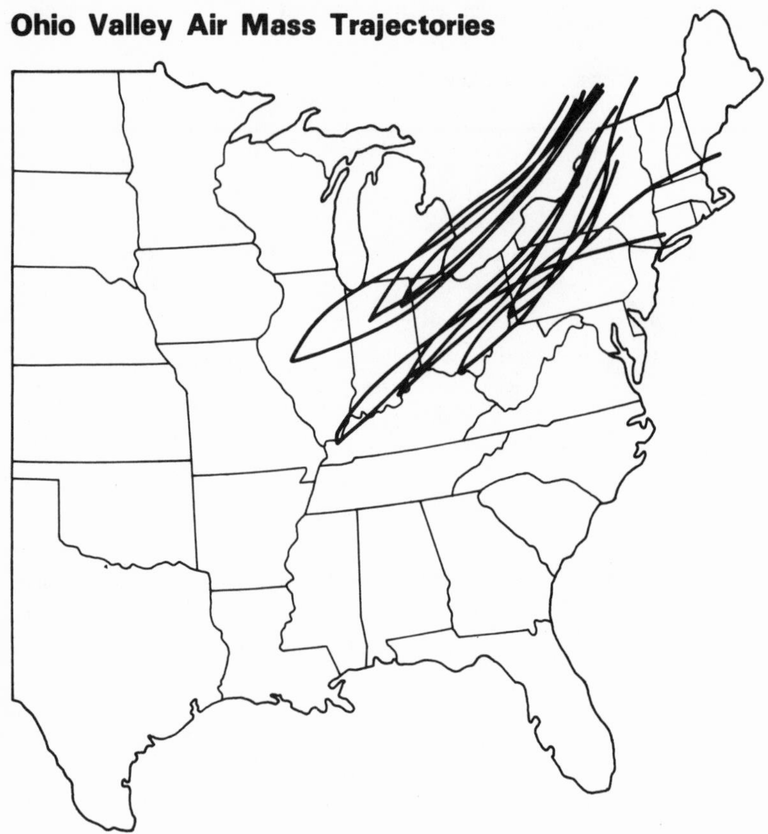

Adapted from *Ohio River Basin Energy Study (ORBES): Main Report*, 1981

various facets of this energy dilemma is one of the most difficult intellectual tasks the human species has ever faced.

While many Ohio Valley residents may view this unprecedented challenge with despair, others may see it as an opportunity for the valley—and the broader basin—to become central actors in a drama perhaps unparalleled in world history. Those wishing to participate in the drama must study the region carefully. They must become knowledgeable as to how massive coal supplies, bountiful water sources, and the availability of land all combined to make the Ohio Valley region an ideal location for power plants. Such producers of energy, in turn, served as magnets for a wide range of industrial installations, particularly in the upper reaches of the Ohio and its tributaries.

ORSANCO

Historical sources suggest that attempts to view the Ohio Valley as an ecosystem began in the 1920s when it was recognized that the mining of coal and its use by industry was contributing to the degradation of rivers and streams in the broader Ohio River Basin. Edward J. Cleary, an authority on the subject, has noted that "a growing advocacy for federal intervention" on pollution questions began to assert itself in several parts of the valley by the 1930s.[4]

Though federal control—or even federal assistance—was not a popular notion sixty years ago, a political event occurred in 1932 that contributed much to institutional innovations for river-basin development: the election of Franklin D. Roosevelt as president in the midst of the Great Depression. Clearly sympathetic to new ideas in a time of national crisis, Roosevelt was convinced of the need for a development authority to remedy economic and natural resource problems centered around the Tennessee River. Congress created the Tennessee Valley Authority (TVA) in 1933.

Leadership at the national level that supported natural resource planning and development such as TVA stimulated local initiatives. Beginning in 1935, efforts of civic leaders in Cincinnati culminated in the formation of the Ohio River Valley Water Sanitation Commission, now known as ORSANCO. This organization has been hailed across the country—even across the world—as the first major intergovernmental effort committed solely to the objective of improving water quality. The attempt has involved transjurisdictional activities across many hundreds of miles and a host of agencies, cities, counties, and states.

In his study of ORSANCO, Cleary credits efforts by valley citizens for bringing about the final step, a formal 1948 meeting of governors in Cincinnati that bound eight states together in an agreement pledging cooperation in water pollution abatement. Prior authorization by the state legislatures and approval from the U.S. Congress made this interstate compact possible. ORSANCO represents a unique grouping: in addition to the six "border" states, it includes New York and Virginia. Unfortunately, Tennessee, with a much larger Ohio watershed than the latter two, has not seen fit to join.

Published in 1967, Cleary's book is particularly useful in presenting the contrast between approaches taken in the Ohio Valley and in the Tennessee Valley to solve environmental and natural resources problems from the 1930s into the 1960s. Unlike TVA, whose foundations were based on federal leadership for an entire region and for multiple issues that extended far beyond pollution control, those early leaders in Ohio Valley planning exhibited confidence that strengthening existing state-oriented institutions (including ORSANCO) would be adequate to meet future challenges. The Ohio Valley leaders of the 1950s and 1960s seemed to acknowledge that large coal corporations, chemical firms, and giant electric utilities were major contributors to the area's pollution. But few of them—in government, industry, or academia—seriously questioned the prevailing view that these corporations were also the best hope for improving the area's quality of life.

Though the word "ecosystem" was not used, the boundaries set by ORSANCO for improving water quality may be viewed as the first effort to define the Ohio Valley area as such an entity. Over the years, its mandate has broadened to permit the organization to address other river-related problems that have mushroomed since 1948.

From its earliest days, ORSANCO's leaders were forced to become students of "ecopolitical systems" in order to keep the organization healthy amid the host of political dynamics surrounding its operation. Joseph L. Fisher, former president of Resources for the Future, Inc., has written:

> The interstate compact has long offered a possible basis for establishing an interstate agency to deal with problems of a regional nature, but the device has seldom been utilized successfully to deal with complex problems. ORSANCO is an outstanding exception: an interstate compact agency with a long and successful record of dealing with a complex day-to-day planning and operation task . . . (it) is of special interest to students of American government interested in the evolution of the federal system.[5]

Though Fisher was writing in 1967, few knowledgeable government officials or industrial leaders would dispute his assessment. The ORSANCO annals contain many proposals for the management of the Ohio River area. One of the most creative has been an offer to formally aid public utilities and governments in the selection of sites for industrial facilities, particularly electric power plants. The year 1991 marks the forty-third year of ORSANCO's existence as a viable entity.

Cleary, who long served as ORSANCO's director, was one of the few who occasionally pondered the possibility that ORSANCO might expand its interests into related areas. There are indications that he anticipated the political convulsions—some of them related to ecological awareness—of the late 1960s. But in retrospect his ORSANCO leadership seems less representative of today's ecologists than of the sanitary engineers and public health specialists of previous decades who, alarmed over the condition of America's rivers and streams, called themselves conservationists. To illustrate, neither "environment" nor "ecology" appears in Cleary's carefully prepared index.

THE ENVIRONMENTAL MOVEMENT

In the late 1960s, a more militant group of conservation advocates emerged who preferred to be known as environmentalists. Far less optimistic about the future than Cleary and his cohorts, some were brutally critical of prevailing notions of future planning for the Ohio River, its valley, and its basin. These individuals often claimed that ownership of corporations in the Ohio Valley—whether their products were coal, steel, chemicals, glass, or electric power—was most often centered outside the broader basin. A prime example was the export of electric power, particularly to large metropolitan areas outside the valley and the basin. This outside or absentee ownership of resources and the export of products contributed to a deteriorating environment.

Among the most vociferous critics was John Flynn, a journalist on valley newspapers and later a free-lance environmental writer who characterized the Ohio River and its basin as the "packhorse of the East." In a recent essay, he wrote:

> For the first half of this century, this area labored as the packhorse of the steel industry, shipping its hand-loaded coal primarily by rail to northern production centers. On one occasion, in 1948, in Donora, Pennsylvania, combustion of this coal resulted in human deaths from a prolonged episode of acidic fog. But pollution from the earlier open fires, and later the short stacks of the steel mills, generally fell locally in the form of sooty particulants. Pittsburgh, the capital of the interlocked coal and steel industries, earned a reputation as one of the dirtiest places in America.[6]

In what might be seen as a twentieth century miracle, the city once known as "hell with the lid taken off" is now described by the media as one of the most desirable American cities in which to live. Flynn and others in the environmental movement concur, acknowledging that the post–World War II decline of steel and abandonment of coal as a home heating source caused "the soot . . . to disappear from Pittsburgh skies."[7] But new kinds of environmental problems in the broader Ohio River Basin have emerged, including abuses to the land and water from strip mining of coal, erosion of topsoil, chemical plant pollution, and the formation of acid rain.

Vast amounts of energy were required for all of the major industries that developed in the valley. Coal provided the fuel necessary to generate electric power. But a new realization became more prevalent across the nation following World War II that greater concern for air quality was essential.

By the early 1970s, environmental pressures were contributing to two significant and related developments which are critical to understanding complexities now surrounding the Ohio Basin ecopolitical system: (1) oil and natural gas, much of it imported from the Middle East, were replacing basin coal in many industrial processes, including the generating of electric power; and (2) the federal government was encouraging the construction of tall smokestacks at new power plants to protect nearby communities from air pollution.

Use of foreign oil and natural gas was supported by environmentalists because they contained less sulfur than most Ohio Basin coal. But the 1973 Arab oil embargo demonstrated that dependence upon foreign fossil fuels could threaten our national security. Also relevant was that, even at that early date, a significant portion of the American population was suspicious of nuclear-generated electric power. Thus, concerns over nuclear power and risks associated with utilization of foreign oil and gas in 1973 and 1974 made Ohio Basin coal a more attractive fuel, particularly for use in electric power plants. Coal industry leaders in all six states bordering the Ohio River began to argue effectively that their product was the best available fuel source for the nation's future. As they put it, Ohio Basin coal was our country's "ace in the hole."

However, as memories of the embargo faded and national concerns over air quality mounted, the issue of coal burning in the Ohio Basin gradually became almost an obsession with national policymakers during the mid and late 1980s. Mainly responsible for the Ohio Basin's prominent role in the national air quality debate was the concentration of electric power generating stations in the area, particularly along the Ohio River itself.

Central to the debate are the scientific uncertainties that remain in regard to generation of electric power through the burning of fossil fuels. A majority of scientists now agree that the tall stacks of massive electric power plants in the Ohio Valley are definitely involved in the formation of acid rain, emitting pollutants in the form of sulfur dioxide and nitrogen oxides which are carried by prevailing winds toward the Northeast. These compounds presumably undergo further chemical reactions in the atmosphere while traveling long distances, becoming chemical actors in the process whereby acid rain falls on the northeastern states and Canada.

In September 1990 a report was released by the National Acid Precipitation Assessment Program (NAPAP). A decade-long project mandated by Congress, this $537 million study has concluded that acid rain is a long-term problem but not a "flat-out" environmental crisis. The report supports many concerns expressed by scientists about acid rain—that it affects visibility, erodes buildings, damages trees, reduces soil nutrients, and kills fish and other forms of aquatic life. The study notes that a 10-million-ton cut in sulfur dioxide emissions would reverse the trend. This is the approximate amount of reduction contained in the 1990 Clean Air Act which was passed shortly before this volume went to press.[8]

While an extensive analysis of the impact of the Clean Air legislation cannot be undertaken here, one reality is clear in even a cursory examination of the atmospheric process whereby Ohio Valley power plants affect "downwind" states. An ecopolitical system has developed from the combination of ecological phenomena and legal/political realities. Americans have been given graphic descriptions of the workings of this ecopolitical system almost daily by the media over recent years. The issue was framed in terms of region with lawmakers in the East and the West resisting attempts to have them share the cost of cleaning up the power plants with the nine Midwestern and Ohio Valley states. The controversy suggests that ecologists like Bedford and Levin are correct in warning that students of ecosystems should not draw rigid boundaries around a given area.

Another reality is that the Ohio River ecopolitical system is not just a single entity. It is many systems which have been subjectively defined at various times in history. Little attention has been given to maintaining a careful history of ecopolitical dynamics. The recent action to revise the Clean Air Act is but one issue in understanding the ecopolitics of the Ohio Valley—and the broader basin; the region is replete with other examples, one of the most important of which is the ecopolitical system known as the Tennessee Valley.

THE TENNESSEE VALLEY AUTHORITY AND OAK RIDGE

While somewhat remote from the six "border" or valley states, Tennessee is essential for understanding the broader basin's ecopolitical system; this state is intertwined politically and sociologically with its neighbors in the entire Ohio River Basin, which includes portions of fourteen states. The Tennessee River is a major tributary of the Ohio which delays its approach into the larger Ohio until it reaches a point near Paducah, Kentucky, only thirty-five miles upstream from the Ohio's mouth at Cairo. The state of Tennessee contains a major portion of the land and water managed by the Tennessee Valley Authority, whose area, defined by the Tennessee River Basin, is undoubtedly the nation's most controversial regional entity.

The Tennessee River, then, is both an ecopolitical system and a part of the larger ecopolitical system represented by the overall Ohio River Basin. TVA is the only genuine regional natural resource corporation to which Congress has delegated many functional responsibilities and/or powers normally administered by the seven states involved: Tennessee, the state which contains by far the largest portion of the Tennessee River Basin; Kentucky; Alabama; Mississippi; Georgia; North Carolina; and Virginia. While Kentucky is the only one that borders the Ohio River, portions of all the other TVA states are located in the Ohio River Basin.

Even before the first self-sustaining nuclear reaction was achieved at the University of Chicago in December of 1942, TVA was destined for a unique role in America's victory in World War II. Months before the momentous Chicago event, plans were being made to exploit the natural and human-made resources in the Tennessee Valley. Nuclear policymakers, lodged in the fabled Manhattan Project, identified the TVA region as the site for what some were beginning to call the world's first "atomic bomb factory."

The search for a location for a full-size, functional industrial installation had led to the Knoxville area, where several streams rolled out of the Appalachian mountains. Because TVA had harnessed the power of these streams, it could guarantee the hundreds of millions of watts of electricity needed for the atomic factory. There were many other advantages to this location: it had valleys where buildings could be constructed, a relatively sparse population, much land which had not been cultivated, and a secure setting in the interior. Within a few weeks acquisition by the federal government of the 56,000-acre site—a part of which would soon become the town of Oak Ridge—was complete.

Both the drama and the technological significance of the choice of Oak Ridge for bomb production are seen in this description by two historians of the period:

> On a muggy morning in September, 1942, General [Lester R.] Groves stood at a vantage point near the hamlet of Elza, Tennessee, and looked southwest over the terrain where the race for the atomic bomb might well be won or lost. . . . In the weeks following the General's visit, local residents abandoned their churches, homes, schools, and roads, as the Army quickly acquired the entire area as a military reservation. . . . With no thought of building a permanent or ideal community, the Army set out to construct a temporary, low-cost housing development.[9]

The 1942 Oak Ridge siting decision may have been the most influential step toward placing the broader Ohio River Basin at the center of the world's nuclear fuel cycle "ecopolitical system" for the next half century. Oak Ridge is located on the Clinch River, a tributary of the Tennessee. With the Tennessee itself a tributary of the Ohio, a large area within the broader Ohio River Basin became central to the Manhattan Project. Atomic power management was first introduced to the world as a result of a wide variety of activities performed at Oak Ridge, particularly by the massive uranium enrichment plant there. Later, we shall note the significance of the Oak Ridge "reservation" for the present controversy over nuclear weapons waste. Undoubtedly ecopolitical diplomats of the future, whether in advanced or developing countries, will discover some helpful lessons from this Ohio Basin experience.

OTHER NUCLEAR FACILITIES

Few Ohio Basin residents fully understand the extent of the role played by their area in management of the nuclear fuel cycle. While the community of Oak Ridge may seem remote from the mainstem of the Ohio River, it was the first critical industrial link in this complicated uranium-based development. Later, other nuclear installations for both power generation and weapons production were built in the upper portion of the Ohio River Basin.

Attempts to discuss nuclear weapons plants in this country have been discouraged, if not prohibited, until recently. Little information has been made public regarding the relationship of these facilities and nuclear weapons. Perhaps one of the most desirable results of this chapter would be to encourage Americans—in the Ohio Valley and elsewhere—to understand our country's complex nuclear fuel cycle. For some years, at least, the broader Ohio basin was apparently the region of the country in which *all* basic uranium enrichment processes—both for weapons and for power plants—was carried out. Today, the number of nuclear materials plants in the region still makes it a prime region for educating citizens about this ill-understood technology.

The lifting of the veil of secrecy surrounding nuclear weapons installations is relevant, of course, to such an educational effort. An apparent new "openness" by the U.S. Department of Energy, now manager of all nuclear facilities—whether weapons oriented or dedicated to commercial fuel preparation—now permits an understanding of the cycle not previously possible. It also allows us to sort out the difference between the preparation and refining of uranium for weapons and the processing required for commercial power plant fuel. Once we gain such an understanding from our own Ohio Basin nuclear materials segment, a broader perspective on the nation's total nuclear sector is possible. This in turn may enable us to learn lessons of use for other countries on Planet Earth.

The story of the expansion of nuclear plants in the Ohio basin has its beginnings in August 1945 when, following the dropping of atomic bombs on Hiroshima and Nagasaki, the Japanese surrendered. Though no map of our nation's nuclear complex was available to the public at the time, such a map of major installations would have shown: (1) residual facilities of the old Metallurgical Laboratory in the Chicago area; (2) the Ohio Basin's Oak Ridge installation which included its uranium enrichment plant; (3) a bomb production plant at Hanford, Washington; and (4) the Los Alamos facility in New Mexico. The enormity of these projects and the haste with which they were built are now almost impossible to imagine.

Under the AEC, progress in developing reactors for commercial use required that steps be taken to provide additions to the gaseous diffusion capability provided at Oak Ridge. In November 1950 the commission approved construction of a new gaseous diffusion uranium enrichment plant near Paducah, Kentucky, not far from the banks of the Ohio River. From the beginning it was clear that the new plant would be operated in close cooperation with Oak Ridge. Indeed the site was selected because so many of Oak Ridge's advantages were present at Paducah. Though these decisions were made in secret, the broader basin characteristics, in particular the abundance of river water, were responsible for the choice of both sites.

To supply immense amounts of electric power for the proposed Paducah facility, the AEC resorted to a scheme which allowed the agency to partially avoid direct confrontation in an ongoing battle between investor-owned utilities and TVA. The Paducah area is within the TVA service area. But the private utilities and their supporters—mainly individuals in the Republican party—successfully argued that a group of electric power companies across the river in Illinois should share in providing power to the new plant. The AEC awarded one contract for plant construction to TVA and another contract to private utilities. This unusual AEC compromise still contains political imagery that is helpful in making meaningful distinctions between the methods for delivering electric power in the Ohio River Valley, which still favors the "private" sector, and in its most prominent tributary, the Tennessee, which remains wedded to "public" power.

Union Carbide apparently served the nation well in managing the Oak Ridge uranium enrichment facility in its early years and probably did the same at Paducah. But given the environmental abuses which have allegedly occurred at several nuclear weapons sites, the management of such facilities is a proper question for examination by the general public in a democratic society.

As the Paducah plant was nearing completion in 1952, President Harry S Truman cited production rates projected for nuclear weapons which would require increased gaseous-diffusion capacity for uranium enrichment. Once more the U.S. government turned to an Ohio River Basin site, one located about eighty-five miles upriver from Cincinnati near Portsmouth. Again, ample water supplies and the availability of massive amounts of electric power were critical factors in site selection.

With the completion of this new installation in the mid-1950s, all three of the nation's uranium enrichment facilities—at Oak Ridge, Paducah, and Portsmouth—were located in the Ohio Basin, the latter two squarely in the valley not far from the Ohio River itself. Little information is available as to whether the Portsmouth decision was preceded by considerations of environmental effects from the plant. In 1952, when plans were being made for the facility, the nation was still nearly twenty years away from the advent of federally mandated impact statements.

Aspiring ecopolitical diplomats would find the Portsmouth facility and its linkages to other energy-related installations on a 200-mile reach of the Ohio River a stimulating case study. Such a study would support John Flynn's argument that the "packhorse" of the eastern United States has been saddled with complex and subtle burdens.

The Oak Ridge enrichment plant site was ideal because of electric power generated by TVA hydroelectric facilities. The power supply required for the Paducah installation came equally from TVA generating stations and privately owned and operated plants. During the 1950s, more than half of the electric power generated by TVA went to these two uranium enrichment plants. As a part of the Portsmouth construction job, the federal government contracted with a consortium of midwestern utilities to build two gigantic new coal-fired plants which would provide the immense amount of electric power needed. The new stations were the Clifty Creek plant near Madison, Indiana (nearly 150 miles to the west of Portsmouth), and the Kyger Creek plant, near Cheshire, Ohio (about 50 miles to the east). Probably no other two power plants in the nation have received more publicity as likely sources of emissions involved in acid rain formation from the Ohio Valley corridor. The subtle linking of one phase of the nuclear fuel cycle with acid rain ironically illustrates the complexity of ecopolitical analysis.

Today, virtually all facilities associated with the nuclear fuel cycle are being viewed critically because of serious waste management difficulties. The Portsmouth plant still enriches atomic fuel for commercial nuclear reactors and the defense industry. In 1979, the U.S. Department of Energy (DOE) began building a new facility for an enrichment process known formally as "gas centrifuge" at nearby Piketon, which was expected to modernize uranium enrichment procedures. After spending $3 billion for the new system, the DOE decided in 1985 that a new laser technology was superior and closed the Piketon facility shortly after it was opened. Federal officials later admitted its construction had been a costly mistake, blaming the error on lack of foresight in the development of atomic technology. The DOE plans to move ahead with the new technology, known as Atomic Vapor Laser Separation (AVLS). The Piketon installation, along with DOE sites at Paducah and Oak Ridge, is a prominent candidate for a new plant which will utilize the AVLS process. DOE expects to approve a preferred site by November of 1992. Thus the Ohio Basin could provide the locale for the next act in the uranium enrichment ecopolitical drama.

The early 1950s also saw the construction of another Ohio DOE facility which the public understood to be a "feed materials production center." Built near Fernald, a small town about twenty miles northwest of Cincinnati, it in fact was a uranium processing plant. An almost unprecedented disclosure in 1987–88 revealed extensive radiation and hazardous waste emanating from the Fernald plant, only a few miles from the Ohio River. Even DOE officials acknowledge that it was an environmental disaster of extreme proportions. The DOE suspended production at Fernald in 1989 to concentrate on the cleanup of uranium contamination and the removal of hazardous wastes. These include wastes from the early Chicago experiments that have apparently been stored for more than three decades on the plant's 1,050-acre site. The DOE has recently announced that lifetime medical monitoring will be provided as part of a $78 million court settlement for 14,000 Fernald residents living within five miles of the plant.

In emphasizing the problems at Fernald, it should not be overlooked that other less prominent, nuclear weapons–related installations were placed in Ohio during the same period. These include the Mound facility near Dayton, inside the Ohio Basin, and the facility at Ashtabula, outside the basin near Cleveland.

COMMERCIAL NUCLEAR PLANTS

The building of commercial nuclear power plants for generation of electric power did not commence until the late 1950s. While no American region has faced a nuclear power plant tragedy to match that which occurred at the Soviet Union's Chernobyl facility, it should be noted that Pennsylvania's Three Mile Island accident occurred within a few miles of the Ohio drainage basin. Also, the broader basin itself contains several commercial nuclear plants, including a number of TVA units at which mishaps have occurred. If our historical scanning of the impact of "atomic energy" in the basin is to have any real meaning, we cannot ignore such generating facilities. But it seems most reasonable to concentrate upon unique nuclear power installations located upon the Ohio River itself.

The world entered the nuclear age when the first sustained nuclear reaction was achieved in that Chicago laboratory in 1942. Not until fifteen years later, at an Ohio River site near Shippingport, Pennsylvania—about twenty-five miles northwest of Pittsburgh—did the first nuclear power plant begin to generate electricity. The facility was jointly owned by the U.S. Atomic Energy Commission (AEC) and the Duquesne Light Company. Pittsburgh, once prominent as a producer of steel made possible by the burning of coal, now became known for its achievements in nuclear technology. In part this was possible because of the presence of the corporate headquarters of Westinghouse which, along with General Electric, dominated the reactor field in the late 1950s and early 1960s.

The bountiful coal supplies in the broader Ohio River Basin have discouraged the location of many nuclear power plants along the mainstem. These few have been plagued by both economic and perceived environmental problems, though fortunately not as severe as those associated with the TMI accident. The pioneer Shippingport plant became the source of one of the most prominent environmental health controversies. In the early 1970s, there was intense debate over possible involvement of Shippingport in apparent increases in cancer, leukemia, and infant mortality all along the Ohio River from Pittsburgh to Cincinnati. Yet, in 1972, Duquesne Light Company claimed that it was the "cleanest, safest nuclear plant in the world." While the company contended that the Shippingport installation had not released one bit of radioactive gas in a year's period, critics claimed that "radioactive wastes . . . greatly exceeded legal discharge limits" and might explain increased health risks.[10] The Shippingport reactor was retired in 1982; debates about its environmental impact still continue.

The Midwest has been described as a "nuclear power plant graveyard" because of the more than $14 billion spent on projects that were never completed. Among these was a plant located on the Ohio River, the Marble Hill nuclear station near Madison, Indiana. The chief owner, Public Service Company of Indiana (PSI), stopped Marble Hill construction in January of 1984 and mothballed the twin-unit power plant, which was almost half complete. The formal cancellation by PSI in November 1984 was accompanied by a statement that $2.34 billion had been spent by the company at Marble Hill. More than $7.7 billion was needed to complete the project as a nuclear plant. About the same time, a power consortium known as the Wabash Valley Association, with a 17 percent share of Marble Hill, announced that it would restructure its own $478.8 million debt in the plant. As of late 1990, the fate of the half-completed structure, plagued by defective concrete, remains uncertain. Much discussion earlier centered on conversion of the facility to enable it to generate electric power by burning coal; this option has apparently been discarded.

In terms of technological innovation, a power plant less than 150 miles east of Madison (about 50 miles upriver from Cincinnati) has probably attracted more attention than any other in the country. This is the Zimmer plant, originally planned as a nuclear facility, but now nearing completion as a coal-burning station. Zimmer's owners, Cincinnati Gas & Electric, Dayton Power & Light, and American Electric Power's Columbus and Southern Ohio Electric subsidiary, plan to do what some scientists and engineers have said is impossible: convert the nuclear reactor-centered facility into an efficient coal-burning plant. According to a *Wall Street Journal* article,

> When the utilities announced in January [1984] that they intended to convert the plant, the announcement was greeted by howls. Making a coal-fired plant out of a nuke made about as much sense as trying to shoe-horn an eight-cylinder engine into a Volkswagen Beetle, engineers warned. . . .
>
> What most of them said was that steam comes rushing out from a coal boiler much hotter and with greater intensity than it DOES from a nuclear reactor. That means the turbines and generators

> that convert the steam to electricity have to be designed very differently. If you just patch on a scaled-down coal boiler, the engineers said, you get a plant with a piddling power capacity that wastes much of the coal's heating power.[11]

Apparently Zimmer's owners believe they have found a way to turn that potential problem into a positive situation. They claim that, by letting the steam first drive a new, higher-powered turbine and generator, and then drive Zimmer's existing, lower-powered machinery, a highly efficient coal-fired plant will result.

The various cooperating utilities in the Zimmer project expect to have the converted plant on line by June 1991. Calling the conversion effort a clear success, company officials cite "modularized construction" as a major factor in what many believe to be a highly significant model for power generating entities around the globe. Throughout this complex political dilemma, leaders of the affected utilities were cognizant of the long-term "coal versus nuclear" arguments. If the Zimmer experiment is indeed successful, the enterprise could be one of the first examples of ecopolitical success available from experiences in the Ohio Valley.

CITIZEN OPPOSITION

In the summer and fall of 1974 while the nation was recovering from the 1973–74 Arab oil embargo, utility leaders joined a great many other Americans who strongly felt the country was too dependent on foreign oil. Indeed, in the early weeks of the embargo, then-President Richard Nixon had called for a massive "Project Independence" effort which would free America of dependence upon oil from overseas by 1980. Central to proposals of Nixon and others was a greater emphasis upon both coal and nuclear energy in the generation of electric power. As leaders in government and industry viewed the national landscape for possible sites for new power stations, portions of the Ohio River Basin seemed to rank near the top—perhaps at the very top—of almost everyone's list.

A number of factors seemed to favor the location of new power plants on the banks of the Ohio River itself. As suggested by the map in Figure 2, two rich coalfields are evident: (1) the Appalachian Coal Province (ranging from western Penn-

Figure 2

ORBES Region, Showing The Two Coalfields

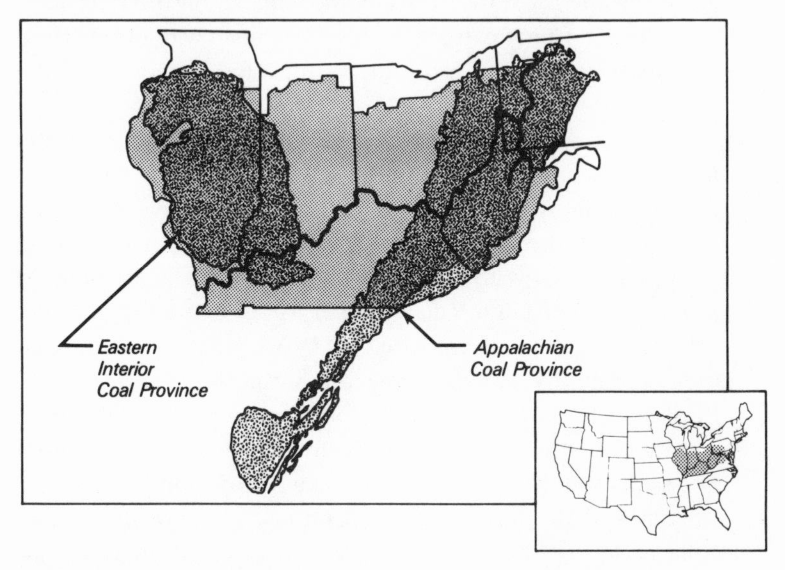

Adapted from *Ohio River Basin Energy Study (ORBES): Main Report*, 1981

sylvania, eastern Ohio, and West Virginia down through eastern Kentucky, Tennessee, and Alabama; and (2) the Eastern Interior Coal Province (underlying a great portion of Illinois and portions of southwestern Indiana and western Kentucky).

To the east, Pittsburgh had long utilized both the Ohio River and coal in the Appalachian Province to build an unprecedented steel industry. The river's water had also been used, along with the nearby coal, to operate large coal-fired power plants near Pittsburgh and throughout most of the northern reaches of the river. Also, pioneering U.S. efforts to use nuclear reactors to generate electric power were centered near Pittsburgh. Thus both coal and nuclear facilities already crowded the northern reaches of the Ohio River in Pennsylvania, and coal plants filled most of the appropriate sites down through Ohio and West Virginia. However, the southern (or lower) portions of the river offered a great many potential sites for power generating facilities. As the embargo ended early in 1974, utilities indicated preferences for sites on open farmland in southern Indiana and northern Kentucky—particularly from Louisville northeast to the Indiana-Ohio border (near Cincinnati).

Citizen opposition to siting new power plants in the lower portion of the Ohio mobilized rapidly. A group of concerned citizens living in and near Madison, Indiana, on the river midway between Cincinnati and Louisville, joined with others from the Kentucky side to form an organization called "Save the Valley" (STV).

It was no accident that this opposition was centered in the Madison area. Only a few miles away, Marble Hill was under construction by late 1974; in addition, a massive coal-fired plant with exceedingly tall stacks, Clifty Creek, had been in operation since the 1950s on the outskirts of the community by a consortium of Ohio Valley utilities. A large number of Madison citizens, long resentful of Clifty Creek and fearing that their community might become a national "sacrifice" area, enthusiastically supported STV's opposition to further encroachments. Probably the most nationally prominent figure within STV ranks was Dr. Harold G. Cassidy, Professor Emeritus of Chemistry, Yale University, and Professor-at-Large at Hanover College, located at Madison. Upon retirement from Yale, Cassidy had moved to Madison, and he provided STV with scientific expertise and credibility helpful in opposing planning by the utilities in the absence of an impact study. In the mid-1970s, Cassidy joined with Fred Hauck, a Kentucky engineer and ardent environmentalist, to provide a team which has been extremely effective in presenting STV's views over a period of fifteen years. The broader community surrounding Madison also has produced an unusual number of environmental strategists. STV's success in organizing, documenting their opposition to the facility, and predicting the fate of Marble Hill represents one of the nation's most revealing case studies of the work of non-paid environmentalists, another example of what may be described as "ecopolitical" scanning.

Early in its development, STV argued that existing plants were already exporting large amounts of electric power from the region. The specific case of the Clifty Creek plant provided a poignant example of technological linkages between coal as a fuel and uranium as a source of fuel for both commercial power plants and nuclear weapons. Clifty Creek was originally built as one of two coal plants which would transmit virtually all of its electric power to the uranium enrichment installation located near Portsmouth, Ohio. The uranium processes at Portsmouth ultimately would be used to produce both commercial fuel rods and nuclear weapons.

As the early months of 1974 passed, a number of Ohio residents joined their Indiana and Kentucky neighbors either in formal STV membership or in sharing concerns. By that summer STV had contacted a great many federal and state agencies, seeking action to delay plans for additional power plant construction until a study could be conducted of the impact of such facilities. But they claimed they were given the "runaround" by all parties.

Frustration was great at STV until an event occurred in 1974 that gave its members the opportunity they had been seeking. Birch Bayh, already a two-term U.S. Senator from Indiana, was in the midst of his bid for reelection. A campaign swing through southern Indiana brought Bayh to the Madison area. He soon discovered that not only STV but a great many of his other southern Indiana constituents were concerned about plans to build several more massive power stations in the area. Bayh therefore arranged a meeting in Washington involving several agencies and STV leadership to pursue the possibility of mounting a study to assess the effects of power plants on the region. Following that meeting, Bayh persuaded colleagues on the Senate Appropriations Committee to attach a provision to EPA's 1975 fiscal year budget directing the agency to conduct the desired study. Upon recommendation of the committee, the U.S. Congress approved legislation for an EPA study of "the proposed concentration of power plants" along the Ohio River in Ohio, Kentucky, Indiana, and Illinois.[12]

ORBES

Since few congressional research directives had been received by EPA, the federal agency clearly viewed the proposed study with trepidation. Adding to its concern, Senate sponsors wanted the project to be undertaken by university researchers within the four designated states rather than by government or industrial scientists. Thus EPA officials were faced with the task of designing a research project—in effect an ecosystem science study—whose vital elements had already been determined by the Congress, a body which, of course, is highly political in nature. This 1975 action may be considered one of the nation's first efforts to create an "ecopolitical system," and the EPA officials who designed the study were likely among the world's first ecopolitical diplomats.

Ecopolitical diplomacy of a sort rarely practiced before was necessary as EPA officials took steps to form boundaries for the study and select university researchers. EPA leadership realized that the very naming of the project was fraught with political sensitivities. Without the advantage of time to consider the subtle distinctions among such terms as valley, basin, and watershed, the Congress had utilized language in the mandate which was contradictory. Eventually EPA chose to call the project the Ohio River Basin Energy Study (ORBES).

While citing four "valley" or "border" states (Ohio, Kentucky, Indiana, and Illinois) as the locale for the study, Congress also spoke of facilities in the "lower Ohio River Basin." As noted earlier, the lower *basin* would be much further to the South than any portions of the four states identified in the directive to EPA. Clearly, Senator Bayh and his fellow sponsors mainly wanted a study of the lower *valley*, not of the basin. Perhaps even more troublesome was the demand from Congress that the study should also "take into account the availability of coal" in the region they had roughly defined. The geologic map shown in Figure 2 illustrates the dilemma faced by EPA in trying to design a research project which would meet the specifications relating to coal reserves in the basin and yet limit it to portions of the four states listed.

In retrospect, the intention of the bill's sponsors was to obtain a study that emphasized *lower* parts of the Eastern Interior Coal Province found in southern Illinois, southwestern Indiana, and western Kentucky. But ecopolitical diplomats at EPA realized very quickly that a strict interpretation of the mandate would not achieve objectives desired by anyone. The project would have little credibility if it used state lines as boundaries for an ecosystem study. If an understanding of the coal situation was as important as the congressional mandate suggested, the study could not focus on the four states while ignoring adjacent coalfields in the neighboring states of Pennsylvania, West Virginia, and Tennessee.

Similarly, as already suggested, the use of the term "basin" proved awkward. Because of the necessity to examine coal production and use, EPA and the university researchers quickly expanded the ORBES study region to include relevant counties in the states north of the basin line. However, the fragility and tentativeness of hastily devised ecosystems were soon demonstrated. Responses from the two Ohio River "border" states excluded from the study—West Virginia and Pennsylvania—

caused EPA to expand the ORBES study region to include the basin portions of those states in the project after the first year.

State governments were not the only ones who complained of the boundaries set for ORBES. A number of other important sectors argued that neither the Ohio River Basin nor the valley was an appropriate "system" for meeting the study's energy-oriented objectives. Prominent in taking this position were the electric power utilities, who claimed that none of the regional study areas considered adequately reflected their power grids and "reliability" systems.

The major point is that Congress created an ORBES ecosystem region that did not match the needs prescribed by Congress itself. Some scientists might cite the ORBES experience in setting boundaries for an ecosystem study as an example of why politicians should not take upon themselves the mandating of such studies. But if we recall the counsel of Bedford and Levin it would seem that politicians and scientists must cooperate in such enterprises. Perhaps the ORBES experience proves their point. STV's original "political" demand for a study focused on a relatively small area led to action at a high level in the federal government. Though Congress clearly failed in its efforts to define the most appropriate ecosystem, it put in place a study that led to much interaction among various sectors. If an acceptable quality of life is to be maintained in this region—and the country as a whole—cooperation among these sectors must be improved.

The ORBES study elements attracting most public attention were those associated with long-range transport of air pollutants, acid rain, and the institutional difficulties inherent in environmental problems that are regional in nature. Central to these difficulties is the complexity of the situation with regard to the area's power plants. Its variety of installations in terms of wattage capability and other characteristics makes generalization very difficult. Many hundreds of generating stations provide electric power in the region, ranging in size from small facilities operated by such diverse entities as towns, hospitals, and other quasi-public organizations to the massive plants of giant investor-owned utility corporations. The latter are most critical, of course, in understanding the broad ecosystems of either the valley or the broader basin. Even these large facilities vary greatly. In illustrating the pervasiveness of "large" installations in the study area, an ORBES survey identified more than seventy plants located on the river itself in "the first two rows of counties" bordering the stream. The criterion utilized in this compilation was "50 megawatts of energy or greater." (See Figure 3.) Several of these "valley" plants are producing nearly 3,000 megawatts, placing them among the most powerful generators in the world. Scores of comparable installations are located at varying distances from the Ohio River and in areas of the basin states distant from the mainstem itself.

The ORBES project itself and subsequent debates surrounding Clean Air Act amendments have demonstrated that great risks are attached to casual comments about the number of power plants in the Ohio River region. We have seen that almost every entity, including the U.S. Congress, has many definitions of the valley and the basin. Thus, allegations of abuses from "Ohio River power plants" are meaningless unless they are accompanied by precise definitions.

The final ORBES report was submitted to EPA, Congress, and President Reagan shortly after the latter's inauguration in January 1981. Approximately forty individual ORBES studies provided its foundation. As an "impact" study, the main report summarized a range of coal-based energy development scenarios for the study region. University researchers conducting the ORBES study projected likely impacts under various scenarios which might be devised by policymakers. But in keeping with EPA's understanding of the congressional mandate, ORBES researchers declined to offer "predictions" for the future, thus arousing the ire of environmental groups.

Through the entire four-year period of ORBES, a forty-member advisory committee met regularly to review the research process. The panel included corporate leadership from power companies and other private sector entities; government officials at all levels; and environmental groups such as STV and the Audubon Society. The final task of the committee members was to provide comments on the study's findings and the research process. The process and the findings alike drew both commendations and criticisms, many of them contradictory. Probably the most critical comments came from a group of utility executives on the ORBES advisory committee who had argued throughout the project that researchers had overstepped their congressional mandate by considering policy questions. According to this group, "the study is infected with a biased, misleading perspective . . . basic errors of science and . . . distorted conclusions." They continued:

the study design and presentation of results frustrate any meaningful evaluation of current policy. . . . The ORBES *Main Report* misleads the reader by failing adequately to point out that the National Ambient Air Quality Standards are protected and the regional air quality is improving . . . ORBES grossly overestimates the radiation induced health effects and fails to acknowledge relevant literature. . . . The ORBES crop damage results are based on incorrect theories, incorrect applications of theory, fail to recognize key scientific studies and greatly overestimate air pollution damage.[13]

One of the signatories, W. S. White, Jr., chairman of the American Electric Power Company, Inc. (AEP), a utility holding company that operates in the broader Ohio Basin, chose to offer additional personal views in a separate comment:

The ORBES Main Report . . . remains a classic example of (i) very bad science and (ii) a one-sided approach to highly complex and controversial subject matters. These two general defects are so fundamental and so infect the entire Main Report as to render it worse than useless as a policy tool—worse than useless in the sense that the Main Report is misleading in many respects. . . . Because the Main Report is so scientifically defective and so warped, we urge that it be withdrawn and discarded. . . . We are confident that the Report's numerous technical weaknesses will not withstand competent peer review by the [EPA] Science Advisory Board or the National Academy of Sciences [NAS].[14]

At the other extreme, Ralph Madison, vice president of the Kentucky Audubon Council, countered by criticizing the failure of the study to make recommendations for action:

It is, in fact, no more than a magnificent example of statistics gathering, dedicated to and destined to be used thoroughly by the utility industry. It will serve only to confuse our so-called political decision makers who will be forced to react only to the demands made by each one's specific constituency.

It is deplorable that this study, costing in excess of $4 million, was not designed to produce a *recommendation* on what should be done. The information was gathered by faculty members of some of our greatest universities in an outstanding and imposing example of in-depth and critical research. Who, better than this group of over 100 investigators could be in a position to make a sound recommendation for the future?

Madison cited the need for specific recommendations setting limits on the number of power plants, emissions, sitings, and political arrangements. Its failure to make them, instead simply

Figure 3

Location Of Plants (50 MWe Or Greater) In The First Two Rows Of Counties Bordering The Ohio River Main Stem In EPA Regions III, IV and V

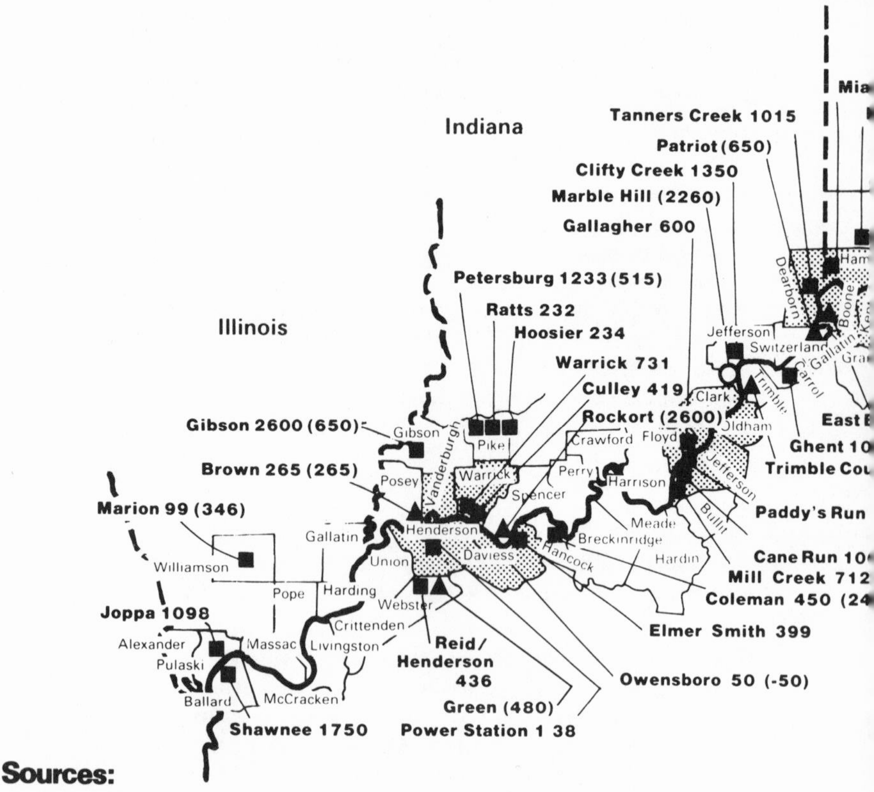

Sources:

(1) Steven D. Jansen, Electrical Generating Unit Inventory, Nov. 1978. Energy Resource Center, Chicago Ill. University of Illinois at Chicago Circle, Prepared for Ohio River Basin Energy Study (ORBES)

(2) ECAR Region Site Inventory 7/18/79, Owen Lentz, Executive Manager

Prepared By:
U.S. Environmental Protection Agency, Region V
Graphic Arts Section

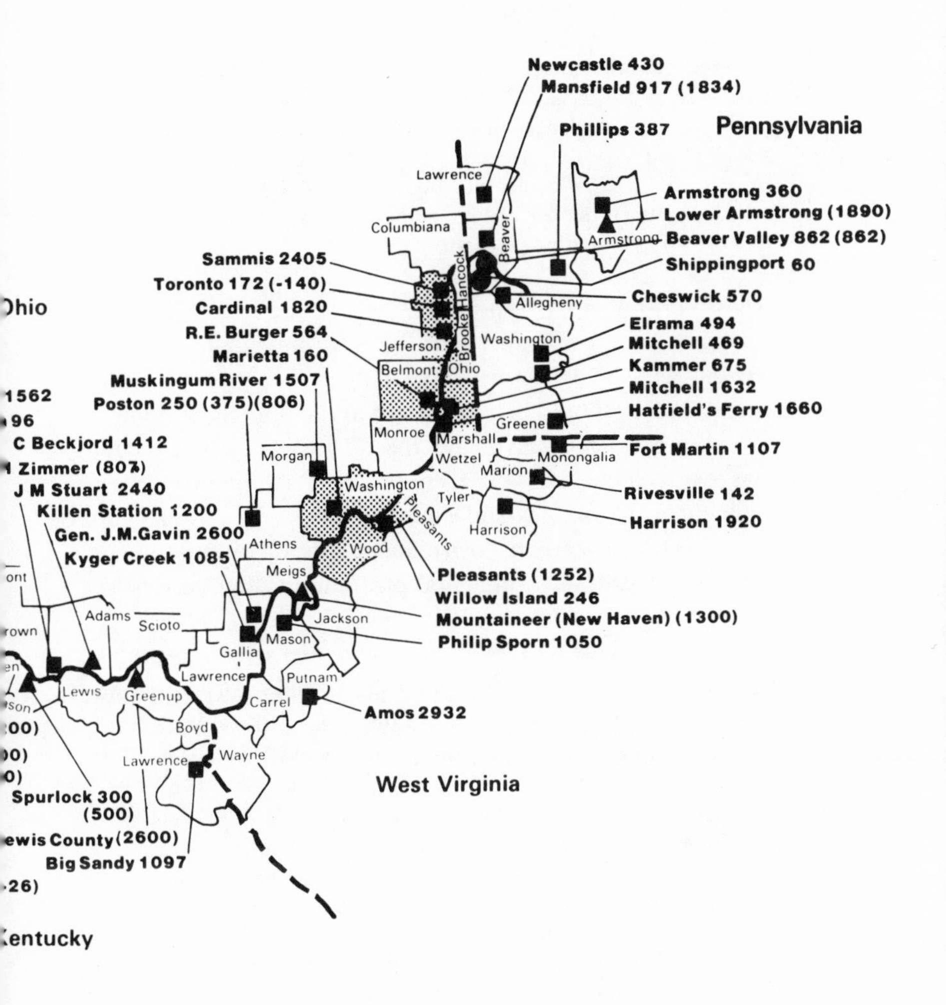

Nuclear

● In service○

○ Under construction or planned through 1986

Coal

■ In service○

▲ Under construction or planned through 1986

SMSA

○ Numbers following plant name indicate total MWe capacity corrected to 1979 where information available. Additions under construction or planned are in parenthesis. Retirements are preceeded by a minus sign. Because of constant change these numbers may not represent current status warning that inaction could drain "much-needed vitality from the region and the nation at large," was

> the most glaring deficiency of the entire report. All the investigators were aware of each piece of research developed, and each piece was discussed. Whether the information was scientifically, socially or politically oriented, it was thoroughly discussed in open sessions. How could they be denied the authority and the responsibility to make carefully authenticated recommendations to solve an admittedly severe problem?[15]

These contradictory responses by representatives of two sectors—the power companies and the environmentalists—illustrate the wide gap between knowledgeable people on how future planning should be carried out in the region. At numerous working sessions involving the advisory committee and ORBES esearchers such differences arose frequently. Most prominent were charges and counter-charges by power company representatives and environmentalists on the nature of future energy and environmental planning in the Ohio Valley area.

A leading spokesman for the environmentalists at these advisory committee meetings was Harold Cassidy. Disappointed that EPA and ORBES researchers did not treat philosophical and ethical questions in its study, he summarized his reactions:

> I gained the impression that there was strong opposition to including this kind of philosophical-technical-boundary condition type of discussion in the Report. It seems to me that such discussion would have been of signal benefit to all sides of this complicated network of issues.
>
> I wish to end on the positive note that this monumental effort by the Core Team and the Project Management Team deserves to bear fruit. It has given us a remarkable example of the value of openness and rational discussion in attacking many difficult and emotionally laden problems.[16]

Cassidy's challenge to develop an understanding of the "complicated network of issues" confronting the Ohio River area relates directly to the theme of this chapter—the opportunity for the region to become a prototype. Every nation on the planet faces similar river basin problems. Indeed, almost every nation shares such basins with one or more countries. Ohio River leadership has an unprecedented opportunity to serve as a model for these nations. But it cannot fulfill this opportunity unless it can inspire the basin's various feuding sectors—energy companies, environmentalists, political leaders, and others—to transcend their differences in mastering the Ohio basin's "complicated network of issues."

One important insight reported by the ORBES researchers is that the Ohio River Basin is far more diverse than they had suspected and probably more so than most public officials realize. This is evidenced in the story of two similarly named citizens' organizations. As we have already seen, Save the Valley (STV), centered around Madison, includes many individuals who fear that power plants and related installations will transform the area into one of heavy industry. STV spokespeople often extol the natural beauty and rural advantages of their section of the valley and talk of a desire to keep it from becoming "another Gary, Indiana, or Youngstown, Ohio," filled with factories and dirty air. Ironically, during the ORBES period a group was formed that was based in Youngstown, in the extreme northern part of the basin. Calling itself Save *Our* Valley (SOV), it had objectives that were diametrically opposed to those of STV. What SOV wanted to "save" were jobs that were being lost owing to the closing of area steel mills. Church leaders and others in Youngstown argued for the development of *more* industry. In its efforts to save jobs and to maintain what it viewed as a desirable quality of life, SOV contended that air quality standards must be relaxed. Equally committed individuals in STV had long called for the imposition of stricter air quality standards.

Research by ORBES scientists ended in 1980; the project itself, which had been funded with a $4.3 million appropriation, was terminated the following year with submission of the final ORBES report to its Washington, D.C., sponsors. There is evidence that ORBES findings have been utilized in a number of ways: (1) by government officials at various levels; (2) by ORBES scientists who continued to conduct research projects; (3) by corporate leaders in various sectors such as electric utilities and the coal industry; and (4) by other scientists who had not been affiliated with ORBES. There was sentiment in some circles to refashion ORBES as a continuing research organization, but no serious effort was mounted to continue the study in any form.

In 1985, five years after completion of the ORBES study, EPA research leadership stated:

> ORBES . . . is probably the largest multi-university, multi-disciplinary study ever undertaken. The sum total of many of the

> ORBES efforts was to bring home to many key midwestern and national political figures the reality of long-range transport of air pollutants, especially acid precipitation. While the ultimate solution to those threats continues to be debated, the 1981 ORBES report advanced the debate significantly toward rational resolution.[17]

For at least four reasons, the ORBES study may assume new significance in the 1990s: (1) the 1990 Clean Air Act, approved by Congress in late 1990, contains amendments focusing heavily upon coal use in the Ohio River Basin; (2) wide differences presently exist as to the possibility of electric power shortages in the coming decade; (3) renewed hostility in the Middle East has led to related concerns about the availability and costs of energy; and (4) the study has potential use as a model for governmental officials and the scientific community for multi-disciplinary approaches to broad global change research.[18]

CHEMICAL PLANTS

The ORBES congressional mandate had specifically directed university researchers to study "social, environmental and economic impacts" from electric power plants. Thus, the large number of chemical plants in the broader Ohio basin were not treated by the ORBES report.

The largest cluster of such facilities is located along West Virginia's Kanawha River, an Ohio tributary, which empties into the mainstem only a few miles to the West. The area surrounds Charleston, the state's capital. Almost four years following completion of the ORBES study, the world's worst industrial disaster occurred halfway around the planet, focusing attention on a specific site within the Kanawha River chemical complex. The tragedy occurred at Bhopal, India, where poison gas from a Union Carbide pesticide plant on December 3, 1984, claimed an estimated 3,000 lives and injured approximately 200,000. The Bhopal installation had been modeled after a "sister" facility located at the small community of Institute, West Virginia. In one of the most succinct summaries of connections between Bhopal and the West Virginia plant, one professional engineering society publication sought possible linkages between risk analysis failure at the older Institute plant and the Indian accident.[19] Since the Bhopal accident, a number of toxic chemical leaks have occurred at plants in the Charleston area, including a second Union Carbide plant five miles east of the Institute plant. Several plant workers and area residents have required hospitalization.

These recurring accidents have produced a great many research and monitoring initiatives at local, state, and national levels. A National Institute for Chemical Studies (NICS) was founded in 1985 by community leaders in the Kanawha Valley to promote understanding and reduction of risks posed by chemical industry operation, while preserving jobs and supporting economic growth. NICS also initiated several research projects, including one conducted by Harvard University's School of Public Health and Kennedy School of Government together with additional participants from Marshall University (Huntington, West Virginia). This study of the impact of chemical manufacturing on the health of valley residents was undertaken with the support of the EPA; its report on "Ambient Exposures to Volatile Organic Compounds in the Kanawha Valley" is forthcoming.

THE CLEAN AIR ACT

Research findings in recent years—to which a majority of scientists seem to subscribe—point to all six of the valley states as major contributors to atmospheric abuses that impact the northeastern United States and portions of Canada. The theory generally accepted is that emissions from massive Ohio Valley electric power generating plants are involved in chemical reactions in the atmosphere which contribute to acid rain.

The complexity of the valley's own ecopolitical system is reflected in 1990 congressional battles over the first major overhaul of the Clean Air Act since 1977. This debate replayed skirmishes staged for more than a decade in the nation's capital. U.S. senators and representatives from the Ohio Valley were leaders in opposing the revisions. For example, former Senate majority leader Robert Byrd of West Virginia almost singlehandedly blocked clean-air legislation for many years because it would hurt miners of high sulfur coal in his home state and neighboring areas. "Clean air is being extracted from the hides of those men and women," Senator Byrd said before voting against a bill approved by the Senate on April 3, 1990.

When a similar bill was being debated in the House of Representatives on May 23, another West Virginian, Congressman Robert Wise, led a successful effort to attach an amendment to the measure which provides $250 million to help those deprived of employment as a result of the new legislation. The Senate and House bills shared generally broad features by outlining action on several environmental fronts including cutting emissions involved in acid rain formation by half, requiring sharp reductions in smog-causing pollutants from automobiles, and demanding that industry control its releases of toxic chemicals. In the fall of 1990 a congressional conference committee blended the House and Senate versions into legislation. President Bush signed the legislation into law on November 15. Some critics argue that quite possibly no other legislation in American history has ever before so clearly targeted a region of the country or specifically focused upon a single industrial sector in that region. This sector, of course, is made up of the Ohio Valley electric utilities which operate some of the largest coal-fired power plants in the country. New requirements to decrease the plants' sulfur dioxide emissions in the region are estimated to cost as much as $46 billion a year and result in rate increases of 15 percent or more for customers of some Ohio Valley and midwestern installations.

THE NEED FOR REGIONAL COOPERATION

The TVA experiment in regional planning, the pioneer work and continuing activities of ORSANCO, and the research of ORBES from 1976 through 1980 are all examples of regional cooperation in the Ohio River Basin. Another is the Ohio River Basin Commission (ORBC), a nine-state planning group that originally included federal participation. Federal funding has been withdrawn, but the commission continues to operate on a limited basis. Other examples are the Association for the Development of Inland Navigation in America's Ohio Valley (DINAMO, which originated in 1895 as the Ohio Valley Improvement Association or OVIA), and the six-state Humanities Councils' "Always a River" project. In this essay many ecopolitical systems have been identified, illustrating the need to avoid rigid definitions of ecosystems.

It has been suggested that the region may possess the strongest foundation for broad planning of any river basin on the planet.

In addition to the fourteen states with territory in the Ohio River Basin, at least a dozen ongoing federal agencies are critical actors in the region, each with differing missions and perspectives. The most important are the U.S. Army Corps of Engineers and the Environmental Protection Agency. These agencies define the region as ecosystems with different boundaries. The newcomer to government and politics will likely respond that such a situation is nonsense. Surely there must be a way to integrate these agencies' activities in the Ohio basin so that at least the majority agree on what represents an ecosystem. But experience suggests such integration is virtually impossible. The upshot? To approach a realistic notion of ecosystem research and management, one must adopt the concept of ecopolitical systems.

Most environmentally oriented federal agencies are filled with professional scientists of good will. But when the forces of "real world" government and politics meet rationally drawn scientific boundaries the same result tends to occur. Social and political forces, which include agency loyalty and understandable bureaucratic inertia, almost always rule the day.

At the beginning of this essay I noted the lack of a vocabulary and concepts to treat challenges which now present themselves at the interface of politics and ecology. I conclude by suggesting that the notion of ecopolitical systems will move us toward the development of such concepts.

The Ohio River Basin contains virtually all the political, economic, social, and environmental problems to be found anywhere on the planet, including, in addition to the subjects we have treated above, oil and chemical spills, topsoil erosion, the preservation of wetlands, and the impact of electrical power transmission lines on the environment and human health. It thus offers the opportunity of confronting regionally some of the most fundamental challenges of the twenty-first century. By treating the broader Ohio River Valley region as an ecosystem among the planet's thousands of such systems, however defined, and raising questions as to its possible significance in future global evolution, given our technological knowledge it may be possible to study, manage, and coordinate our resources in a manner that will provide models for others.

NOTES

1. Georgia Anne Geyer, "Ecological Protests Erupt in the Soviet Union," *Chicago Sun Times*, July 7, 1988.
2. Barbara L. Bedford and Simon A. Levin, "Interfacing Ecosystem Science and Environmental Policy," in Boyd Keenan, et al., *Science, Universities, and the Environment.* Proceedings of Symposium (Urbana, Ill.: University of Illinois, Institute of Government and Public Affairs, 1988), 227, 239–40.
3. Ibid., 242.
4. Edward J. Cleary, *The ORSANCO Story: Water Quality Management in the Ohio Valley Under an Interstate Compact* (Baltimore: Johns Hopkins University Press, 1967), 6–7.
5. Joseph L. Fisher, "Foreword," ibid., v–vi.
6. John Flynn, "Ohio River Basin: Packhorse of the East," *Amicus Journal* (Winter 1989):36.
7. Ibid.
8. *Evansville Courier*, September 16, 1990.
9. Richard G. Hewlitt and Oscar E. Anderson, Jr., *The New World, 1939–1946* (University Park, Pa.: Pennsylvania State University Press, 1962), 116.
10. James Feron, "Professor Warns New Rochelle Atom Plant Would Pose Peril," *New York Times*, May 31, 1973.
11. Geraldine Brooks, "Zimmer Plant's Coal Conversion May Be Model for Nuclear Industry," *Wall Street Journal*, August 3, 1984.
12. The Ohio River Basin Energy Study (ORBES) Core Team, *Ohio River Basin Energy Study (ORBES): Main Report* (Washington, D.C.: Office of Environmental Engineering and Technology, Office of Research and Development, U.S. Environmental Protection Agency, 1981). This mandate appears in U.S. Congress, Appropriations Committee, 94th Congress, 1st Session, Senate, Department of Housing and Urban Development—Independent Agencies (Senate Report 94036, 1975).
13. "Utility Industry Advisors' Comments on ORBES Analyses," in *Comments on the Ohio River Basin Energy Study*, collected by James J. Stukel and Boyd R. Keenan (Washington, D.C.: Office of Research and Development, U.S. Environmental Protection Agency, February 1981), 29, 30.
14. Comments by W. S. White, Jr., Chairman and Chief Executive Officer, American Electric Power Company, Inc., ibid., 115–23.
15. Comments by Ralph Madison, Vice President, Kentucky Audubon Council, Louisville, Kentucky, ibid., 105–106.
16. Comments by Harold Cassidy, Professor of Chemistry Emeritus, Yale University.
17. Dr. Stephen J. Gage, EPA assistant administrator for research and

development during the period in which the ORBES study was carried out, to Patricia S. Curlin, American Association for the Advancement of Science, February 26, 1985.

18. During the 1980s a new university-related consortium was organized under the name of the Ohio River Basin Consortium on Research and Education (ORBCRE), started with seed money provided by the Virginia Environmental Endowment in 1984. Ohio State University Professor William J. Mitsch, ORBCRE executive director, reports a membership of more than forty institutions, including many of the largest universities and corporations in the basin. ORBCRE is concerned with "the totality of the Ohio River, which unifies the entire region ecologically." Alan B. Nichols, "Consortium Champions a Major River Basin," *Journal of Water Pollution Control Federation*, Vol. 61, No. 3 (March 1989):316–19.

19. Gary Stix, "Bhopal: A Tragedy in Waiting," *IEEE Spectrum* (publication of the Institute of Electrical and Electronics Engineers), June 1989, 47–49. It should be noted that the Union Carbide plant at Institute was sold to a French company, Rhone-Polene SA, in 1986.

Notes on the Illustrations

page 1:

"Cave-in-Rock, on the Ohio" by Swiss artist Karl Bodmer. Sketched during Bodmer's travels in America with his patron, Prince Maximilian of Wied, 1832–1834. Indiana Historical Society

page 32:

The "great bridge" under which Reuben Thwaites's party camped. A. C. Warren, "City of Louisville" (from William Cullen Bryant, ed., *Picturesque America,* Vol. II, 1872). Indiana Historical Society

page 67:

"View from Wheeling Hill" (ca. 1850-1855, artist unknown). Shown are the National Road, the town of Wheeling, and the first suspension bridge over the Ohio River. Print by Herrmann J. Meyer. Oglebay Institute Mansion Museum

page 105:

The pilot of the towboat *Ernest T. Weir* going down the Ohio to Cincinnati, June 1942. U.S. Office of War Information. Photo by Arthur Siegel

page 130:

Thomas B. Anshutz, "Steamboat on the Ohio" (ca. 1896). The Carnegie Museum of Art, Pittsburgh; Patrons Art Fund, 1957 *page 180:*

The pilot of the towboat *Twin Cities* maneuvers through the lock of Markland Dam on a recent stormy night. Photo credit: The Cincinnati Enquirer/Glenn Hartong

page 190:

The Corps snagboat *R. E. DeRussy,* built at New Albany in 1867, cleared obstructions from the Ohio and inland rivers. It had two hulls with a windlass between for hoisting snags and wrecks from the channel. RG 77, National Archives

page 194:

Wicket dams built on the Ohio from 1879 to 1929 were raised as shown, one wicket at a time, and propped up to hold a pool during low water. At high water, they were lowered to the bottom, opening passage for boats, floods, and ice. U.S. Army Corps of Engineers, 1904

page 210:

View of the river showing Clifty Creek Station and the town of Madison, Indiana, September 1988. Courtesy Louisville Engineer District, U.S. Army Corps of Engineers

Notes on the Contributors

MICHAEL ALLEN, Assistant Professor of History at the University of Washington, Tacoma, is author of *Western Rivermen, 1763–1861: Ohio and Mississippi Boatmen and the Myth of the Alligator Horse* (Baton Rouge: Louisiana State University Press, 1990). From 1977 to 1981 Allen worked as a towboat deckhand and cook on the Mississippi, Illinois, St. Croix, Ouachita, and Arkansas rivers and the Gulf of Mexico.

DARREL BIGHAM is Professor of History at the University of Southern Indiana. A native of Harrisburg, Pennsylvania, he holds a Ph.D. degree from the University of Kansas. His books include *We Ask Only a Fair Trial* and *An Evansville Album,* both published by Indiana University Press. He serves as Director of the Historic Southern Indiana Project, an alliance of historic sites, agencies, and people.

JOHN JAKLE received his doctorate in geography from Indiana Unversity in 1967. Presently he serves as Head of the Department and Professor of Geography at the University of Illinois, Urbana-Champaign. His major writings include *Images of the Ohio Valley: A Historical Geography of Travel, 1740 to 1860, The Tourist: Travel in Twentieth Century North America,* and *Visual Elements of Landscape.*

LELAND R. JOHNSON, Ph.D., Vanderbilt University, directs Clio Research Company, which performs historical and technical research for governments, businesses and institutions. The author of Engineer District histories and many other publications, he has inspected most Corps projects in the Ohio River Division and canoed many of the streams.

BOYD R. KEENAN is Professor of Political Science at the University of Illinois at Chicago and in the Institute of Government and Public Affairs, which serves both the Chicago and Urbana-Champaign campuses. He grew up in Parkersburg, West Virginia, and holds degrees from the University of Kentucky and the University of Illinois. The author and editor of numerous publications, he was the codirector of the Ohio River Basin Energy Study (ORBES).

ROBERT L. REID is Vice President for Academic Affairs and Professor of History at the University of Southern Indiana. His degrees were earned at St. Olaf College and Northwestern University. A native of Red Wing, Minnesota, he has taught at Miami University (Ohio) and Sangamon State University (Illinois). His books include three edited works based on the Farm Security Administration–Office of War Information photographs: *Back Home Again* (Indiana), *Chicago and Downstate* (Illinois), and *Picturing Minnesota, 1936–1943*. He is a member of the board of directors of the Indiana Humanities Council.

SCOTT RUSSELL SANDERS grew up in the Ohio Valley and has written extensively on the Midwest. His books include *Wilderness Plots* (1983), *Stone Country* (1985), *Bad Man Ballad* (1986), and *The Paradise of Bombs* (1987). Following the completion of his graduate studies at Cambridge University, he began teaching at Indiana University, Bloomington.

HUBERT G. H. WILHELM, who was educated at the University of Illinois and Louisiana State University, is Professor of Geography at Ohio University in Athens. His teaching and research interests center on cultural-historical geography with emphasis on Anglo American landscapes. In addition to numerous papers and articles, he has prepared video documentaries, including his forthcoming "Log Cabins and Castles: Virginia Settlers in Ohio."

Editor: Roberta L. Diehl
Designer: Matthew S. Williamson
Managing editor: Terry L. Cagle
Production coordinator: Harriet Curry
Typeface: Baskerville with Caslon display
Compositor: Shepard Poorman Communications Corp.
Printer: Haddon Craftsmen